Jayson™
Best of the 90s

KRELL

by
Jeff Krell

Ignite!
Entertainment

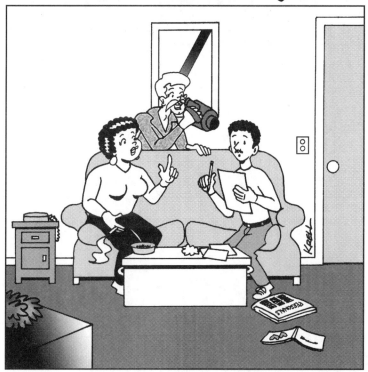

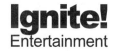

ALSO BY THE AUTHOR:

Jayson: Best of the 80s
Jayson: A New Collection
Maybe...Maybe Not (Translator)
Maybe...Maybe Not Again! (Translator)

Jayson: Best of the 90s
by Jeff Krell

FIRST EDITION
Collection © 2005 by Ignite! Entertainment
Cover illustration and Foreword © 2005 by Jeff Krell
Cartoons © 1990-1997 by Jeff Krell

Library of Congress Control Number: 2005929152
ISBN 0-9656323-7-7 $9.95

Ignite! Entertainment
P.O. Box 641131
Los Angeles, CA 90064
http://ignite-ent.com

Foreword

"Volume 12 will have a science fiction theme," decreed Winston Leyland, publisher of the popular "Meatmen" series of gay male cartoon anthologies. I had happily contributed "Jayson" stories to the first 11 volumes of "Meatmen," so without hesitation I responded, "See you in Volume 13."

I'm not much of a science fiction fan. Early on in life I sank my roots deep into situation comedy, and that's where I remained planted. Plus, the few gay male sci-fi comics I'd ever read were all variations on the theme of "Giant Phalluses In Space!" Not exactly my style.

"Oh, go on and give it a try," Winston implored. I'd like to believe that my publisher was encouraging me to stretch as an artist, but I suspect that he was merely counting on me to contribute my usual twelve pages to a volume he had already committed to publishing.

So I gave the matter some thought. I decided that if I could remain true to my characters while sending them on some sort of wacky sci-fi adventure, I just might end up learning more about them. So I devised a story in which Jayson's universe collided with a PG-rated version of the Giant Phalluses In Space, with ruminations on the AIDS crisis and Jayson and Robyn's inability to hold onto a man. I called the story "Jayson Visits Planet 69." (In retrospect, I find this story such a delicious commentary on my characters' earthly lives that I placed it at the very end of this collection.)

Volume 12 of "Meatmen" was so successful that Winston announced a second sci-fi volume, for which I wrote the sprawling three-part adventure, "Jayson Becomes a Man." I took such delight in crafting these stories that as the 1990s wore on, I even found myself weaving more fantasy elements into Jayson's regular continuity.

The 1990s also saw the weekly syndication of "Jayson." Within the confines of the four-panel format, I still attempted to tell stories – albeit with less detail and more restatement of the plot points, since each new installment represented someone's first encounter with the series. Here I've included Jayson's experiences with video dating, Christian telemarketers, and of course the bar scene. (These stories were also reprinted in the "Meatmen" series, so I've cited those volume numbers for you.)

If you're reading these collections in order, you know that the 1980s ended with a huge cliffhanger: Jayson declared his love for Ed (sort of) on the occasion of his wedding to Arena; Arena stormed out of Jayson's life; and Jayson's mother Bertha moved in. We pick up the story with Jayson deeply committed to Ed, who is about burst onto the scene in Robyn's epic film, "Hung Jury." Action!

Jeff Krell

October 8, 2005

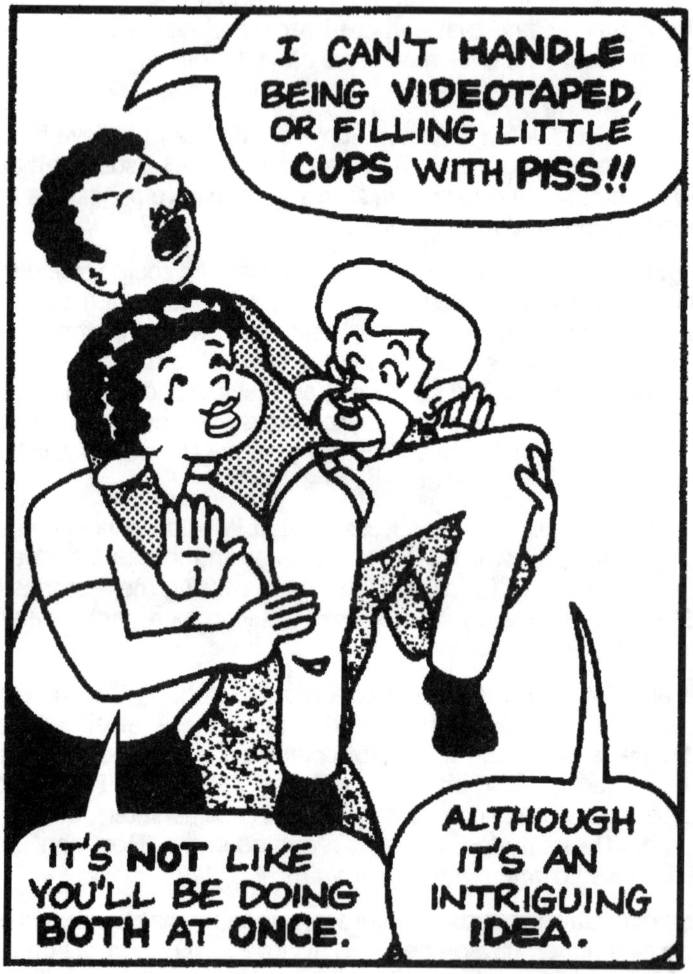
I CAN'T HANDLE BEING VIDEOTAPED, OR FILLING LITTLE CUPS WITH PISS!!
IT'S NOT LIKE YOU'LL BE DOING BOTH AT ONCE.
ALTHOUGH IT'S AN INTRIGUING IDEA.

Table of Contents

Jayson's™ world premiere

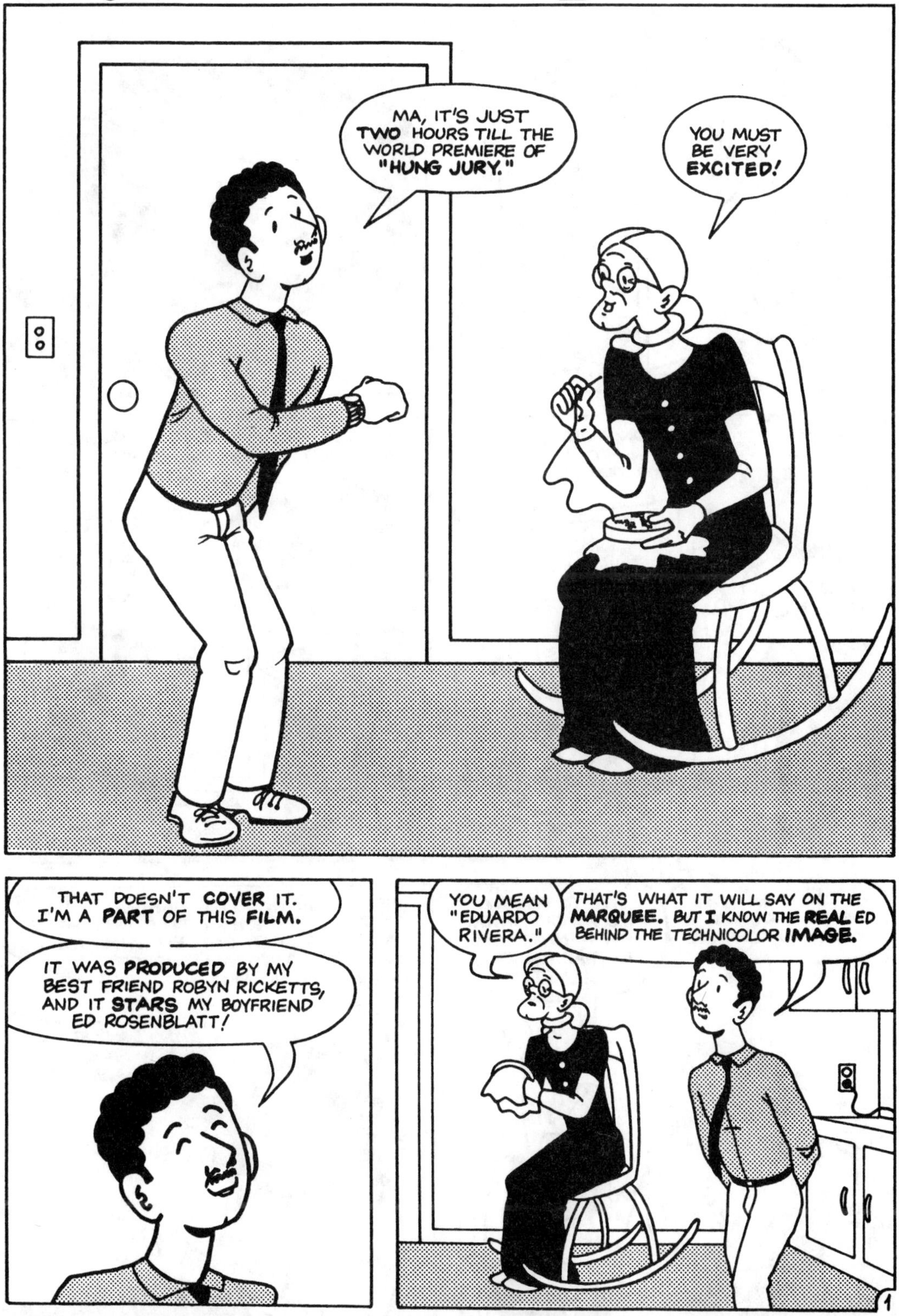

MA, IT'S JUST TWO HOURS TILL THE WORLD PREMIERE OF "HUNG JURY."
YOU MUST BE VERY EXCITED!
THAT DOESN'T COVER IT. I'M A PART OF THIS FILM.
IT WAS PRODUCED BY MY BEST FRIEND ROBYN RICKETTS, AND IT STARS MY BOYFRIEND ED ROSENBLATT!
YOU MEAN "EDUARDO RIVERA."
THAT'S WHAT IT WILL SAY ON THE MARQUEE. BUT I KNOW THE REAL ED BEHIND THE TECHNICOLOR IMAGE.
1

ORIGINALLY PRESENTED IN MEATMEN VOL. 9, 1990

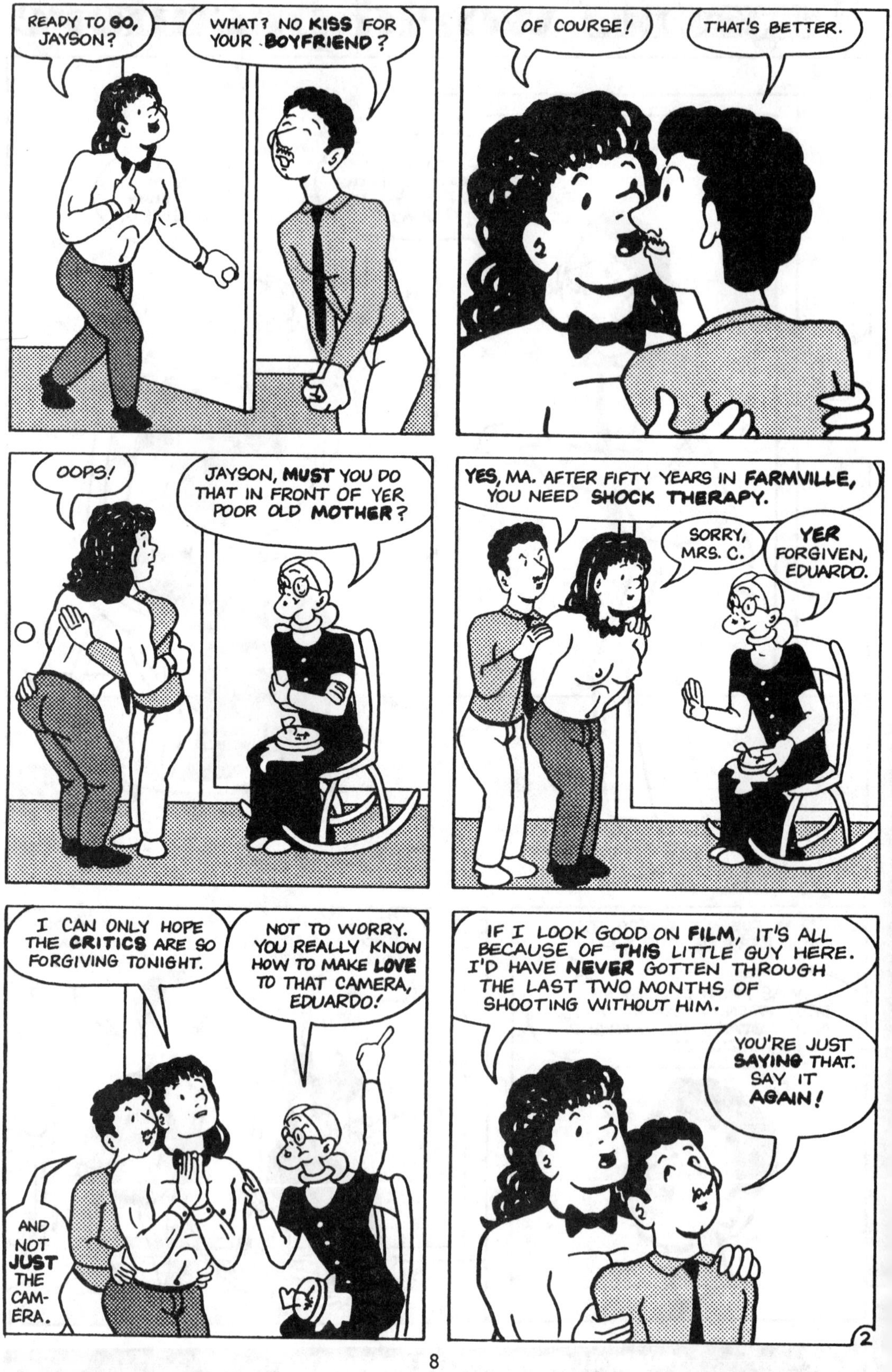
READY TO GO, JAYSON?
WHAT? NO KISS FOR YOUR BOYFRIEND?
OF COURSE!
THAT'S BETTER.
OOPS!
JAYSON, MUST YOU DO THAT IN FRONT OF YER POOR OLD MOTHER?
YES, MA. AFTER FIFTY YEARS IN FARMVILLE, YOU NEED SHOCK THERAPY.
SORRY, MRS. C.
YER FORGIVEN, EDUARDO.
I CAN ONLY HOPE THE CRITICS ARE SO FORGIVING TONIGHT.
NOT TO WORRY. YOU REALLY KNOW HOW TO MAKE LOVE TO THAT CAMERA, EDUARDO!
AND NOT JUST THE CAM-ERA.
IF I LOOK GOOD ON FILM, IT'S ALL BECAUSE OF THIS LITTLE GUY HERE. I'D HAVE NEVER GOTTEN THROUGH THE LAST TWO MONTHS OF SHOOTING WITHOUT HIM.
YOU'RE JUST SAYING THAT. SAY IT AGAIN!
2

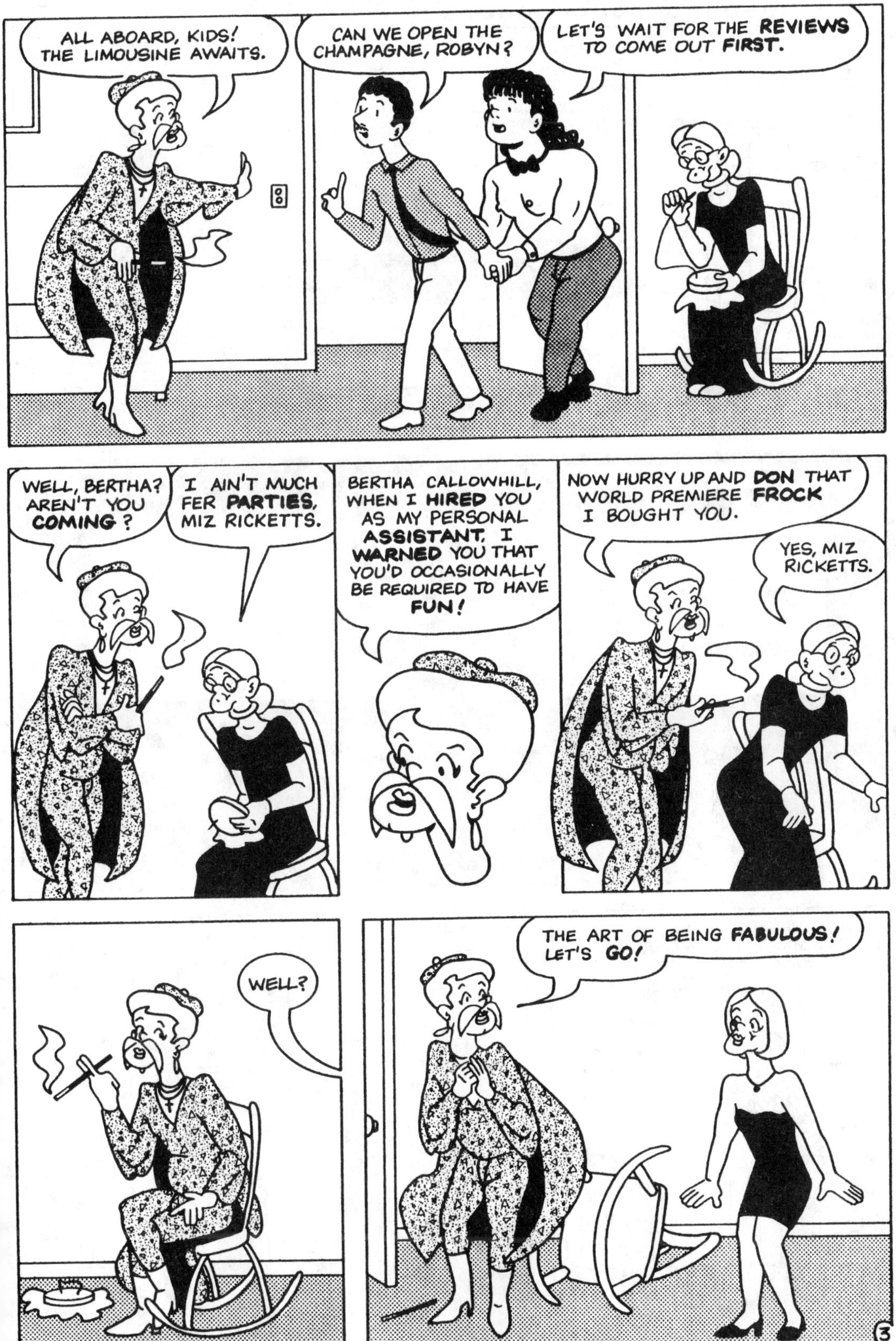
ALL ABOARD, KIDS! THE LIMOUSINE AWAITS.
CAN WE OPEN THE CHAMPAGNE, ROBYN?
LET'S WAIT FOR THE **REVIEWS** TO COME OUT **FIRST**.
WELL, BERTHA? AREN'T YOU **COMING**?
I AIN'T MUCH FER **PARTIES**, MIZ RICKETTS.
BERTHA CALLOWHILL, WHEN I **HIRED** YOU AS MY PERSONAL **ASSISTANT**, I **WARNED** YOU THAT YOU'D OCCASIONALLY BE REQUIRED TO HAVE **FUN**!
NOW HURRY UP AND **DON** THAT WORLD PREMIERE **FROCK** I BOUGHT YOU.
YES, MIZ RICKETTS.
WELL?
THE ART OF BEING **FABULOUS**! LET'S **GO**!
3

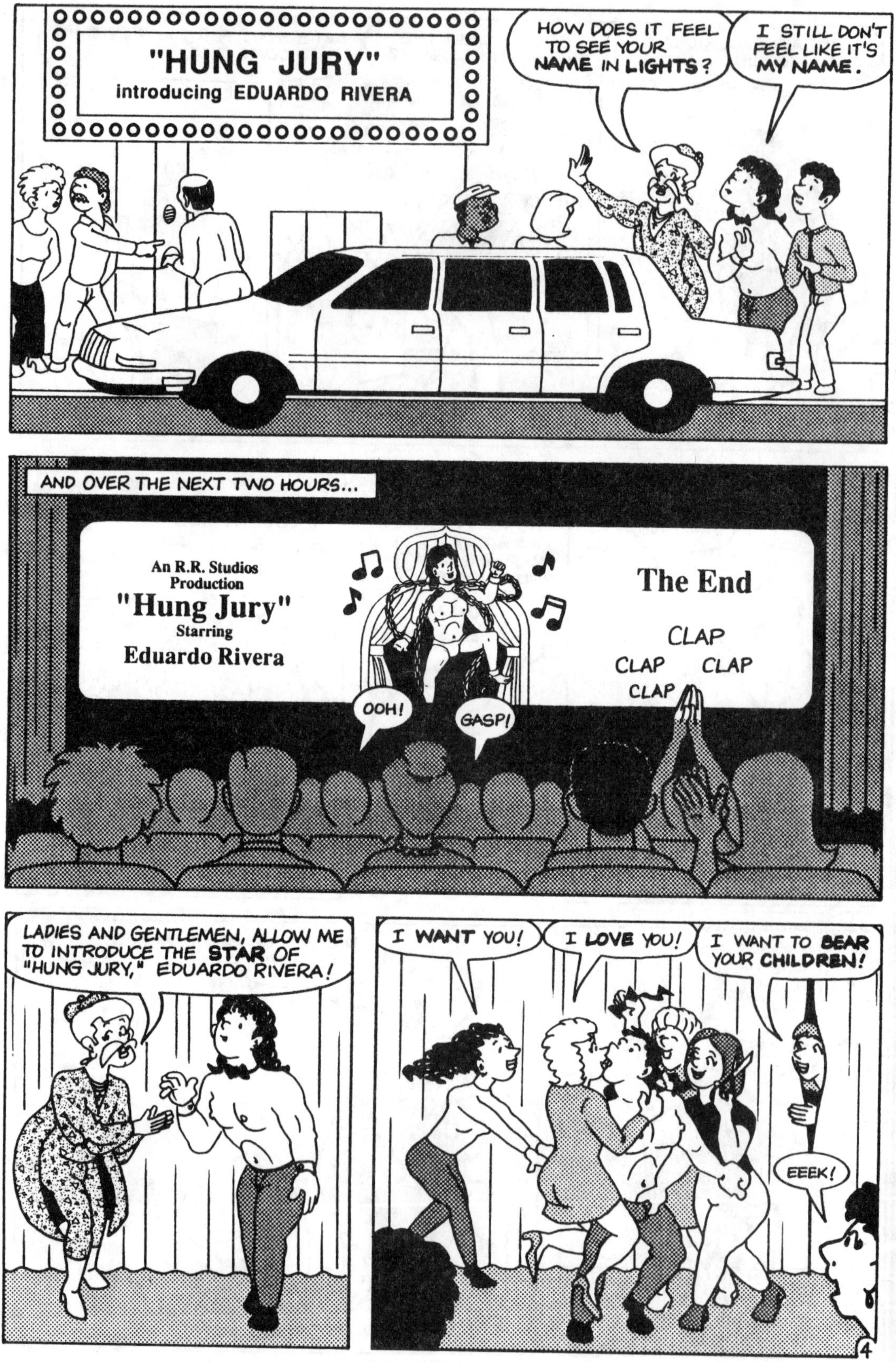
"HUNG JURY"
introducing EDUARDO RIVERA
HOW DOES IT FEEL TO SEE YOUR NAME IN LIGHTS?
I STILL DON'T FEEL LIKE IT'S MY NAME.
AND OVER THE NEXT TWO HOURS...
An R.R. Studios Production
"Hung Jury"
Starring
Eduardo Rivera
The End
CLAP
CLAP CLAP
CLAP
OOH!
GASP!
LADIES AND GENTLEMEN, ALLOW ME TO INTRODUCE THE STAR OF "HUNG JURY," EDUARDO RIVERA!
I WANT YOU!
I LOVE YOU!
I WANT TO BEAR YOUR CHILDREN!
EEEK!
4

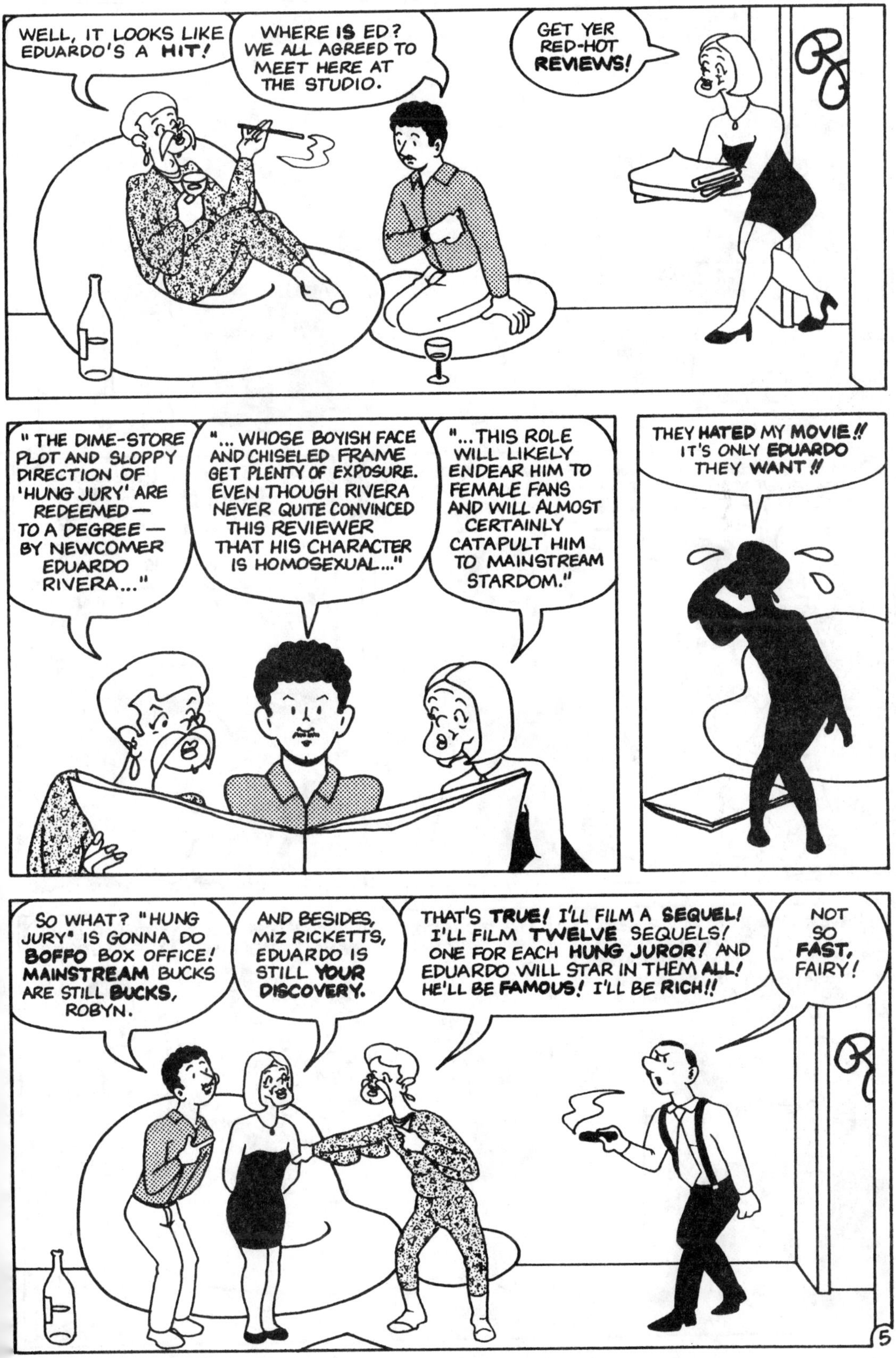
WELL, IT LOOKS LIKE EDUARDO'S A **HIT**!
WHERE **IS** ED? WE ALL AGREED TO MEET HERE AT THE STUDIO.
GET YER RED-HOT **REVIEWS**!
" THE DIME-STORE PLOT AND SLOPPY DIRECTION OF 'HUNG JURY' ARE REDEEMED — TO A DEGREE — BY NEWCOMER EDUARDO RIVERA..."
"... WHOSE BOYISH FACE AND CHISELED FRAME GET PLENTY OF EXPOSURE. EVEN THOUGH RIVERA NEVER QUITE CONVINCED THIS REVIEWER THAT HIS CHARACTER IS HOMOSEXUAL..."
"...THIS ROLE WILL LIKELY ENDEAR HIM TO FEMALE FANS AND WILL ALMOST CERTAINLY CATAPULT HIM TO MAINSTREAM STARDOM."
THEY **HATED** MY **MOVIE**!! IT'S ONLY **EDUARDO** THEY **WANT**!!
SO WHAT? "HUNG JURY" IS GONNA DO **BOFFO** BOX OFFICE! **MAINSTREAM** BUCKS ARE STILL **BUCKS**, ROBYN.
AND BESIDES, MIZ RICKETTS, EDUARDO IS STILL **YOUR DISCOVERY**.
THAT'S **TRUE**! I'LL FILM A **SEQUEL**! I'LL FILM **TWELVE** SEQUELS! ONE FOR EACH **HUNG JUROR**! AND EDUARDO WILL STAR IN THEM **ALL**! HE'LL BE **FAMOUS**! I'LL BE **RICH**!!
NOT SO **FAST**, FAIRY!
5

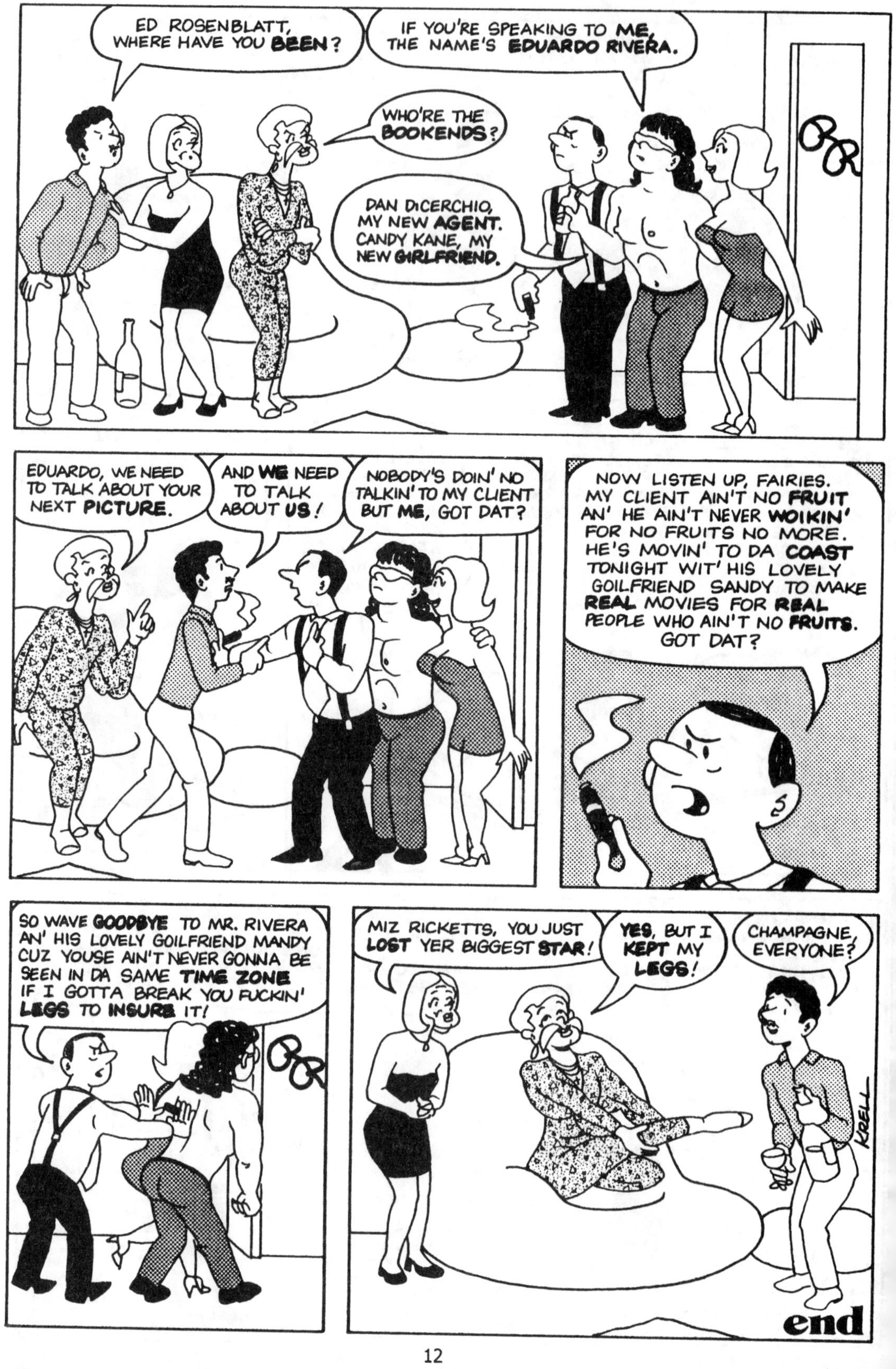
ED ROSENBLATT, WHERE HAVE YOU BEEN?
IF YOU'RE SPEAKING TO ME, THE NAME'S EDUARDO RIVERA.
WHO'RE THE BOOKENDS?
DAN DiCERCHIO, MY NEW AGENT. CANDY KANE, MY NEW GIRLFRIEND.
EDUARDO, WE NEED TO TALK ABOUT YOUR NEXT PICTURE.
AND WE NEED TO TALK ABOUT US!
NOBODY'S DOIN' NO TALKIN' TO MY CLIENT BUT ME, GOT DAT?
NOW LISTEN UP, FAIRIES. MY CLIENT AIN'T NO FRUIT AN' HE AIN'T NEVER WOIKIN' FOR NO FRUITS NO MORE. HE'S MOVIN' TO DA COAST TONIGHT WIT' HIS LOVELY GOILFRIEND SANDY TO MAKE REAL MOVIES FOR REAL PEOPLE WHO AIN'T NO FRUITS. GOT DAT?
SO WAVE GOODBYE TO MR. RIVERA AN' HIS LOVELY GOILFRIEND MANDY CUZ YOUSE AIN'T NEVER GONNA BE SEEN IN DA SAME TIME ZONE IF I GOTTA BREAK YOU FUCKIN' LEGS TO INSURE IT!
MIZ RICKETTS, YOU JUST LOST YER BIGGEST STAR!
YES, BUT I KEPT MY LEGS!
CHAMPAGNE, EVERYONE?
KRELL
end

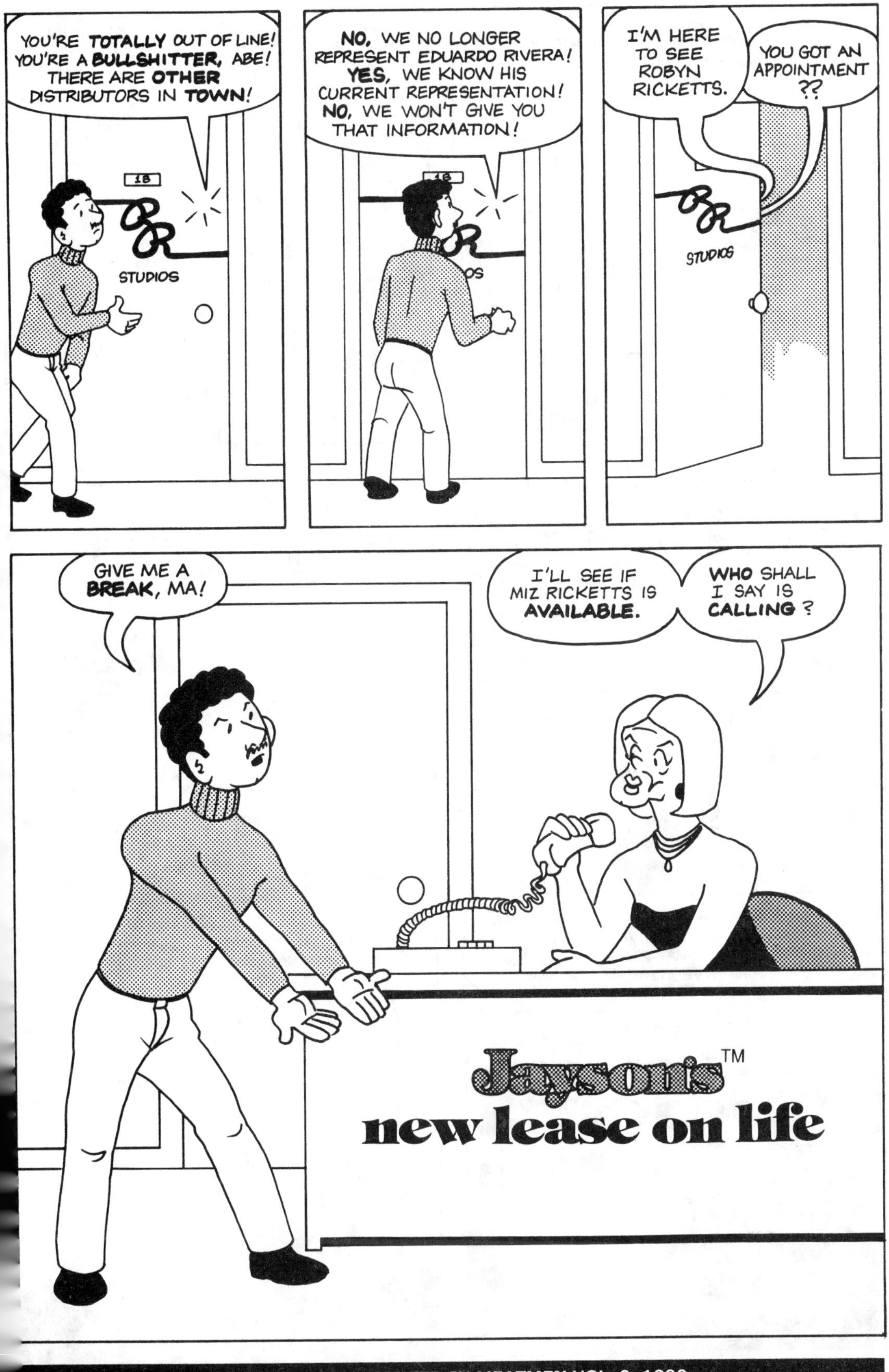
YOU'RE TOTALLY OUT OF LINE! YOU'RE A BULLSHITTER, ABE! THERE ARE OTHER DISTRIBUTORS IN TOWN!
1B
STUDIOS
NO, WE NO LONGER REPRESENT EDUARDO RIVERA! YES, WE KNOW HIS CURRENT REPRESENTATION! NO, WE WON'T GIVE YOU THAT INFORMATION!
I'M HERE TO SEE ROBYN RICKETTS.
YOU GOT AN APPOINTMENT ??
STUDIOS
GIVE ME A BREAK, MA!
WHO SHALL I SAY IS CALLING ?
I'LL SEE IF MIZ RICKETTS IS AVAILABLE.
Jaysons™
new lease on life

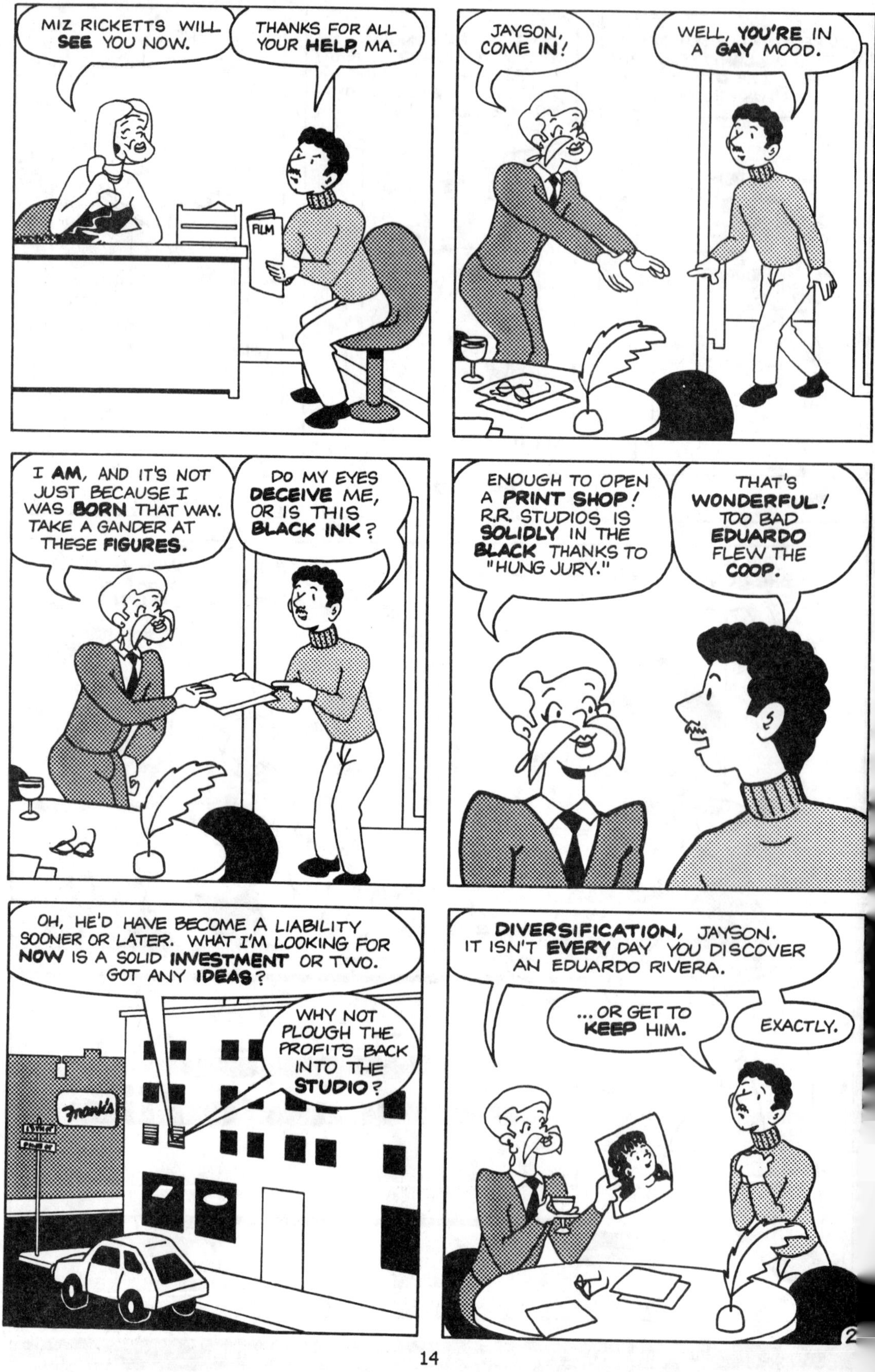
MIZ RICKETTS WILL SEE YOU NOW.
THANKS FOR ALL YOUR HELP, MA.
FILM
JAYSON, COME IN!
WELL, YOU'RE IN A GAY MOOD.
I AM, AND IT'S NOT JUST BECAUSE I WAS BORN THAT WAY. TAKE A GANDER AT THESE FIGURES.
DO MY EYES DECEIVE ME, OR IS THIS BLACK INK?
ENOUGH TO OPEN A PRINT SHOP! R.R. STUDIOS IS SOLIDLY IN THE BLACK THANKS TO "HUNG JURY."
THAT'S WONDERFUL! TOO BAD EDUARDO FLEW THE COOP.
OH, HE'D HAVE BECOME A LIABILITY SOONER OR LATER. WHAT I'M LOOKING FOR NOW IS A SOLID INVESTMENT OR TWO. GOT ANY IDEAS?
WHY NOT PLOUGH THE PROFITS BACK INTO THE STUDIO?
Frank's
DIVERSIFICATION, JAYSON. IT ISN'T EVERY DAY YOU DISCOVER AN EDUARDO RIVERA.
...OR GET TO KEEP HIM.
EXACTLY.

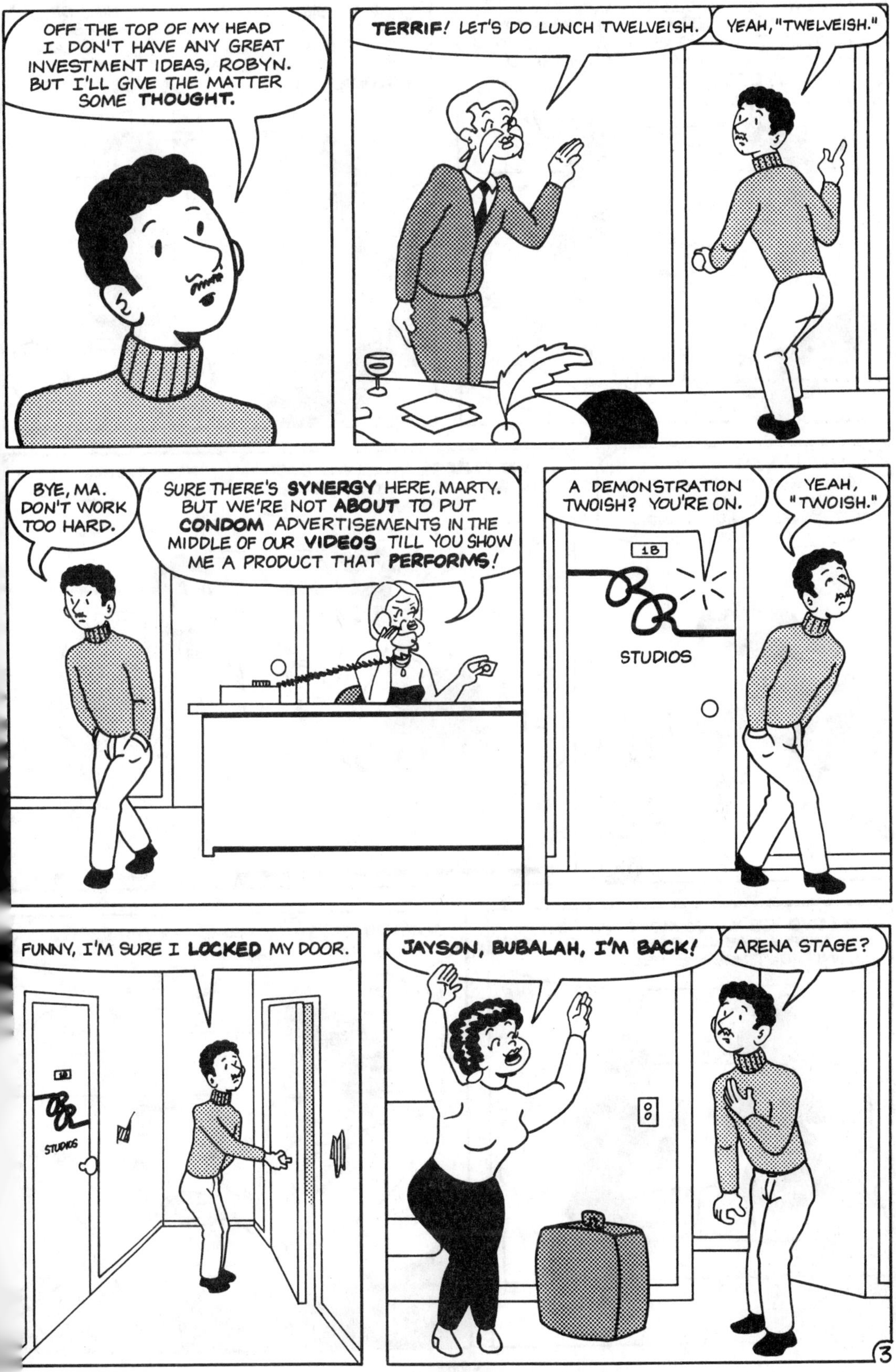
OFF THE TOP OF MY HEAD I DON'T HAVE ANY GREAT INVESTMENT IDEAS, ROBYN. BUT I'LL GIVE THE MATTER SOME THOUGHT.
TERRIF! LET'S DO LUNCH TWELVEISH.
YEAH, "TWELVEISH."
BYE, MA. DON'T WORK TOO HARD.
SURE THERE'S SYNERGY HERE, MARTY. BUT WE'RE NOT ABOUT TO PUT CONDOM ADVERTISEMENTS IN THE MIDDLE OF OUR VIDEOS TILL YOU SHOW ME A PRODUCT THAT PERFORMS!
A DEMONSTRATION TWOISH? YOU'RE ON.
1B
STUDIOS
YEAH, "TWOISH."
FUNNY, I'M SURE I LOCKED MY DOOR.
STUDIOS
JAYSON, BUBALAH, I'M BACK!
ARENA STAGE?
3

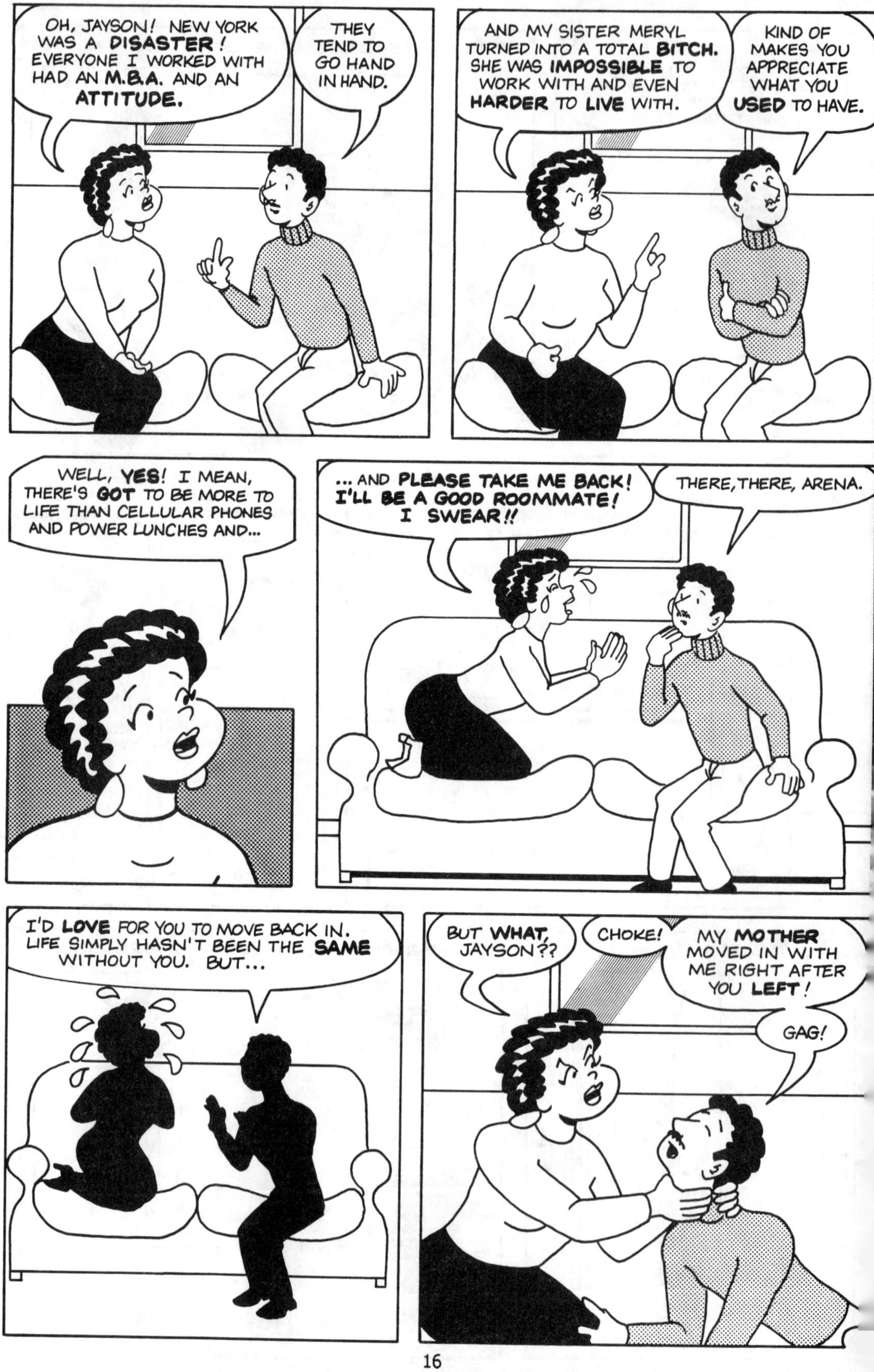
OH, JAYSON! NEW YORK WAS A **DISASTER**! EVERYONE I WORKED WITH HAD AN **M.B.A.** AND AN **ATTITUDE.**
THEY TEND TO GO HAND IN HAND.
AND MY SISTER MERYL TURNED INTO A TOTAL **BITCH.** SHE WAS **IMPOSSIBLE** TO WORK WITH AND EVEN **HARDER** TO **LIVE** WITH.
KIND OF MAKES YOU APPRECIATE WHAT YOU **USED** TO HAVE.
WELL, **YES**! I MEAN, THERE'S **GOT** TO BE MORE TO LIFE THAN CELLULAR PHONES AND POWER LUNCHES AND...
...AND **PLEASE TAKE ME BACK! I'LL BE A GOOD ROOMMATE! I SWEAR!!**
THERE, THERE, ARENA.
I'D **LOVE** FOR YOU TO MOVE BACK IN. LIFE SIMPLY HASN'T BEEN THE **SAME** WITHOUT YOU. BUT...
BUT **WHAT**, JAYSON??
CHOKE!
MY **MOTHER** MOVED IN WITH ME RIGHT AFTER YOU **LEFT**!
GAG!

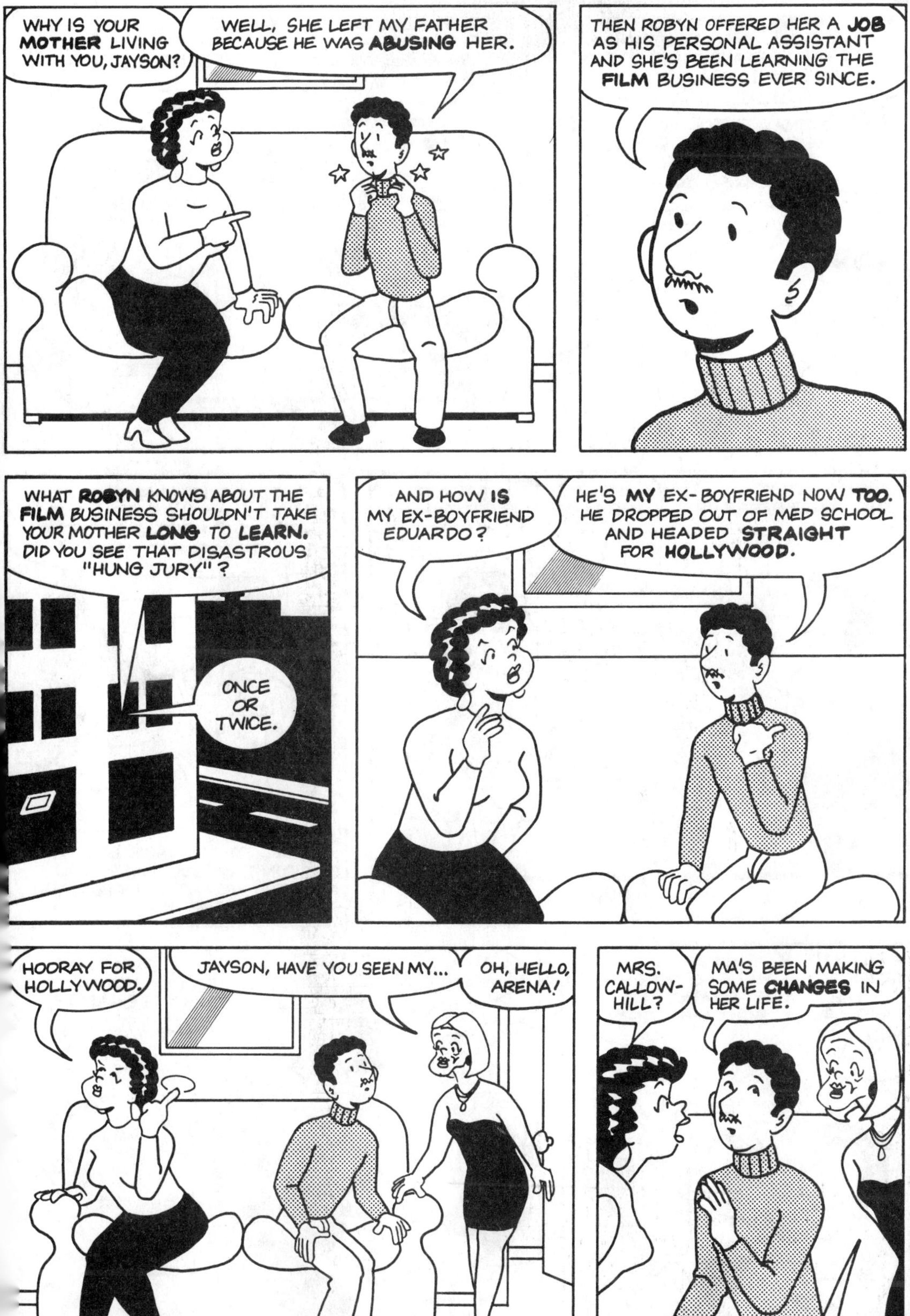
WHY IS YOUR **MOTHER** LIVING WITH YOU, JAYSON?
WELL, SHE LEFT MY FATHER BECAUSE HE WAS **ABUSING** HER.
THEN ROBYN OFFERED HER A **JOB** AS HIS PERSONAL ASSISTANT AND SHE'S BEEN LEARNING THE **FILM** BUSINESS EVER SINCE.
WHAT **ROBYN** KNOWS ABOUT THE **FILM** BUSINESS SHOULDN'T TAKE YOUR MOTHER **LONG** TO **LEARN.** DID YOU SEE THAT DISASTROUS "HUNG JURY"?
ONCE OR TWICE.
AND HOW **IS** MY EX-BOYFRIEND EDUARDO?
HE'S **MY** EX-BOYFRIEND NOW **TOO.** HE DROPPED OUT OF MED SCHOOL AND HEADED **STRAIGHT** FOR **HOLLYWOOD.**
HOORAY FOR HOLLYWOOD.
JAYSON, HAVE YOU SEEN MY...
OH, HELLO, ARENA!
MRS. CALLOW-HILL?
MA'S BEEN MAKING SOME **CHANGES** IN HER LIFE.
ARE YOU BACK FOR **GOOD,** ARENA?
5

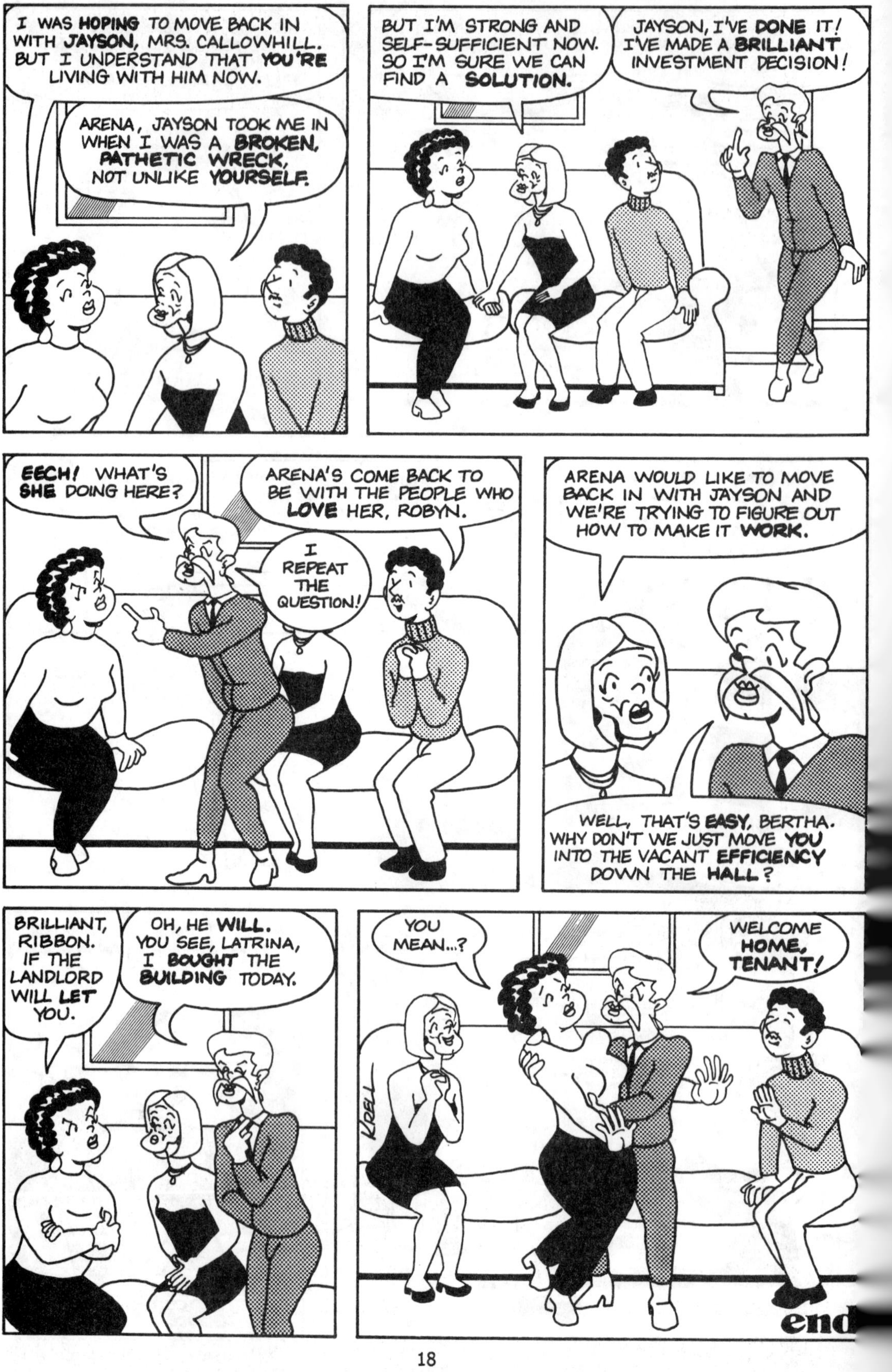
I WAS HOPING TO MOVE BACK IN WITH JAYSON, MRS. CALLOWHILL. BUT I UNDERSTAND THAT YOU'RE LIVING WITH HIM NOW.
ARENA, JAYSON TOOK ME IN WHEN I WAS A BROKEN, PATHETIC WRECK, NOT UNLIKE YOURSELF.
BUT I'M STRONG AND SELF-SUFFICIENT NOW. SO I'M SURE WE CAN FIND A SOLUTION.
JAYSON, I'VE DONE IT! I'VE MADE A BRILLIANT INVESTMENT DECISION!
EECH! WHAT'S SHE DOING HERE?
ARENA'S COME BACK TO BE WITH THE PEOPLE WHO LOVE HER, ROBYN.
I REPEAT THE QUESTION!
ARENA WOULD LIKE TO MOVE BACK IN WITH JAYSON AND WE'RE TRYING TO FIGURE OUT HOW TO MAKE IT WORK.
WELL, THAT'S EASY, BERTHA. WHY DON'T WE JUST MOVE YOU INTO THE VACANT EFFICIENCY DOWN THE HALL?
BRILLIANT, RIBBON. IF THE LANDLORD WILL LET YOU.
OH, HE WILL. YOU SEE, LATRINA, I BOUGHT THE BUILDING TODAY.
YOU MEAN...?
WELCOME HOME, TENANT!
KRELL
end

Jayson™ paints the town

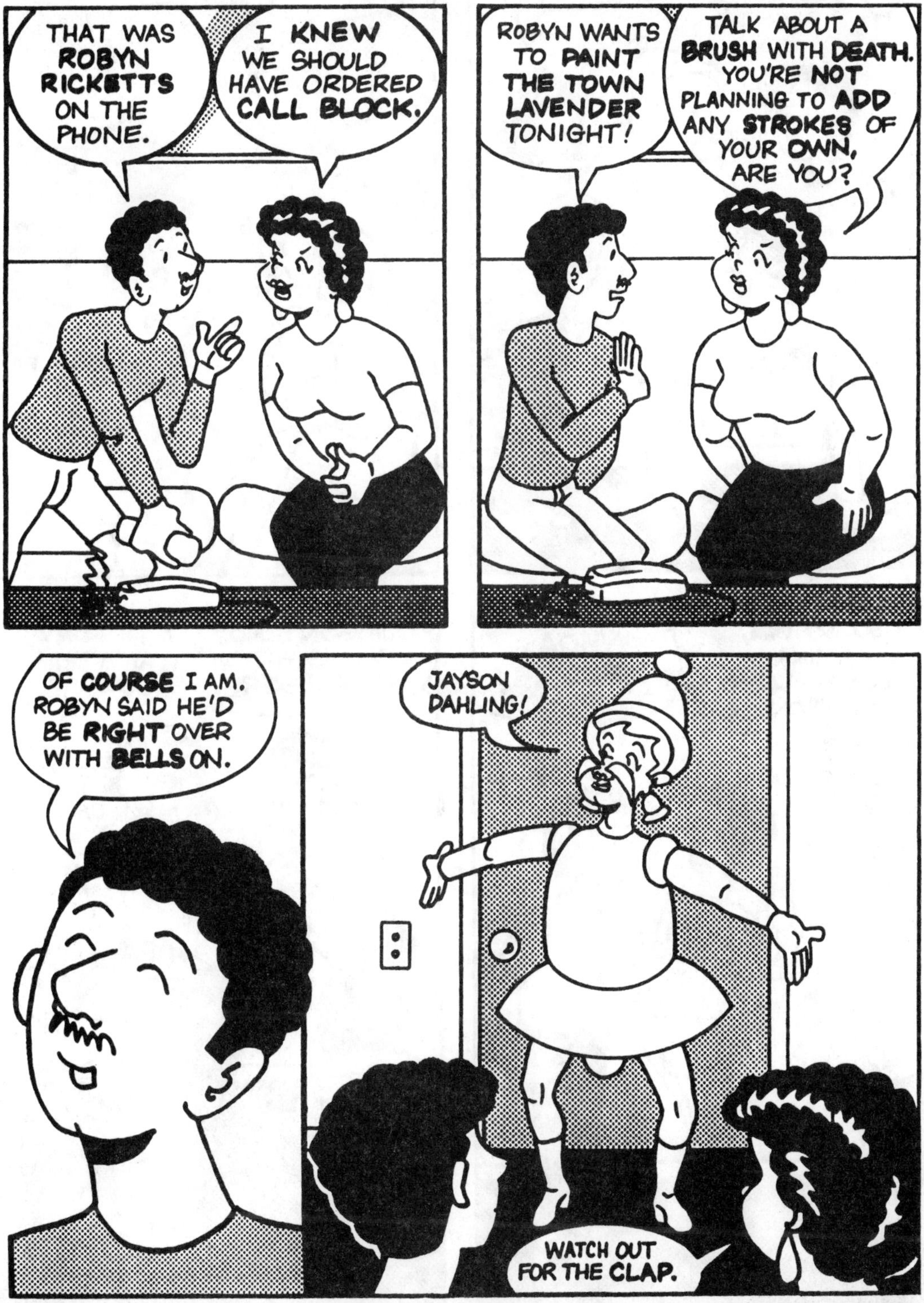
THAT WAS ROBYN RICKETTS ON THE PHONE.
I KNEW WE SHOULD HAVE ORDERED CALL BLOCK.
ROBYN WANTS TO PAINT THE TOWN LAVENDER TONIGHT!
TALK ABOUT A BRUSH WITH DEATH. YOU'RE NOT PLANNING TO ADD ANY STROKES OF YOUR OWN, ARE YOU?
OF COURSE I AM. ROBYN SAID HE'D BE RIGHT OVER WITH BELLS ON.
JAYSON DAHLING!
WATCH OUT FOR THE CLAP.

ORIGINALLY PRESENTED IN MEATMEN VOL. 13, 1992

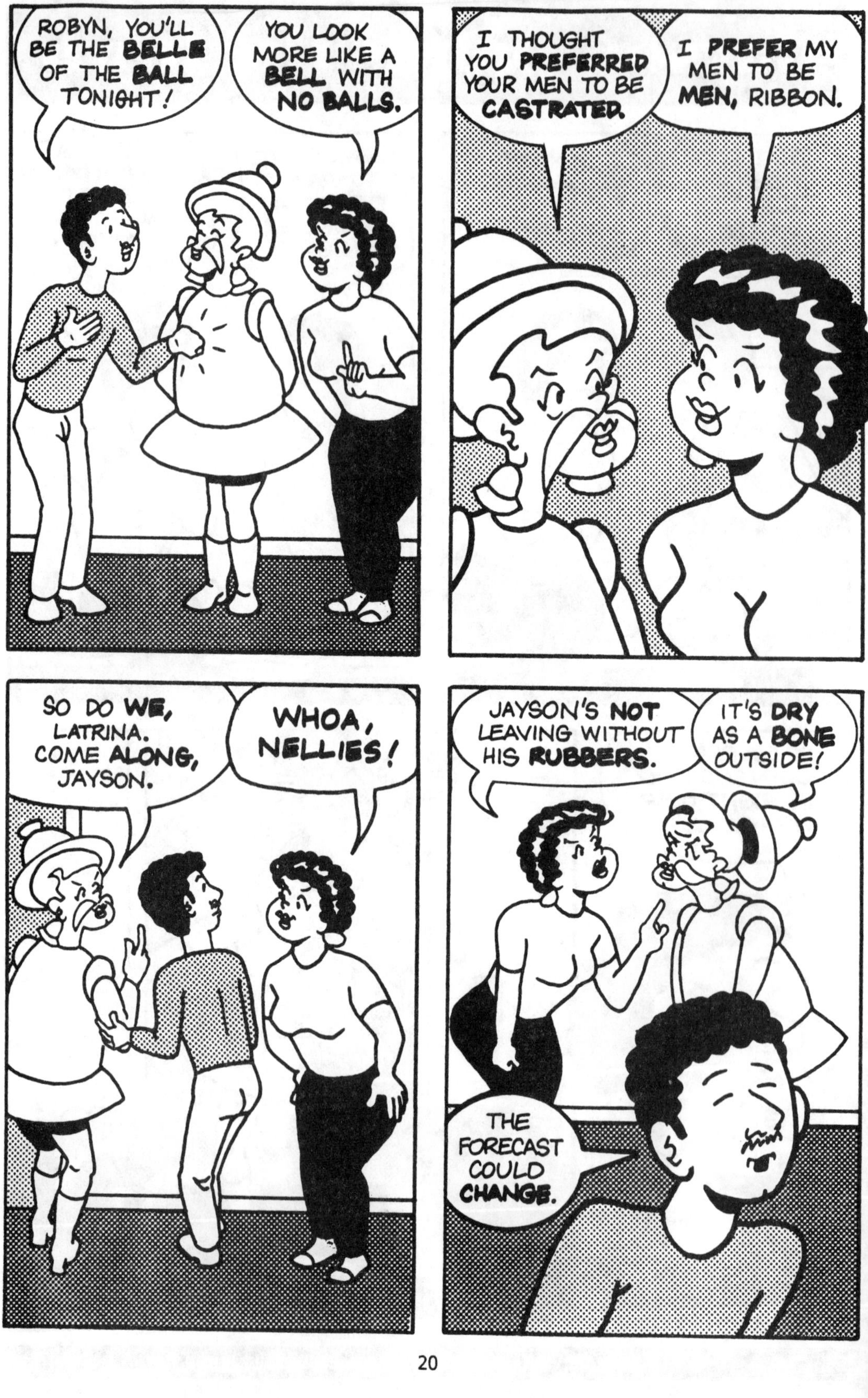
ROBYN, YOU'LL BE THE BELLE OF THE BALL TONIGHT!
YOU LOOK MORE LIKE A BELL WITH NO BALLS.
I THOUGHT YOU PREFERRED YOUR MEN TO BE CASTRATED.
I PREFER MY MEN TO BE MEN, RIBBON.
SO DO WE, LATRINA. COME ALONG, JAYSON.
WHOA, NELLIES!
JAYSON'S NOT LEAVING WITHOUT HIS RUBBERS.
IT'S DRY AS A BONE OUTSIDE!
THE FORECAST COULD CHANGE.

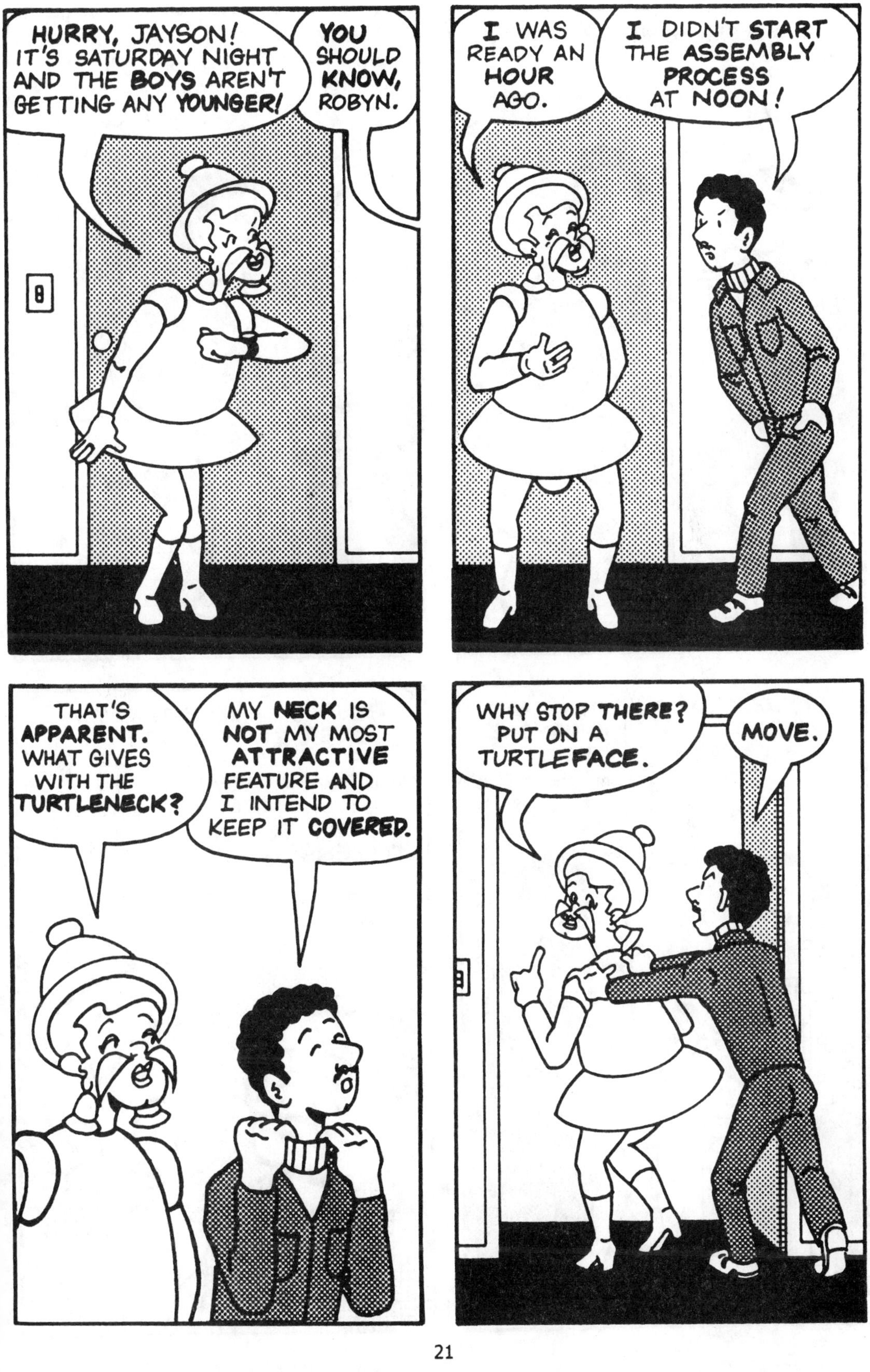
HURRY, JAYSON! IT'S SATURDAY NIGHT AND THE BOYS AREN'T GETTING ANY YOUNGER!
YOU SHOULD KNOW, ROBYN.
8
I WAS READY AN HOUR AGO.
I DIDN'T START THE ASSEMBLY PROCESS AT NOON!
THAT'S APPARENT. WHAT GIVES WITH THE TURTLENECK?
MY NECK IS NOT MY MOST ATTRACTIVE FEATURE AND I INTEND TO KEEP IT COVERED.
WHY STOP THERE? PUT ON A TURTLEFACE.
MOVE.

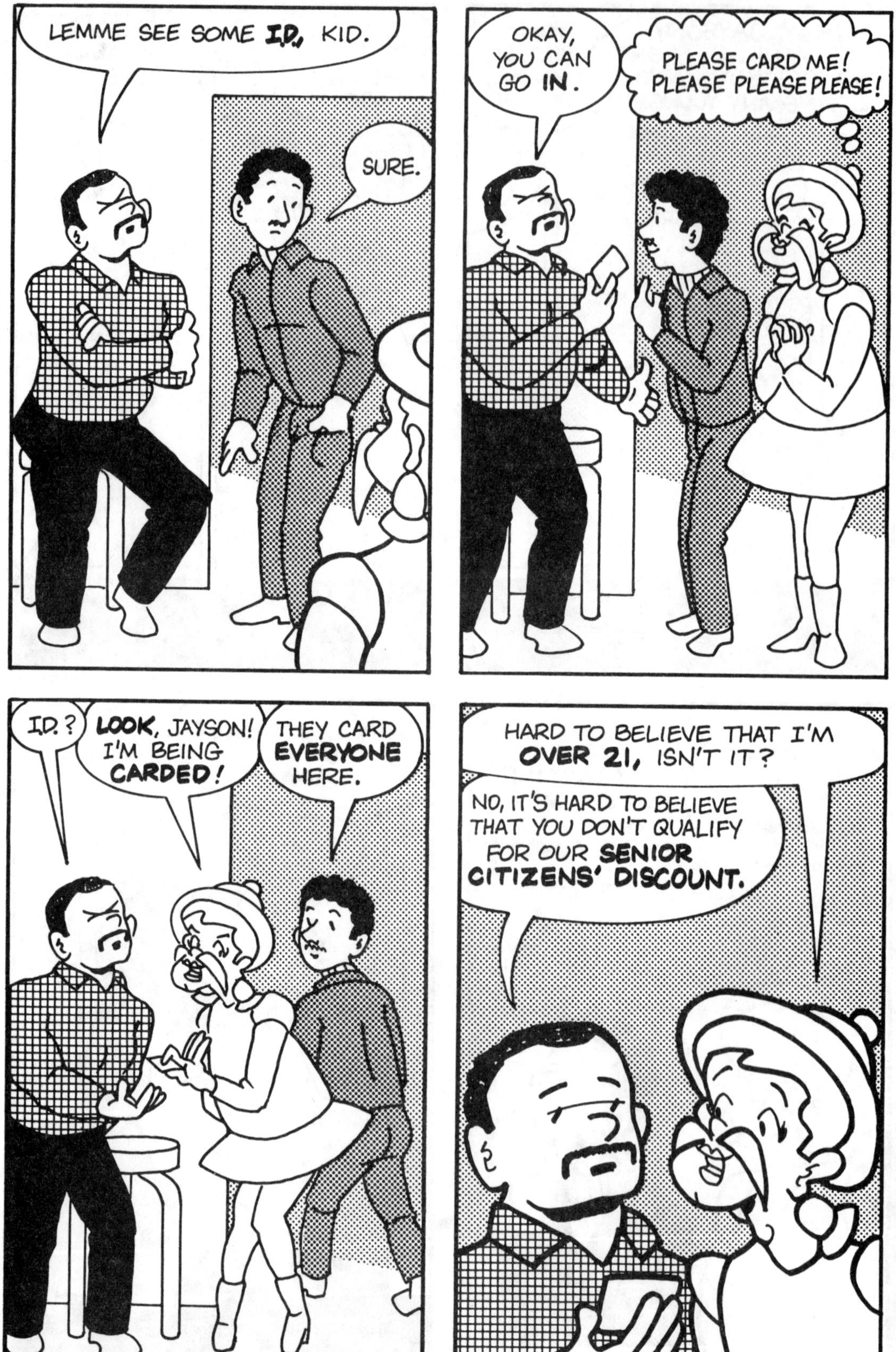
LEMME SEE SOME I.D., KID.
SURE.
OKAY, YOU CAN GO IN.
PLEASE CARD ME! PLEASE PLEASE PLEASE!
I.D.?
LOOK, JAYSON! I'M BEING CARDED!
THEY CARD EVERYONE HERE.
HARD TO BELIEVE THAT I'M OVER 21, ISN'T IT?
NO, IT'S HARD TO BELIEVE THAT YOU DON'T QUALIFY FOR OUR SENIOR CITIZENS' DISCOUNT.

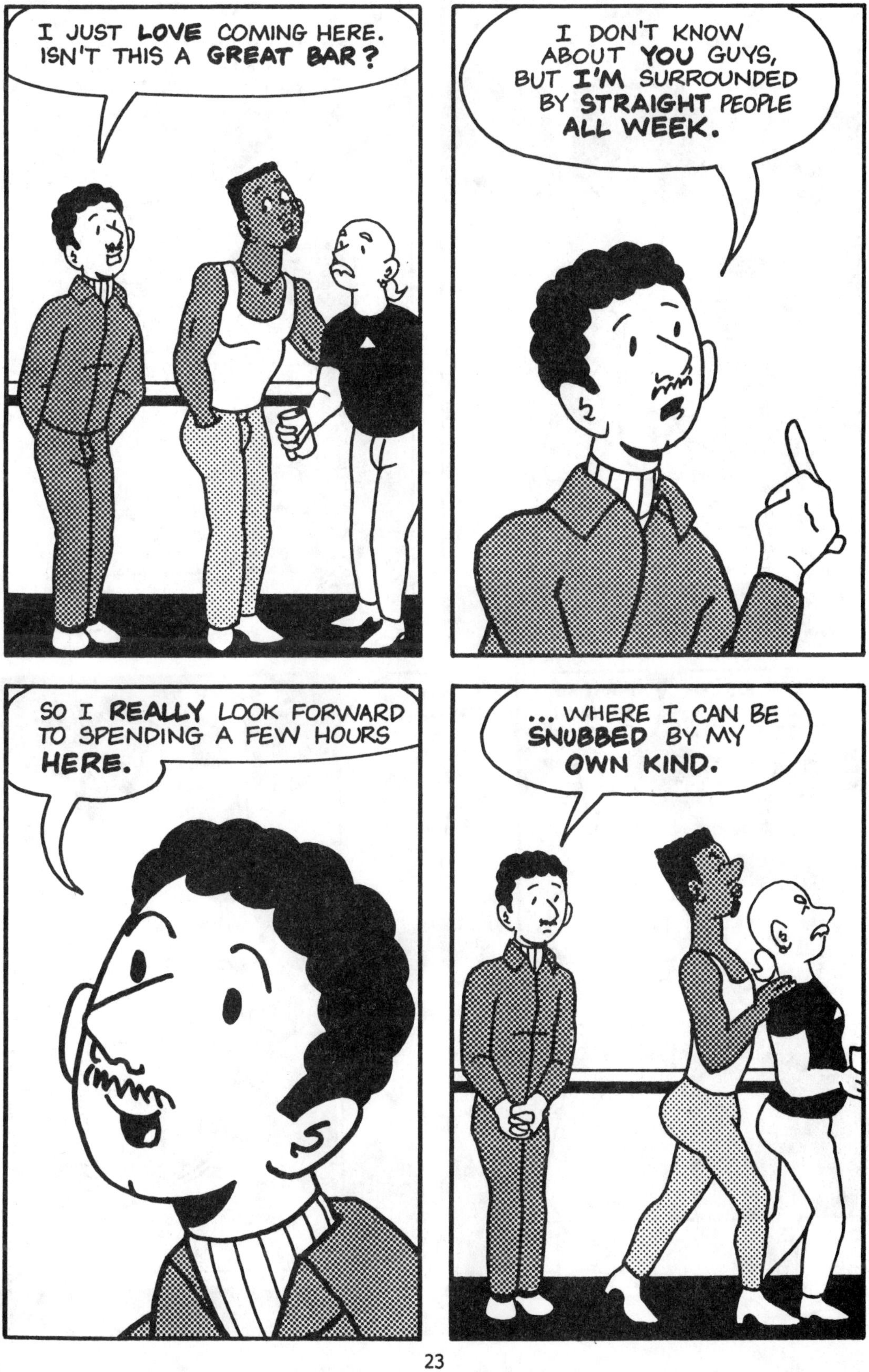
I JUST LOVE COMING HERE. ISN'T THIS A GREAT BAR?
I DON'T KNOW ABOUT YOU GUYS, BUT I'M SURROUNDED BY STRAIGHT PEOPLE ALL WEEK.
SO I REALLY LOOK FORWARD TO SPENDING A FEW HOURS HERE.
... WHERE I CAN BE SNUBBED BY MY OWN KIND.

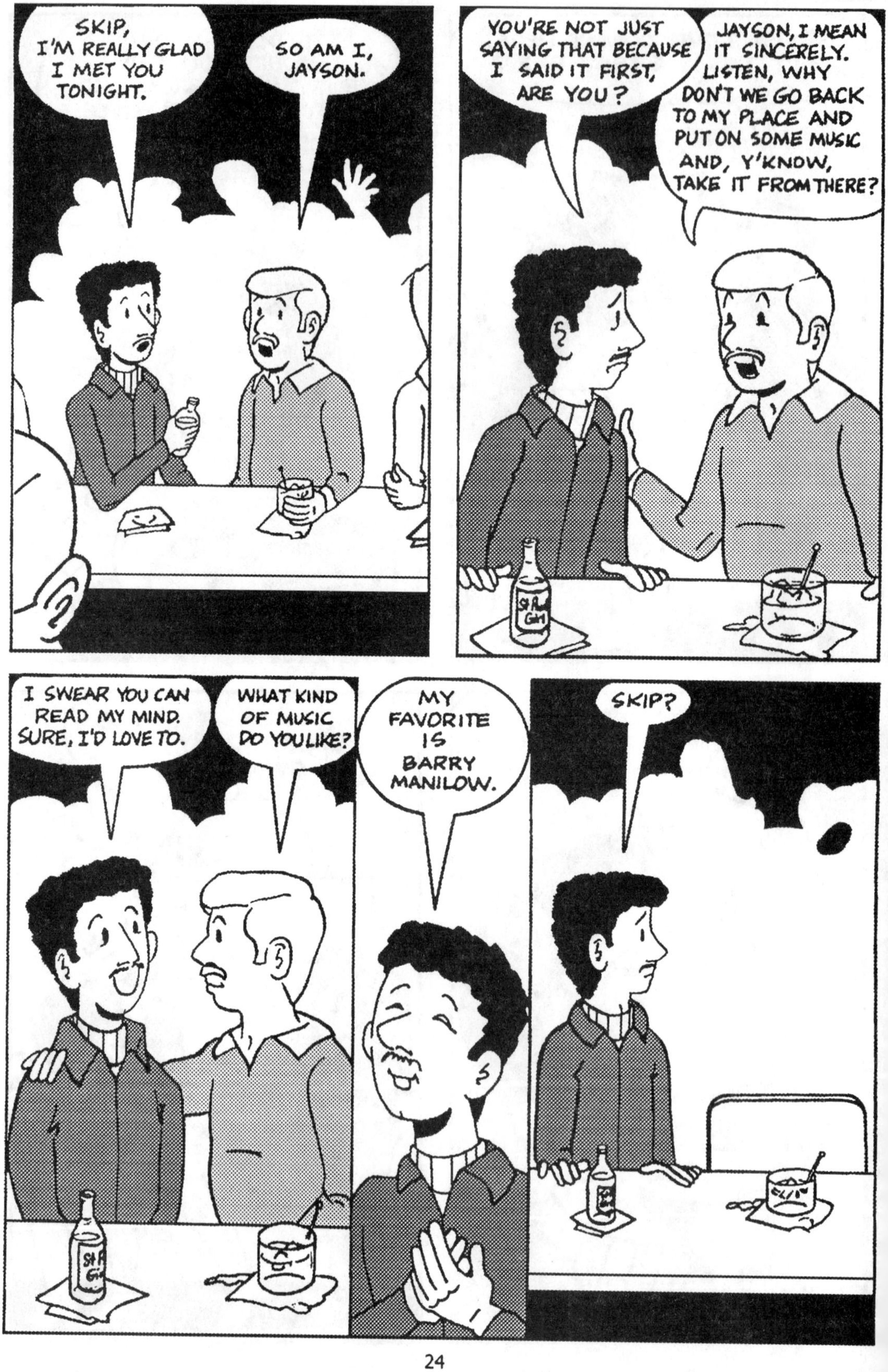
SKIP, I'M REALLY GLAD I MET YOU TONIGHT.
SO AM I, JAYSON.
YOU'RE NOT JUST SAYING THAT BECAUSE I SAID IT FIRST, ARE YOU?
JAYSON, I MEAN IT SINCERELY. LISTEN, WHY DON'T WE GO BACK TO MY PLACE AND PUT ON SOME MUSIC AND, Y'KNOW, TAKE IT FROM THERE?
I SWEAR YOU CAN READ MY MIND. SURE, I'D LOVE TO.
WHAT KIND OF MUSIC DO YOU LIKE?
MY FAVORITE IS BARRY MANILOW.
SKIP?

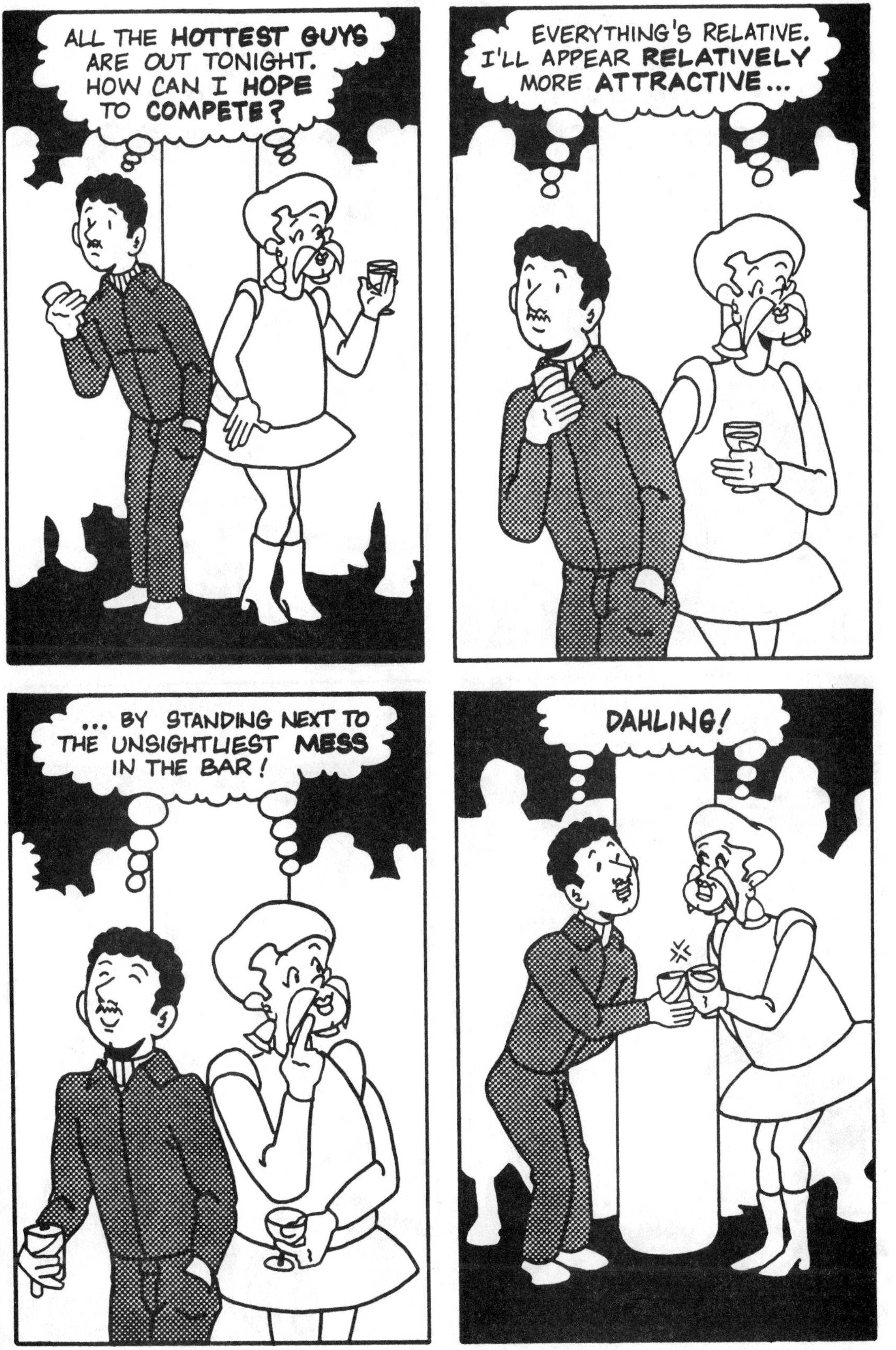
ALL THE HOTTEST GUYS ARE OUT TONIGHT. HOW CAN I HOPE TO COMPETE?
EVERYTHING'S RELATIVE. I'LL APPEAR RELATIVELY MORE ATTRACTIVE...
... BY STANDING NEXT TO THE UNSIGHTLIEST MESS IN THE BAR!
DAHLING!

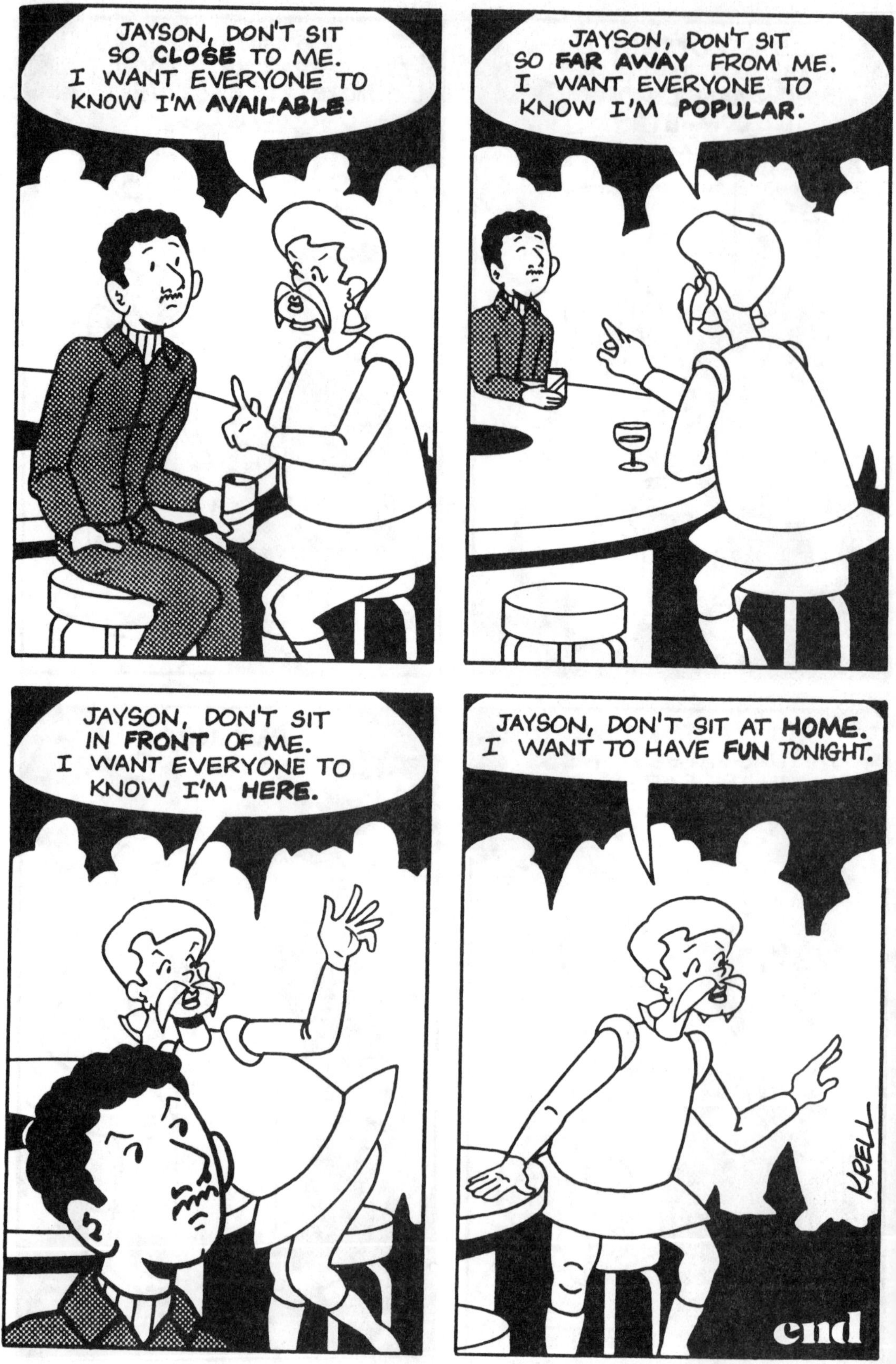
JAYSON, DON'T SIT SO CLOSE TO ME. I WANT EVERYONE TO KNOW I'M AVAILABLE.
JAYSON, DON'T SIT SO FAR AWAY FROM ME. I WANT EVERYONE TO KNOW I'M POPULAR.
JAYSON, DON'T SIT IN FRONT OF ME. I WANT EVERYONE TO KNOW I'M HERE.
JAYSON, DON'T SIT AT HOME. I WANT TO HAVE FUN TONIGHT.
KRELL
end

Jayson's™ video date

WHAT'RE YOU DOING, JAYSON?
WRITING A PERSONAL AD.
"WANTED: ONE CYNICAL OPTIMIST, IVY LEAGUE EDUCATED, WITH A SARDONIC WIT, AN ARTISTIC SOUL, AND A TRUCKDRIVER'S BODY."
THIS READS JUST LIKE A DESCRIPTION OF YOU — EXCEPT PHYSICALLY, OF COURSE.
So?
SO IF YOU LOOKED LIKE A TRUCKDRIVER, YOU COULD GO FUCK YOURSELF.
YOU CAN GO FUCK YOURSELF RIGHT NOW.
1

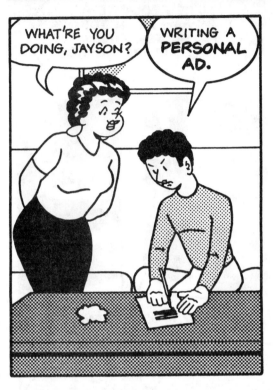

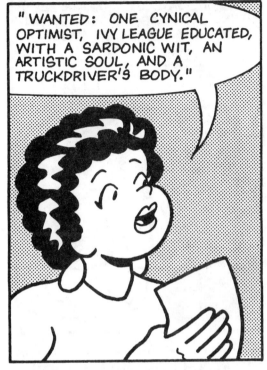

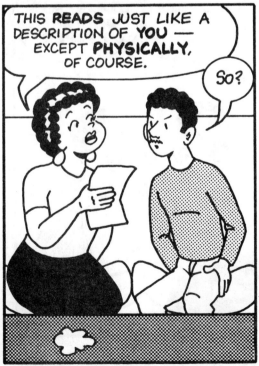

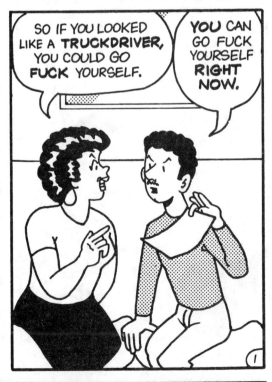

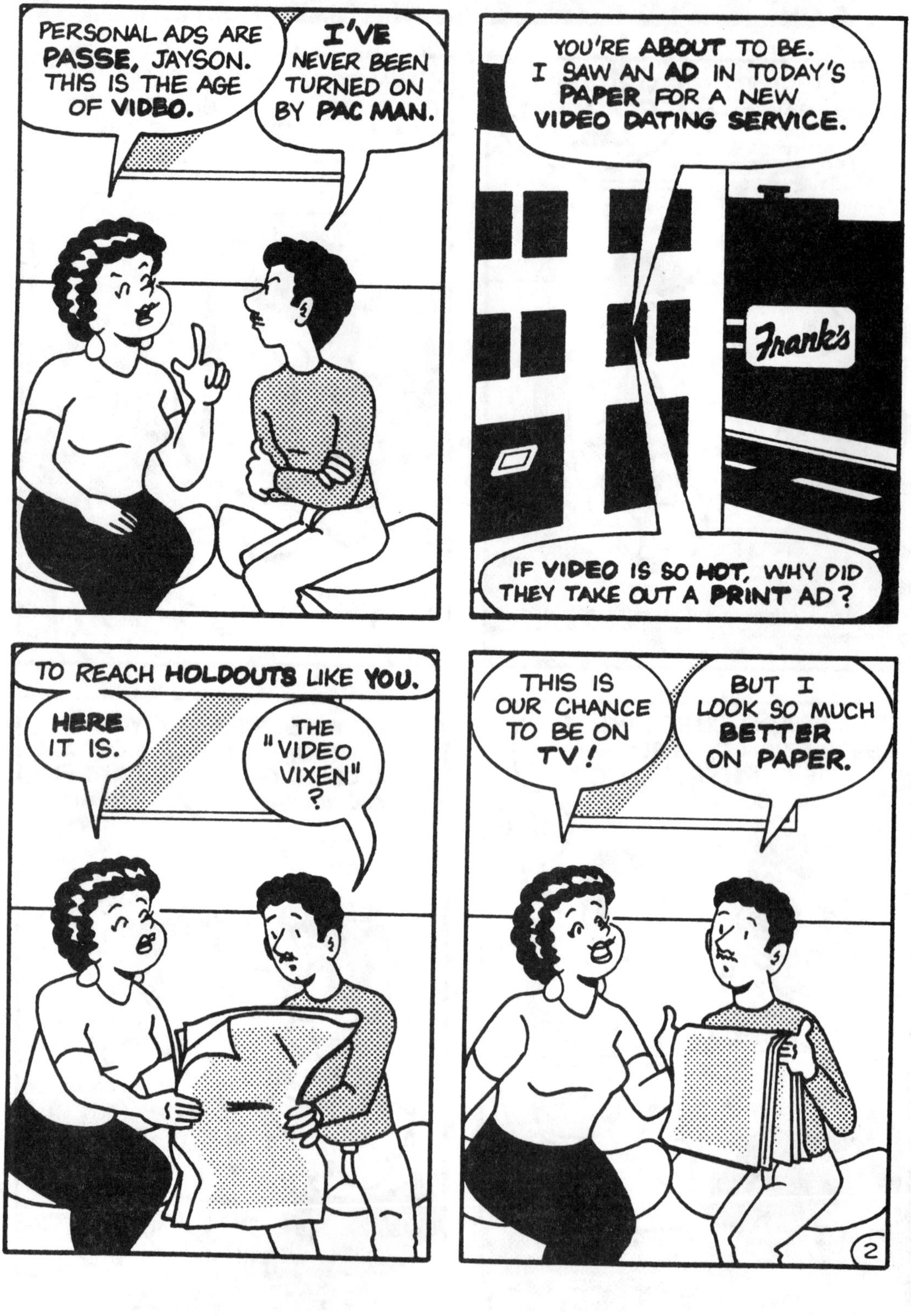
PERSONAL ADS ARE PASSE, JAYSON. THIS IS THE AGE OF VIDEO.
I'VE NEVER BEEN TURNED ON BY PAC MAN.
YOU'RE ABOUT TO BE. I SAW AN AD IN TODAY'S PAPER FOR A NEW VIDEO DATING SERVICE.
Frank's
IF VIDEO IS SO HOT, WHY DID THEY TAKE OUT A PRINT AD?
TO REACH HOLDOUTS LIKE YOU.
HERE IT IS.
THE "VIDEO VIXEN"?
THIS IS OUR CHANCE TO BE ON TV!
BUT I LOOK SO MUCH BETTER ON PAPER.
2

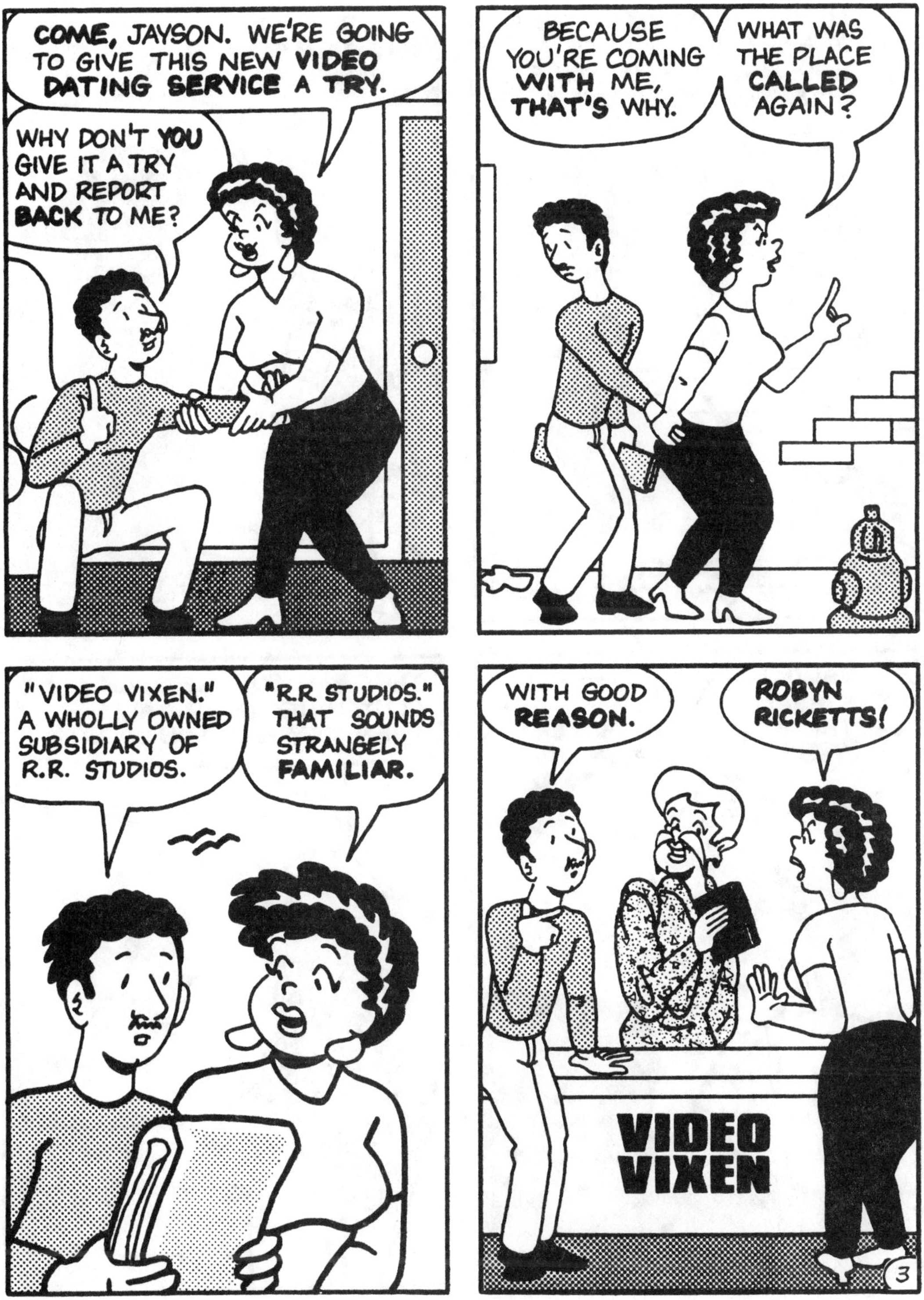

COME, JAYSON. WE'RE GOING TO GIVE THIS NEW VIDEO DATING SERVICE A TRY.
WHY DON'T YOU GIVE IT A TRY AND REPORT BACK TO ME?
BECAUSE YOU'RE COMING WITH ME, THAT'S WHY.
WHAT WAS THE PLACE CALLED AGAIN?
"VIDEO VIXEN." A WHOLLY OWNED SUBSIDIARY OF R.R. STUDIOS.
"R.R. STUDIOS." THAT SOUNDS STRANGELY FAMILIAR.
WITH GOOD REASON.
ROBYN RICKETTS!
VIDEO VIXEN
3

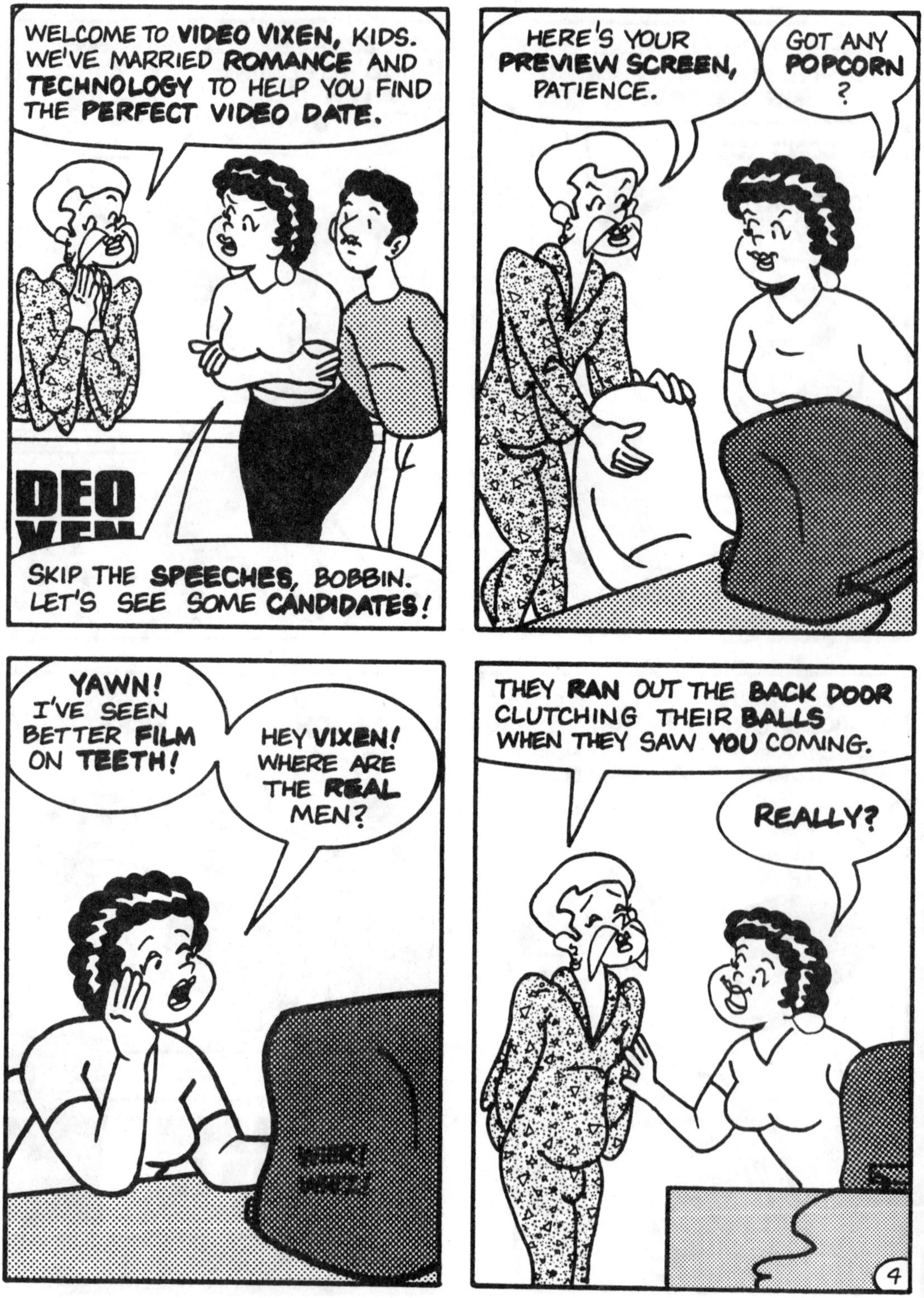
WELCOME TO VIDEO VIXEN, KIDS. WE'VE MARRIED ROMANCE AND TECHNOLOGY TO HELP YOU FIND THE PERFECT VIDEO DATE.
DEO
SKIP THE SPEECHES, BOBBIN. LET'S SEE SOME CANDIDATES!
HERE'S YOUR PREVIEW SCREEN, PATIENCE.
GOT ANY POPCORN ?
YAWN! I'VE SEEN BETTER FILM ON TEETH!
HEY VIXEN! WHERE ARE THE REAL MEN?
THEY RAN OUT THE BACK DOOR CLUTCHING THEIR BALLS WHEN THEY SAW YOU COMING.
REALLY?

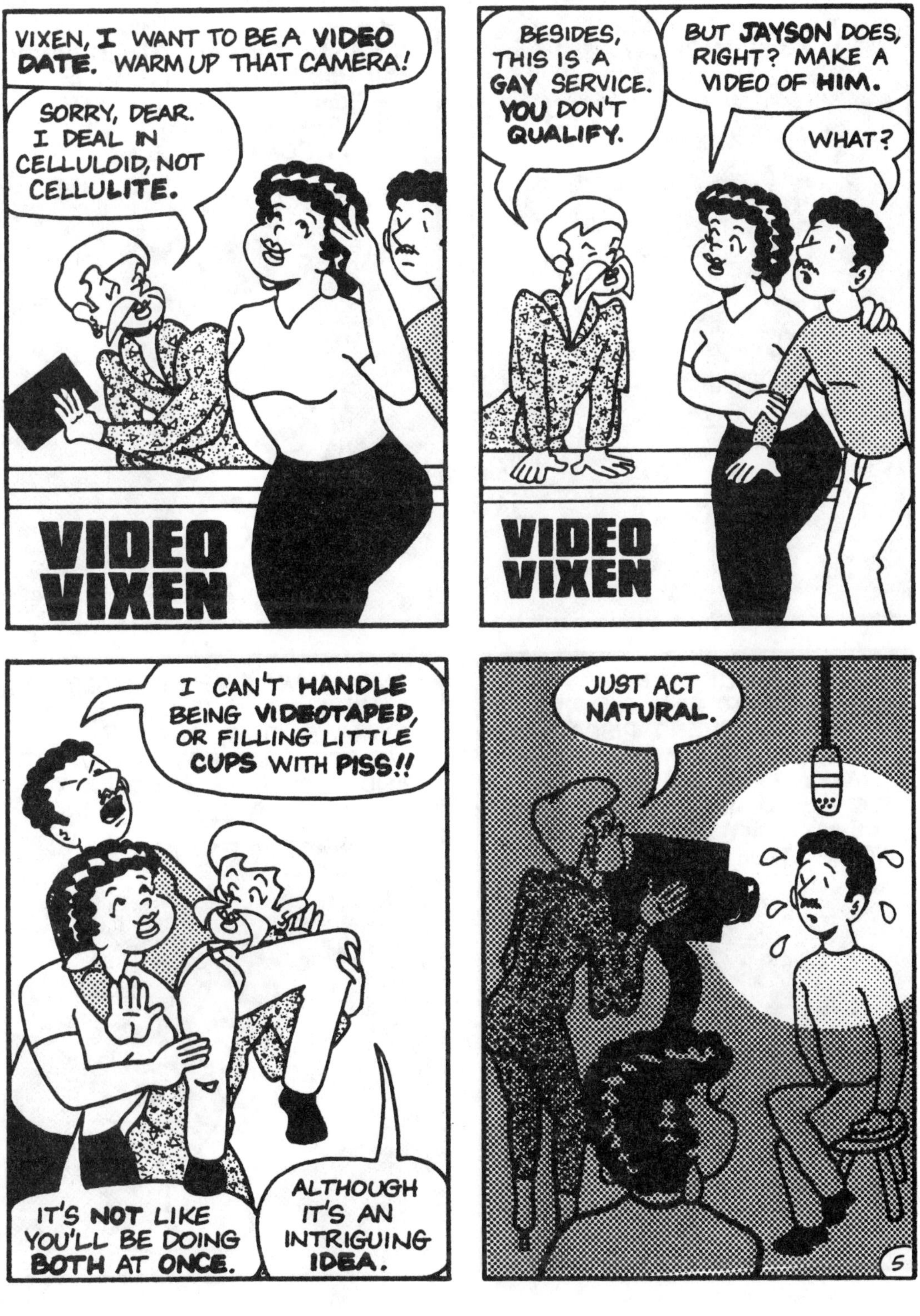
VIXEN, I WANT TO BE A VIDEO DATE. WARM UP THAT CAMERA!
SORRY, DEAR. I DEAL IN CELLULOID, NOT CELLULITE.
VIDEO VIXEN
BESIDES, THIS IS A GAY SERVICE. YOU DON'T QUALIFY.
BUT JAYSON DOES, RIGHT? MAKE A VIDEO OF HIM.
WHAT?
VIDEO VIXEN
I CAN'T HANDLE BEING VIDEOTAPED, OR FILLING LITTLE CUPS WITH PISS!!
IT'S NOT LIKE YOU'LL BE DOING BOTH AT ONCE.
ALTHOUGH IT'S AN INTRIGUING IDEA.
JUST ACT NATURAL.
5

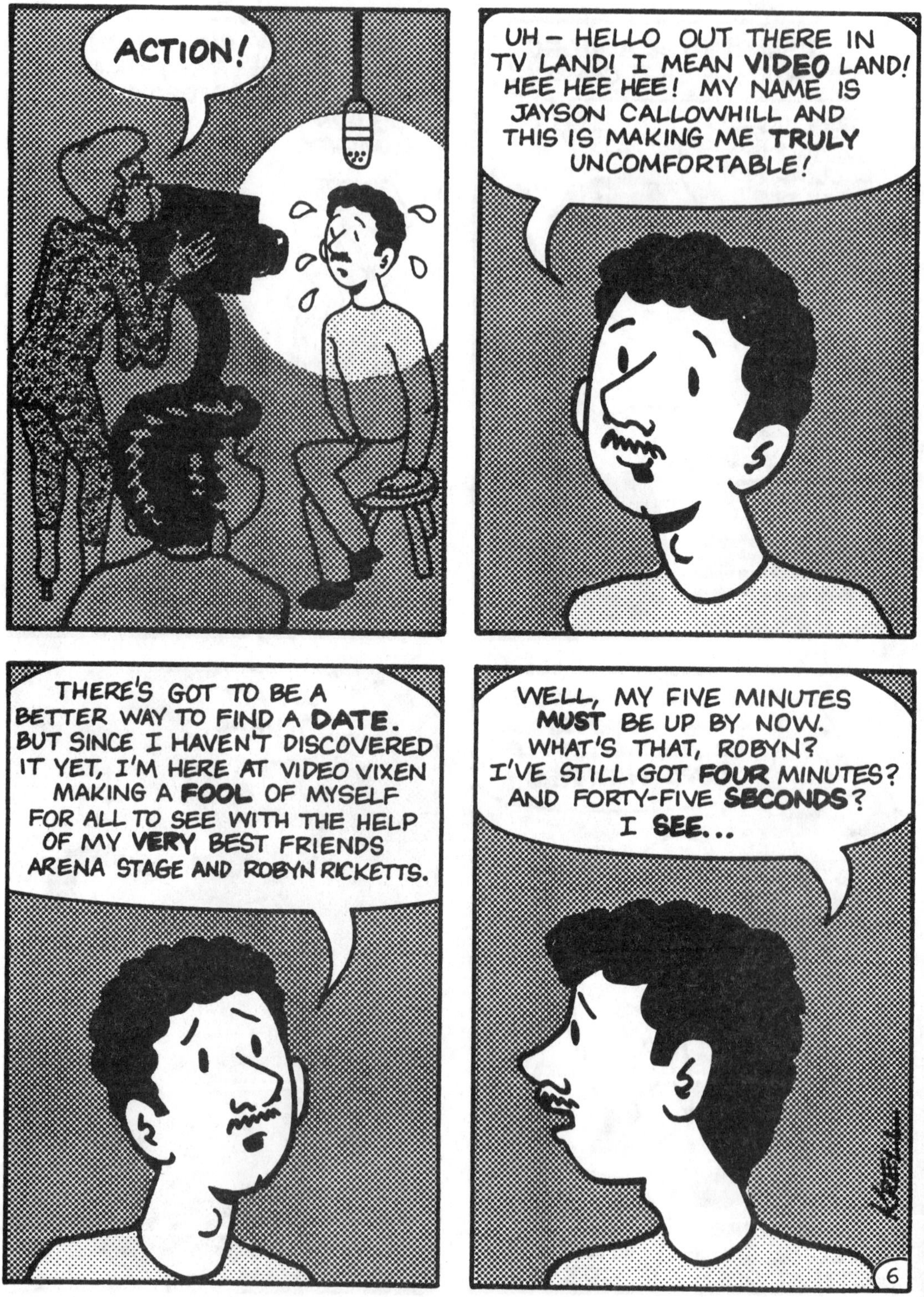
ACTION!
UH – HELLO OUT THERE IN TV LAND! I MEAN VIDEO LAND! HEE HEE HEE! MY NAME IS JAYSON CALLOWHILL AND THIS IS MAKING ME TRULY UNCOMFORTABLE!
THERE'S GOT TO BE A BETTER WAY TO FIND A DATE. BUT SINCE I HAVEN'T DISCOVERED IT YET, I'M HERE AT VIDEO VIXEN MAKING A FOOL OF MYSELF FOR ALL TO SEE WITH THE HELP OF MY VERY BEST FRIENDS ARENA STAGE AND ROBYN RICKETTS.
WELL, MY FIVE MINUTES MUST BE UP BY NOW. WHAT'S THAT, ROBYN? I'VE STILL GOT FOUR MINUTES? AND FORTY-FIVE SECONDS? I SEE...
6

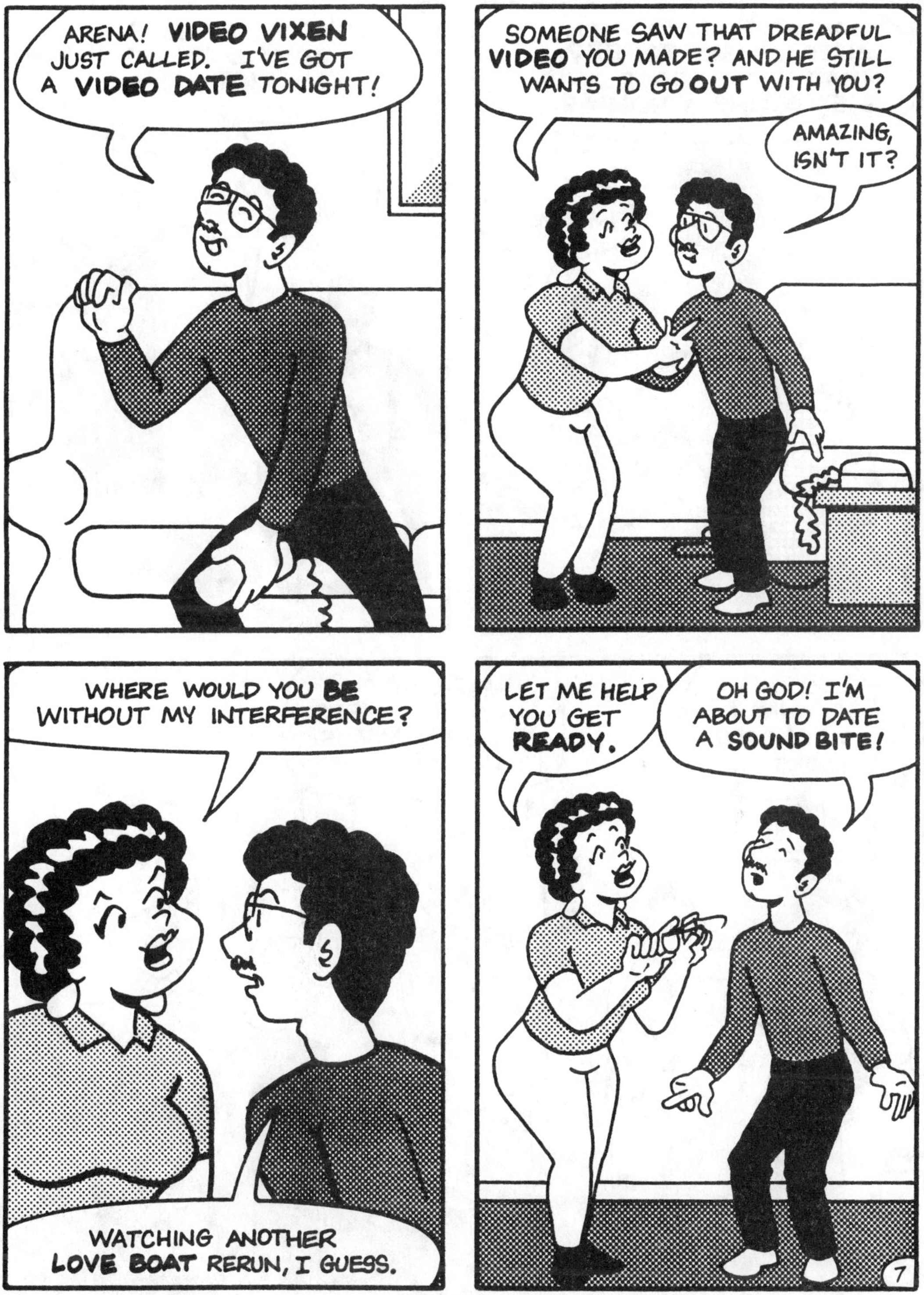
ARENA! VIDEO VIXEN JUST CALLED. I'VE GOT A VIDEO DATE TONIGHT!
SOMEONE SAW THAT DREADFUL VIDEO YOU MADE? AND HE STILL WANTS TO GO OUT WITH YOU?
AMAZING, ISN'T IT?
WHERE WOULD YOU BE WITHOUT MY INTERFERENCE?
WATCHING ANOTHER LOVE BOAT RERUN, I GUESS.
LET ME HELP YOU GET READY.
OH GOD! I'M ABOUT TO DATE A SOUND BITE!
7

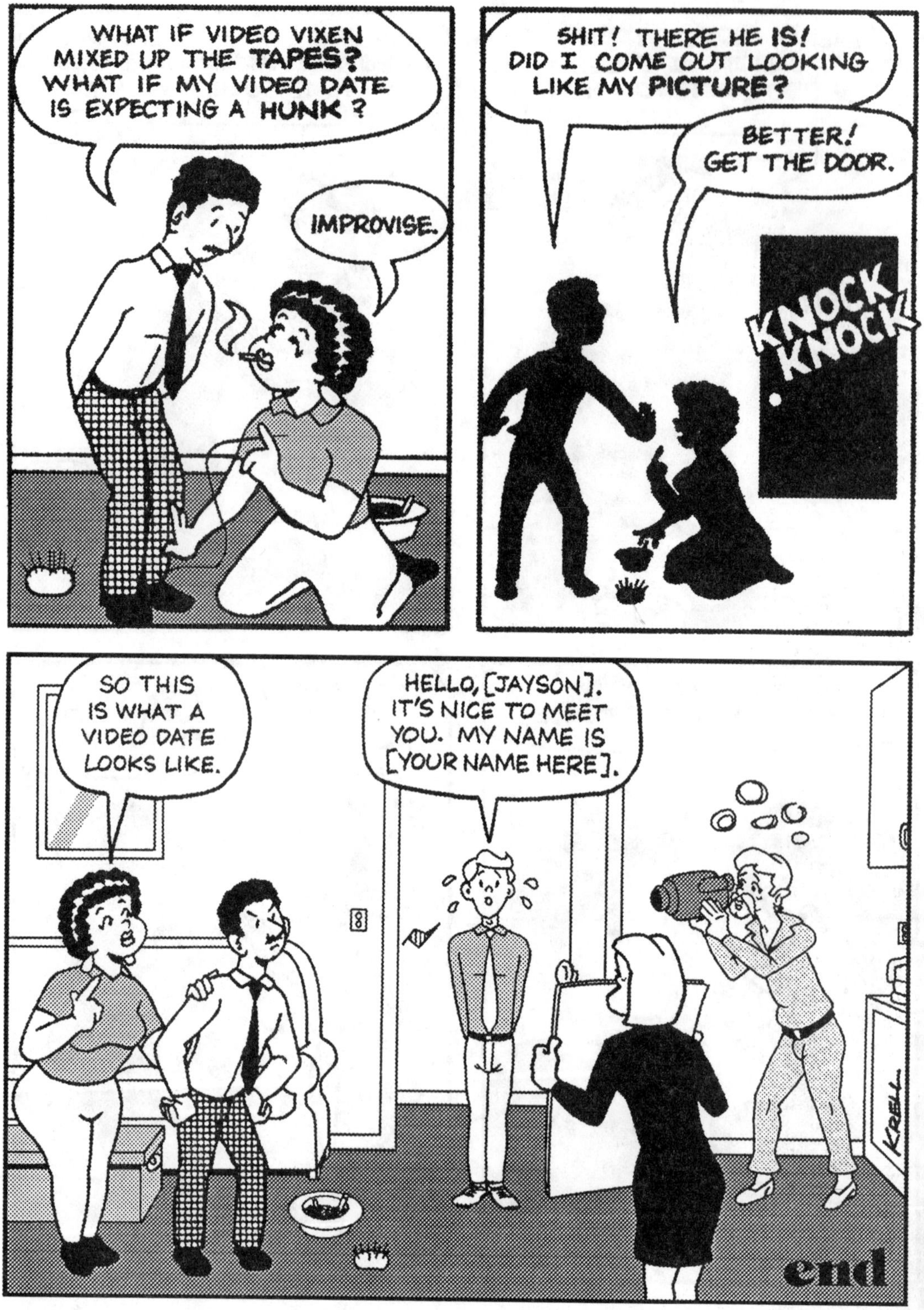
WHAT IF VIDEO VIXEN MIXED UP THE TAPES? WHAT IF MY VIDEO DATE IS EXPECTING A HUNK?
IMPROVISE.
SHIT! THERE HE IS! DID I COME OUT LOOKING LIKE MY PICTURE?
BETTER! GET THE DOOR.
KNOCK KNOCK
SO THIS IS WHAT A VIDEO DATE LOOKS LIKE.
HELLO, [JAYSON]. IT'S NICE TO MEET YOU. MY NAME IS [YOUR NAME HERE].
KRELL
end

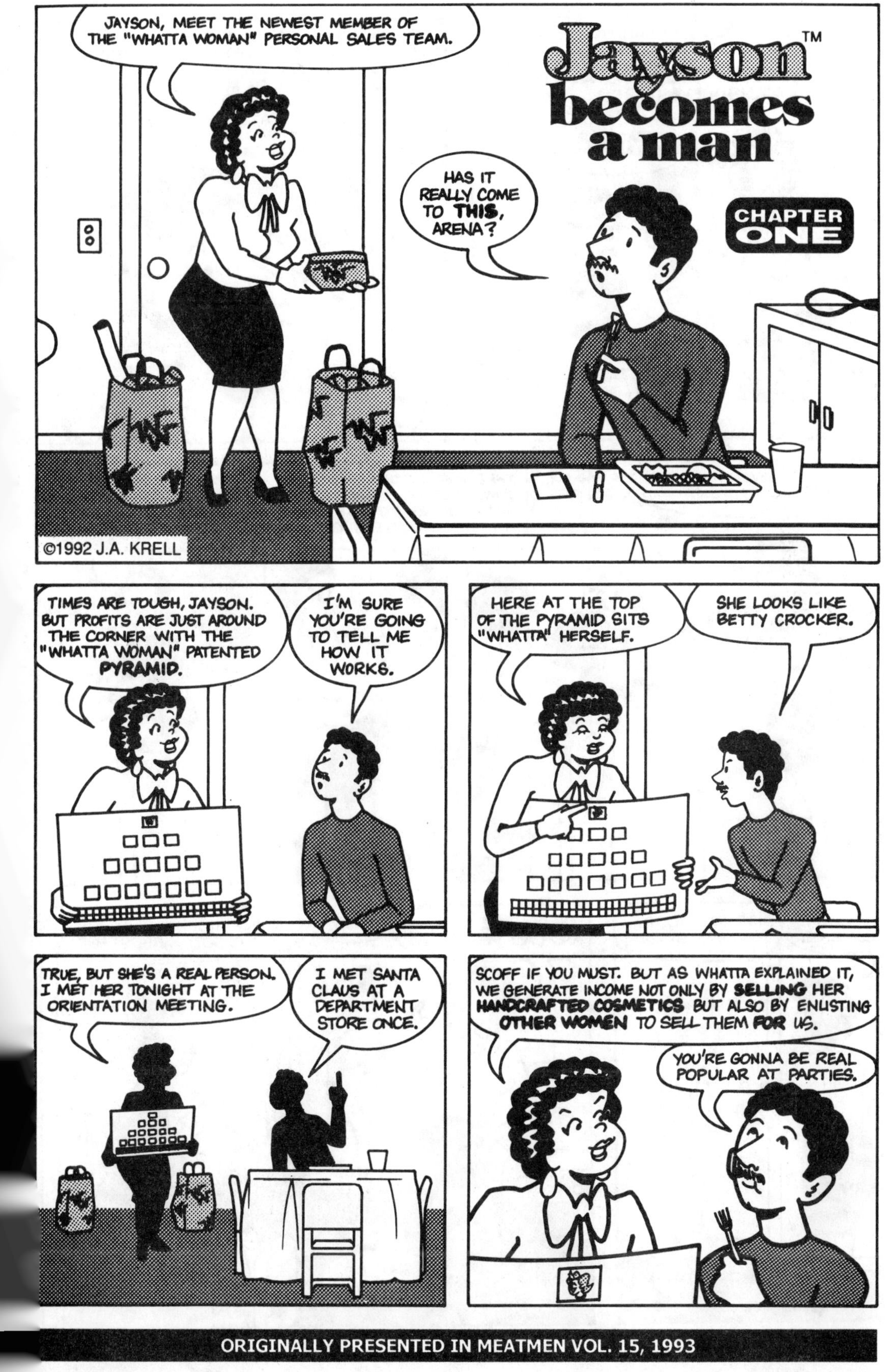

JAYSON, MEET THE NEWEST MEMBER OF THE "WHATTA WOMAN" PERSONAL SALES TEAM.
Jayson™ becomes a man
CHAPTER ONE
HAS IT REALLY COME TO THIS, ARENA?
©1992 J.A. KRELL
TIMES ARE TOUGH, JAYSON. BUT PROFITS ARE JUST AROUND THE CORNER WITH THE "WHATTA WOMAN" PATENTED PYRAMID.
I'M SURE YOU'RE GOING TO TELL ME HOW IT WORKS.
HERE AT THE TOP OF THE PYRAMID SITS "WHATTA" HERSELF.
SHE LOOKS LIKE BETTY CROCKER.
TRUE, BUT SHE'S A REAL PERSON. I MET HER TONIGHT AT THE ORIENTATION MEETING.
I MET SANTA CLAUS AT A DEPARTMENT STORE ONCE.
SCOFF IF YOU MUST. BUT AS WHATTA EXPLAINED IT, WE GENERATE INCOME NOT ONLY BY SELLING HER HANDCRAFTED COSMETICS BUT ALSO BY ENLISTING OTHER WOMEN TO SELL THEM FOR US.
YOU'RE GONNA BE REAL POPULAR AT PARTIES.

ORIGINALLY PRESENTED IN MEATMEN VOL. 15, 1993

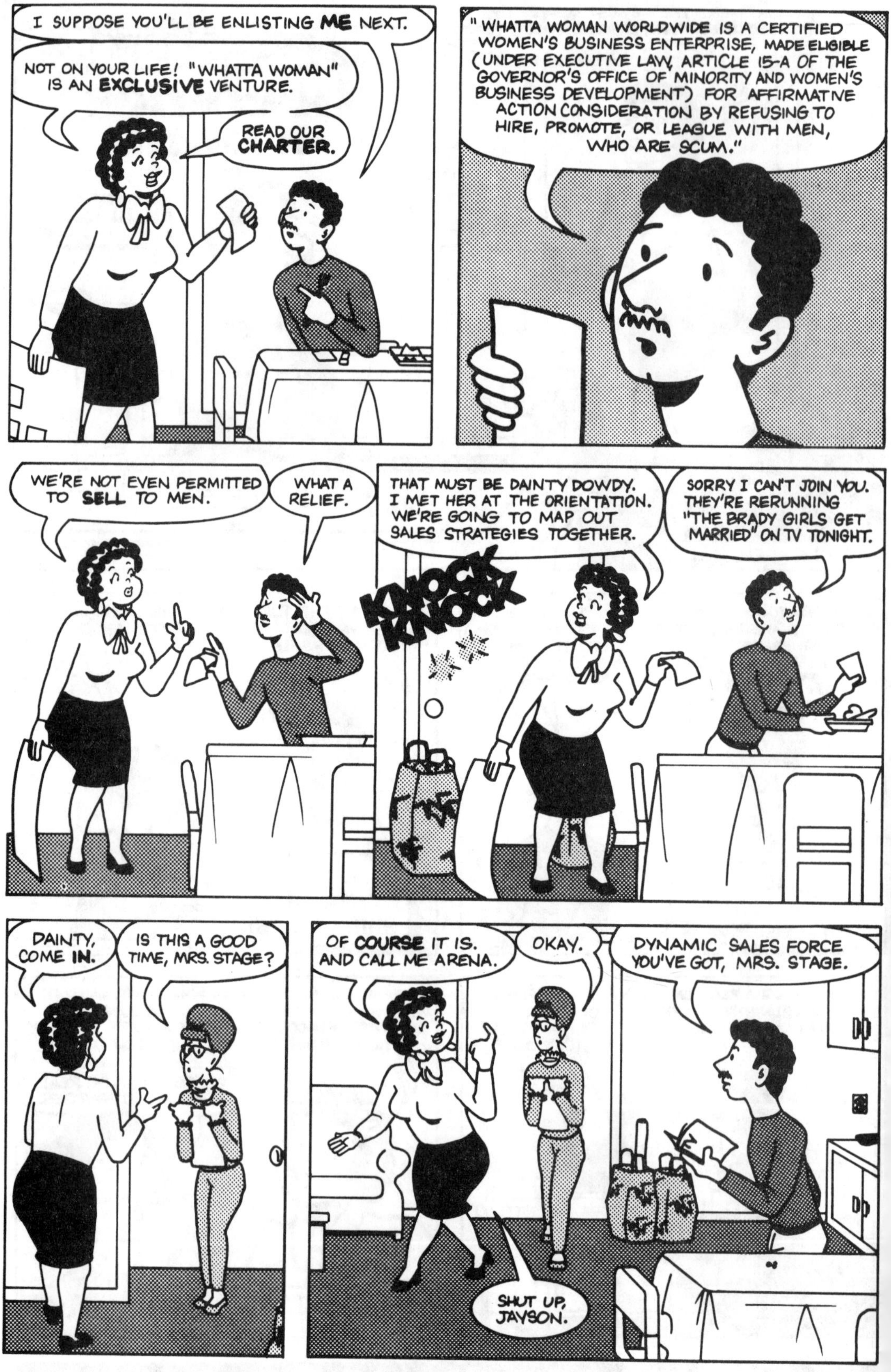
I SUPPOSE YOU'LL BE ENLISTING ME NEXT.
NOT ON YOUR LIFE! "WHATTA WOMAN" IS AN EXCLUSIVE VENTURE.
READ OUR CHARTER.
" WHATTA WOMAN WORLDWIDE IS A CERTIFIED WOMEN'S BUSINESS ENTERPRISE, MADE ELIGIBLE (UNDER EXECUTIVE LAW, ARTICLE 15-A OF THE GOVERNOR'S OFFICE OF MINORITY AND WOMEN'S BUSINESS DEVELOPMENT) FOR AFFIRMATIVE ACTION CONSIDERATION BY REFUSING TO HIRE, PROMOTE, OR LEAGUE WITH MEN, WHO ARE SCUM."
WE'RE NOT EVEN PERMITTED TO SELL TO MEN.
WHAT A RELIEF.
THAT MUST BE DAINTY DOWDY. I MET HER AT THE ORIENTATION. WE'RE GOING TO MAP OUT SALES STRATEGIES TOGETHER.
KNOCK KNOCK
SORRY I CAN'T JOIN YOU. THEY'RE RERUNNING "THE BRADY GIRLS GET MARRIED" ON TV TONIGHT.
DAINTY, COME IN.
IS THIS A GOOD TIME, MRS. STAGE?
OF COURSE IT IS. AND CALL ME ARENA.
OKAY.
DYNAMIC SALES FORCE YOU'VE GOT, MRS. STAGE.
SHUT UP, JAYSON.

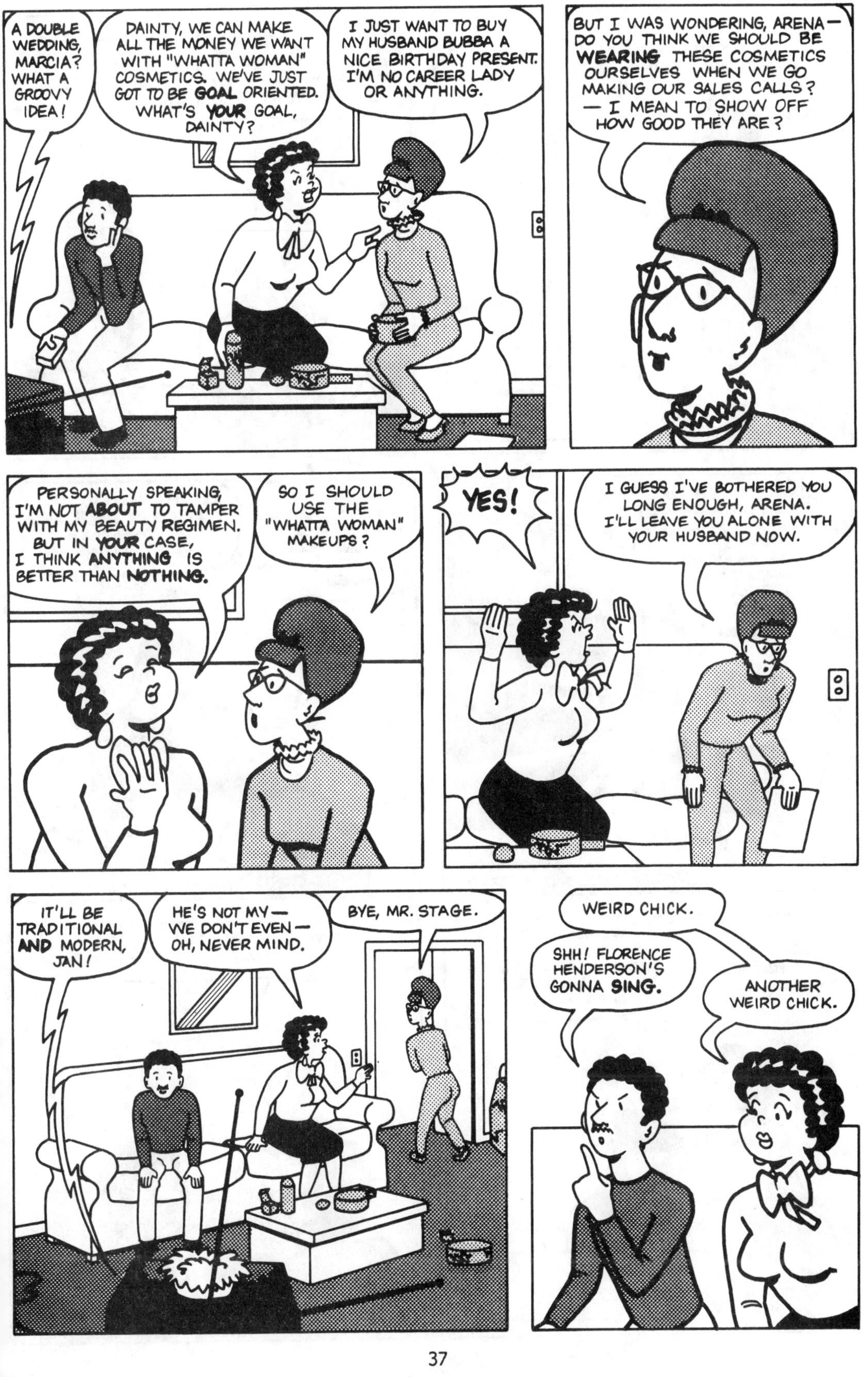
A DOUBLE WEDDING, MARCIA? WHAT A GROOVY IDEA!
DAINTY, WE CAN MAKE ALL THE MONEY WE WANT WITH "WHATTA WOMAN" COSMETICS. WE'VE JUST GOT TO BE GOAL ORIENTED. WHAT'S YOUR GOAL, DAINTY?
I JUST WANT TO BUY MY HUSBAND BUBBA A NICE BIRTHDAY PRESENT. I'M NO CAREER LADY OR ANYTHING.
BUT I WAS WONDERING, ARENA— DO YOU THINK WE SHOULD BE WEARING THESE COSMETICS OURSELVES WHEN WE GO MAKING OUR SALES CALLS? — I MEAN TO SHOW OFF HOW GOOD THEY ARE?
PERSONALLY SPEAKING, I'M NOT ABOUT TO TAMPER WITH MY BEAUTY REGIMEN. BUT IN YOUR CASE, I THINK ANYTHING IS BETTER THAN NOTHING.
SO I SHOULD USE THE "WHATTA WOMAN" MAKEUPS?
YES!
I GUESS I'VE BOTHERED YOU LONG ENOUGH, ARENA. I'LL LEAVE YOU ALONE WITH YOUR HUSBAND NOW.
IT'LL BE TRADITIONAL AND MODERN, JAN!
HE'S NOT MY— WE DON'T EVEN— OH, NEVER MIND.
BYE, MR. STAGE.
WEIRD CHICK.
SHH! FLORENCE HENDERSON'S GONNA SING.
ANOTHER WEIRD CHICK.

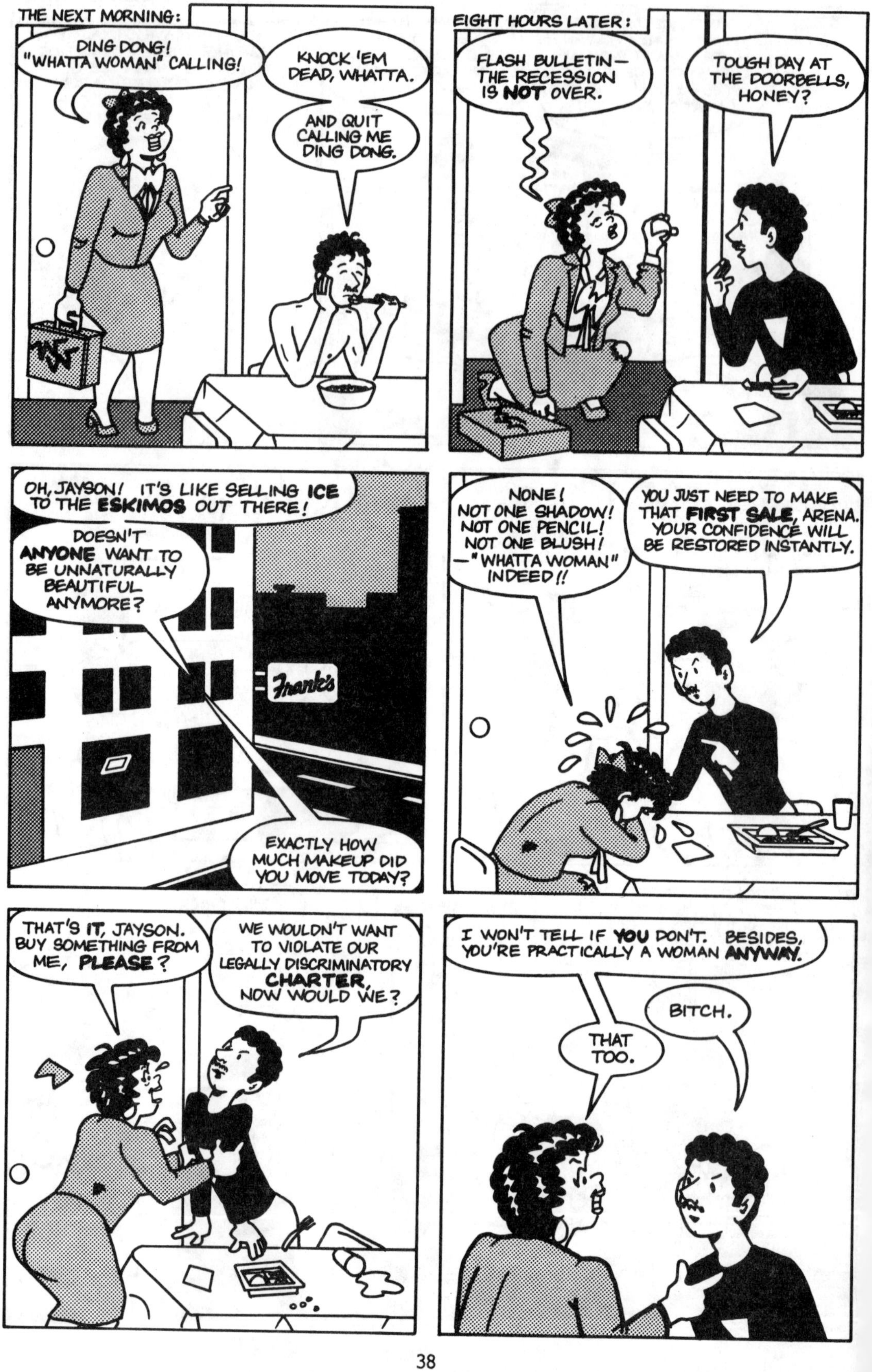
THE NEXT MORNING:
DING DONG! "WHATTA WOMAN" CALLING!
KNOCK 'EM DEAD, WHATTA.
AND QUIT CALLING ME DING DONG.
EIGHT HOURS LATER:
FLASH BULLETIN— THE RECESSION IS NOT OVER.
TOUGH DAY AT THE DOORBELLS, HONEY?
OH, JAYSON! IT'S LIKE SELLING ICE TO THE ESKIMOS OUT THERE!
DOESN'T ANYONE WANT TO BE UNNATURALLY BEAUTIFUL ANYMORE?
Frank's
EXACTLY HOW MUCH MAKEUP DID YOU MOVE TODAY?
NONE! NOT ONE SHADOW! NOT ONE PENCIL! NOT ONE BLUSH! —"WHATTA WOMAN" INDEED!!
YOU JUST NEED TO MAKE THAT FIRST SALE, ARENA. YOUR CONFIDENCE WILL BE RESTORED INSTANTLY.
THAT'S IT, JAYSON. BUY SOMETHING FROM ME, PLEASE?
WE WOULDN'T WANT TO VIOLATE OUR LEGALLY DISCRIMINATORY CHARTER, NOW WOULD WE?
I WON'T TELL IF YOU DON'T. BESIDES, YOU'RE PRACTICALLY A WOMAN ANYWAY.
BITCH.
THAT TOO.

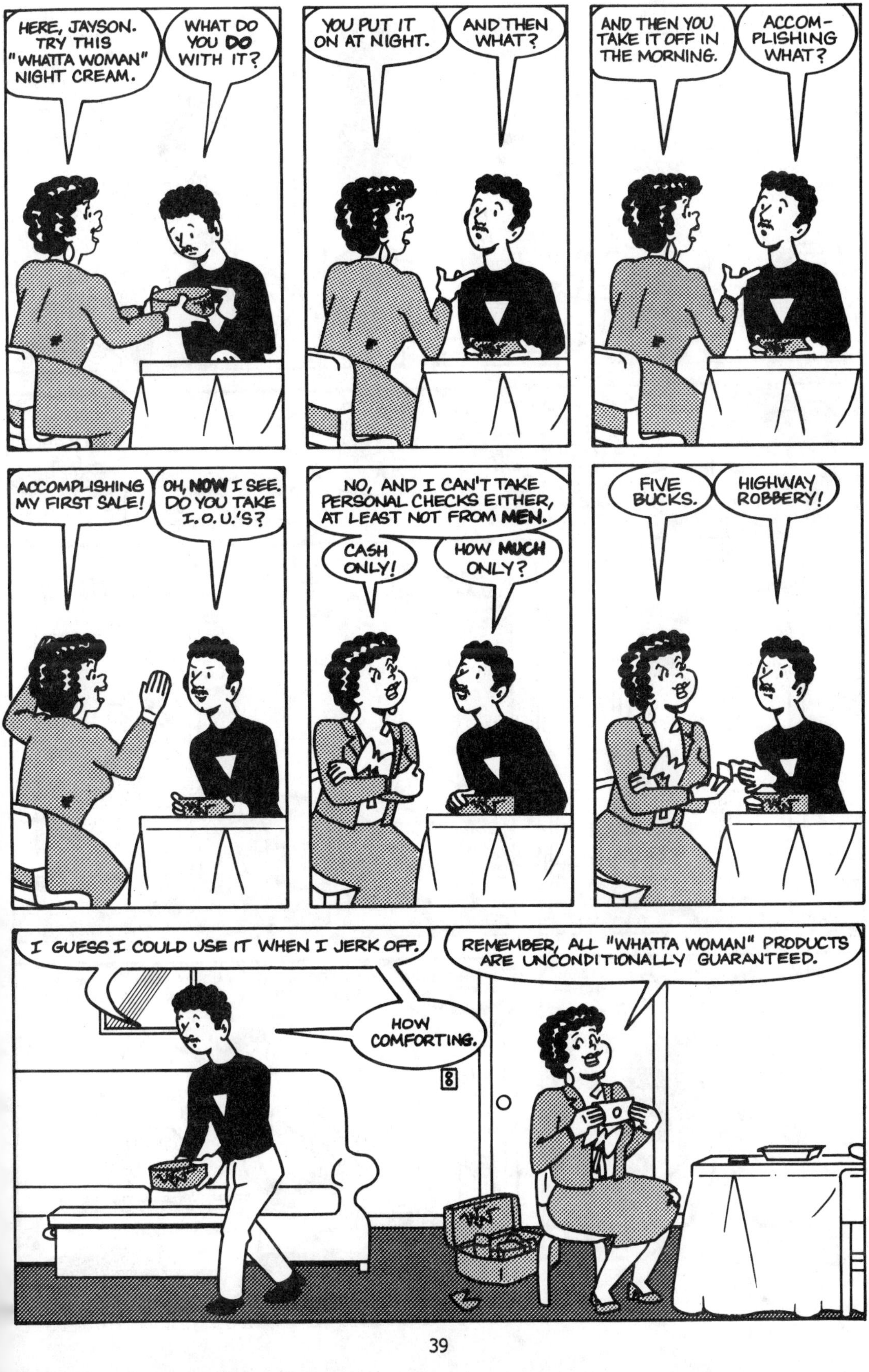
HERE, JAYSON. TRY THIS "WHATTA WOMAN" NIGHT CREAM.
WHAT DO YOU DO WITH IT?
YOU PUT IT ON AT NIGHT.
AND THEN WHAT?
AND THEN YOU TAKE IT OFF IN THE MORNING.
ACCOM-PLISHING WHAT?
ACCOMPLISHING MY FIRST SALE!
OH, NOW I SEE. DO YOU TAKE I.O.U.'S?
NO, AND I CAN'T TAKE PERSONAL CHECKS EITHER, AT LEAST NOT FROM MEN.
CASH ONLY!
HOW MUCH ONLY?
FIVE BUCKS.
HIGHWAY ROBBERY!
I GUESS I COULD USE IT WHEN I JERK OFF.
REMEMBER, ALL "WHATTA WOMAN" PRODUCTS ARE UNCONDITIONALLY GUARANTEED.
HOW COMFORTING.

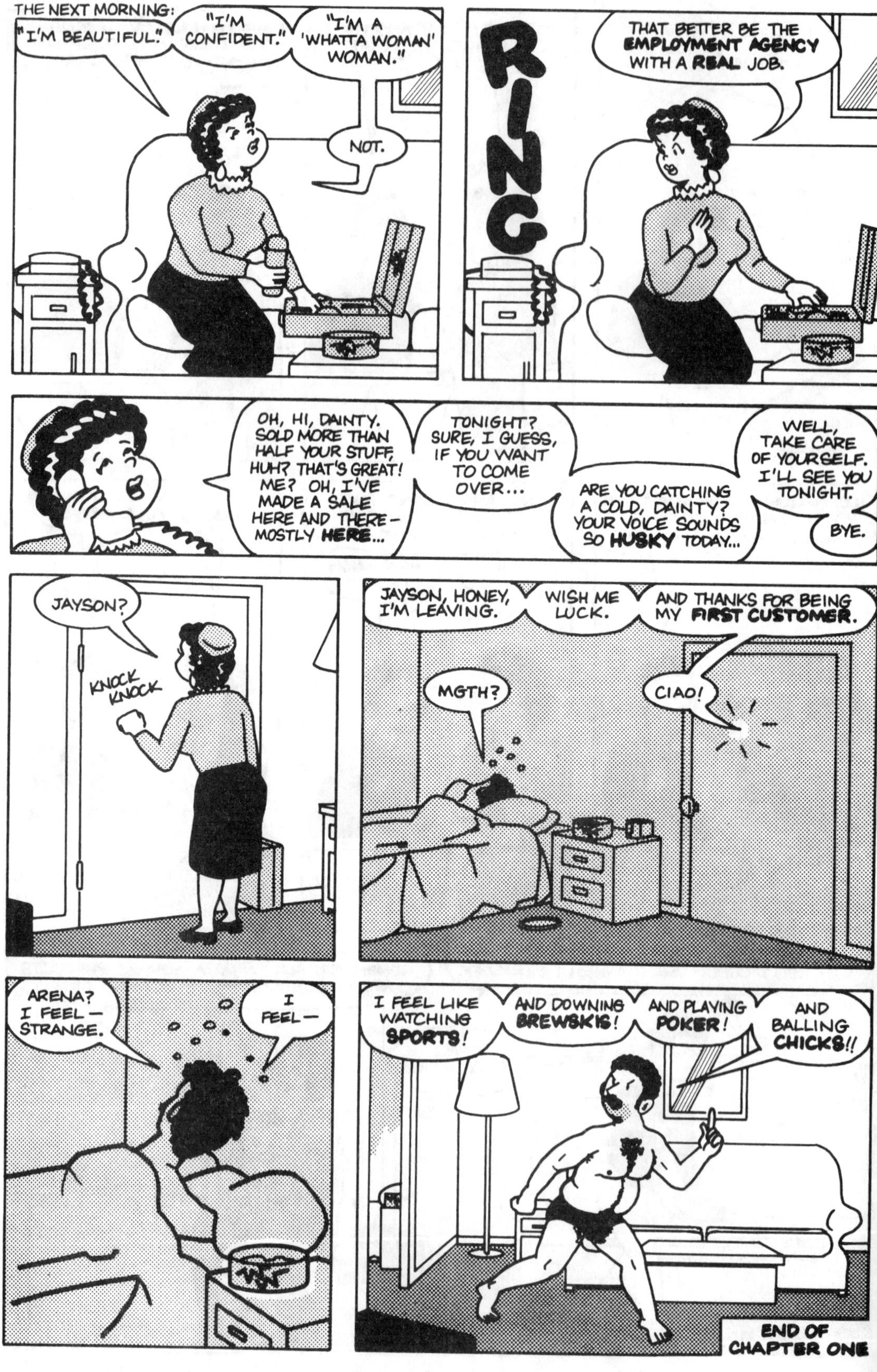
THE NEXT MORNING:
"I'M BEAUTIFUL."
"I'M CONFIDENT."
"I'M A 'WHATTA WOMAN' WOMAN."
NOT.
RING
THAT BETTER BE THE EMPLOYMENT AGENCY WITH A REAL JOB.
OH, HI, DAINTY. SOLD MORE THAN HALF YOUR STUFF, HUH? THAT'S GREAT! ME? OH, I'VE MADE A SALE HERE AND THERE— MOSTLY HERE...
TONIGHT? SURE, I GUESS, IF YOU WANT TO COME OVER...
ARE YOU CATCHING A COLD, DAINTY? YOUR VOICE SOUNDS SO HUSKY TODAY...
WELL, TAKE CARE OF YOURSELF. I'LL SEE YOU TONIGHT.
BYE.
JAYSON?
KNOCK KNOCK
JAYSON, HONEY, I'M LEAVING.
WISH ME LUCK.
AND THANKS FOR BEING MY FIRST CUSTOMER.
MGTH?
CIAO!
ARENA? I FEEL— STRANGE.
I FEEL—
I FEEL LIKE WATCHING SPORTS!
AND DOWNING BREWSKIS!
AND PLAYING POKER!
AND BALLING CHICKS!!
END OF CHAPTER ONE

Jayson™ becomes a man CHAPTER TWO

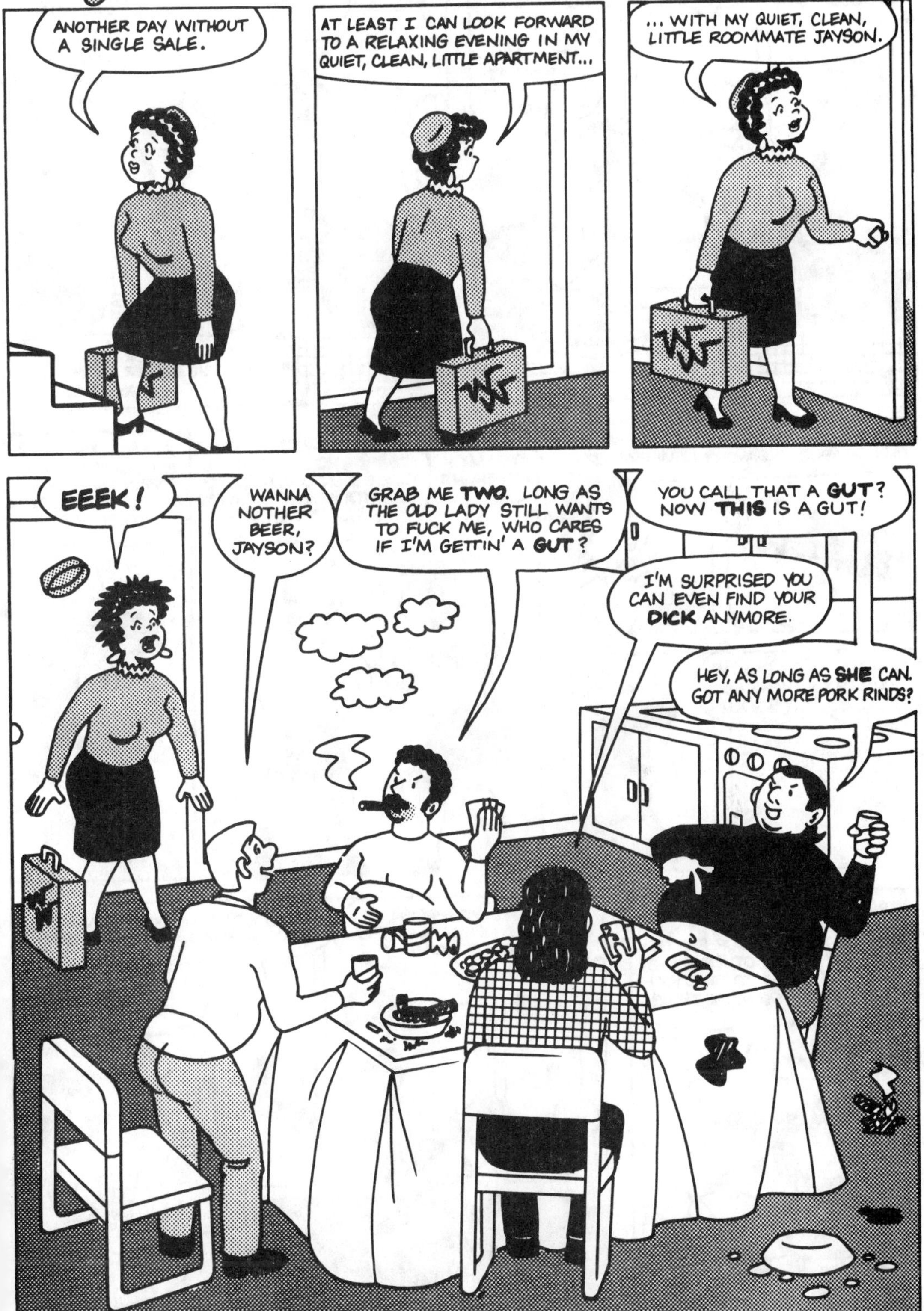

ANOTHER DAY WITHOUT A SINGLE SALE.
AT LEAST I CAN LOOK FORWARD TO A RELAXING EVENING IN MY QUIET, CLEAN, LITTLE APARTMENT...
... WITH MY QUIET, CLEAN, LITTLE ROOMMATE JAYSON.
EEEK!
WANNA NOTHER BEER, JAYSON?
GRAB ME TWO. LONG AS THE OLD LADY STILL WANTS TO FUCK ME, WHO CARES IF I'M GETTIN' A GUT?
YOU CALL THAT A GUT? NOW THIS IS A GUT!
I'M SURPRISED YOU CAN EVEN FIND YOUR DICK ANYMORE.
HEY, AS LONG AS SHE CAN. GOT ANY MORE PORK RINDS?

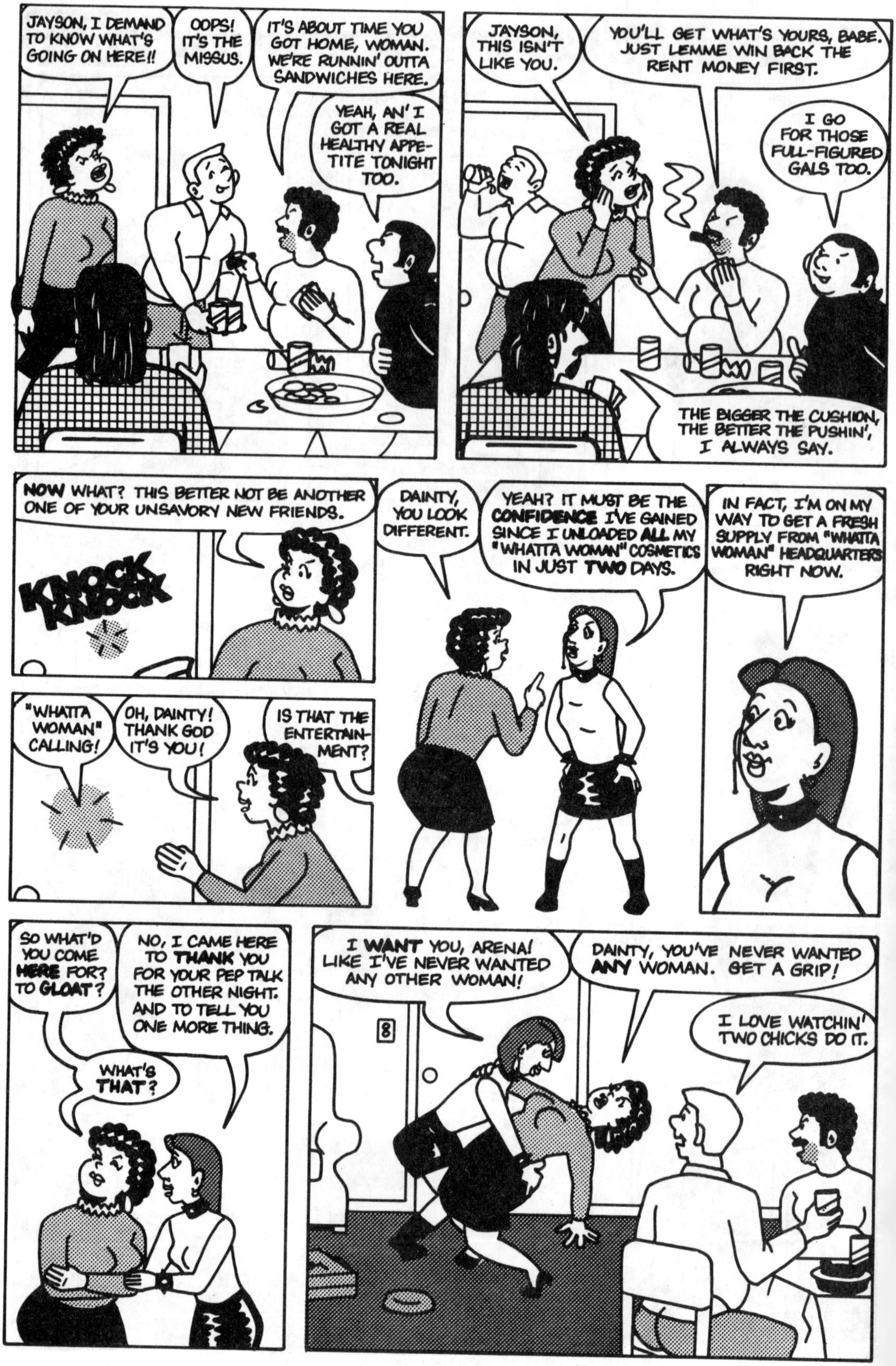
JAYSON, I DEMAND TO KNOW WHAT'S GOING ON HERE!!
OOPS! IT'S THE MISSUS.
IT'S ABOUT TIME YOU GOT HOME, WOMAN. WE'RE RUNNIN' OUTTA SANDWICHES HERE.
YEAH, AN' I GOT A REAL HEALTHY APPE-TITE TONIGHT TOO.
JAYSON, THIS ISN'T LIKE YOU.
YOU'LL GET WHAT'S YOURS, BABE. JUST LEMME WIN BACK THE RENT MONEY FIRST.
I GO FOR THOSE FULL-FIGURED GALS TOO.
THE BIGGER THE CUSHION, THE BETTER THE PUSHIN', I ALWAYS SAY.
NOW WHAT? THIS BETTER NOT BE ANOTHER ONE OF YOUR UNSAVORY NEW FRIENDS.
KNOCK KNOCK
"WHATTA WOMAN" CALLING!
OH, DAINTY! THANK GOD IT'S YOU!
IS THAT THE ENTERTAIN-MENT?
DAINTY, YOU LOOK DIFFERENT.
YEAH? IT MUST BE THE CONFIDENCE I'VE GAINED SINCE I UNLOADED ALL MY "WHATTA WOMAN" COSMETICS IN JUST TWO DAYS.
IN FACT, I'M ON MY WAY TO GET A FRESH SUPPLY FROM "WHATTA WOMAN" HEADQUARTERS RIGHT NOW.
SO WHAT'D YOU COME HERE FOR? TO GLOAT?
NO, I CAME HERE TO THANK YOU FOR YOUR PEP TALK THE OTHER NIGHT. AND TO TELL YOU ONE MORE THING.
WHAT'S THAT?
I WANT YOU, ARENA! LIKE I'VE NEVER WANTED ANY OTHER WOMAN!
DAINTY, YOU'VE NEVER WANTED ANY WOMAN. GET A GRIP!
I LOVE WATCHIN' TWO CHICKS DO IT.
8

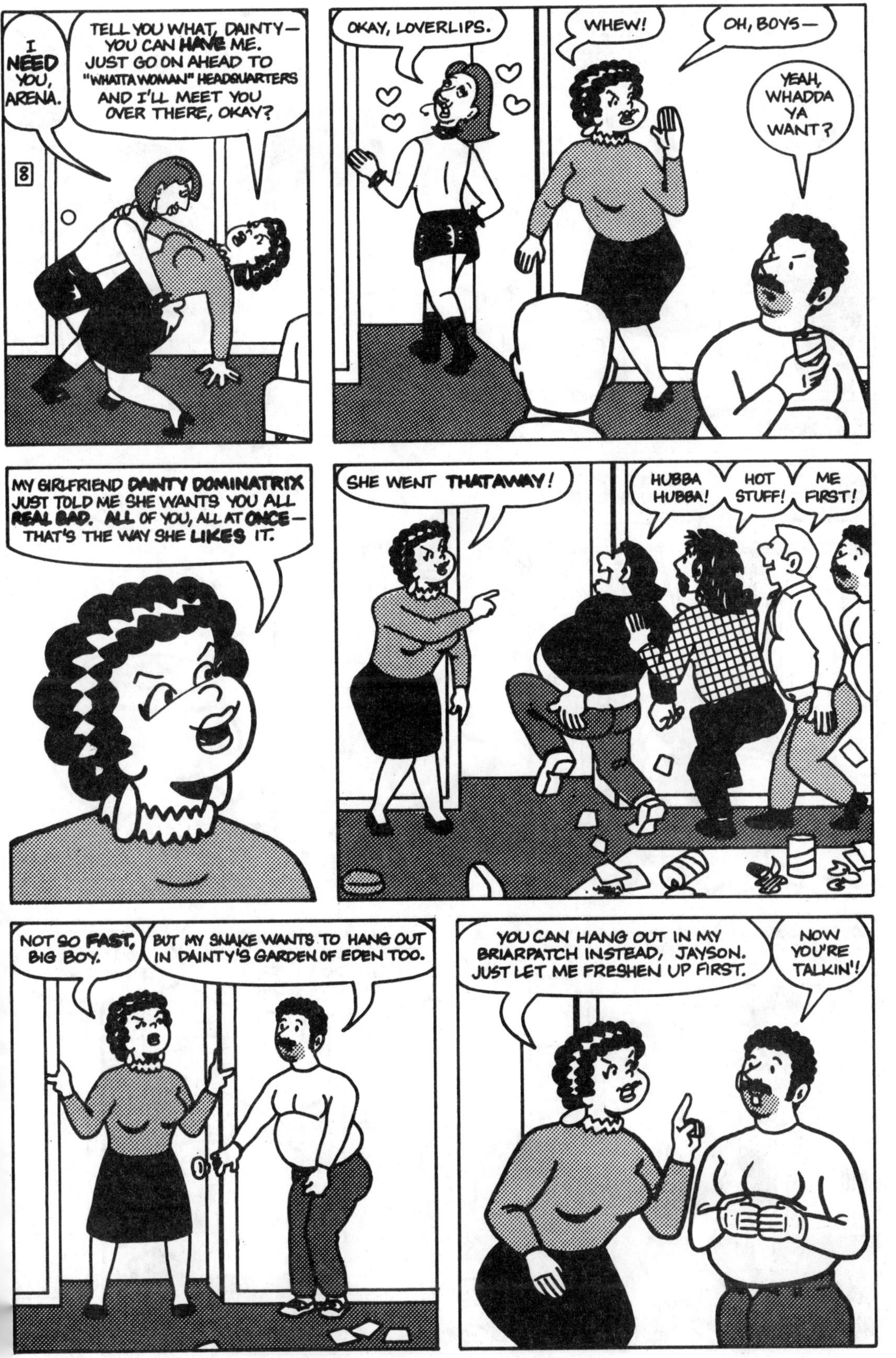
I NEED YOU, ARENA.
TELL YOU WHAT, DAINTY— YOU CAN HAVE ME. JUST GO ON AHEAD TO "WHATTA WOMAN" HEADQUARTERS AND I'LL MEET YOU OVER THERE, OKAY?
8
OKAY, LOVERLIPS.
WHEW!
OH, BOYS—
YEAH, WHADDA YA WANT?
MY GIRLFRIEND DAINTY DOMINATRIX JUST TOLD ME SHE WANTS YOU ALL REAL BAD. ALL OF YOU, ALL AT ONCE— THAT'S THE WAY SHE LIKES IT.
SHE WENT THATAWAY!
HUBBA HUBBA!
HOT STUFF!
ME FIRST!
NOT SO FAST, BIG BOY.
BUT MY SNAKE WANTS TO HANG OUT IN DAINTY'S GARDEN OF EDEN TOO.
YOU CAN HANG OUT IN MY BRIARPATCH INSTEAD, JAYSON. JUST LET ME FRESHEN UP FIRST.
NOW YOU'RE TALKIN'!

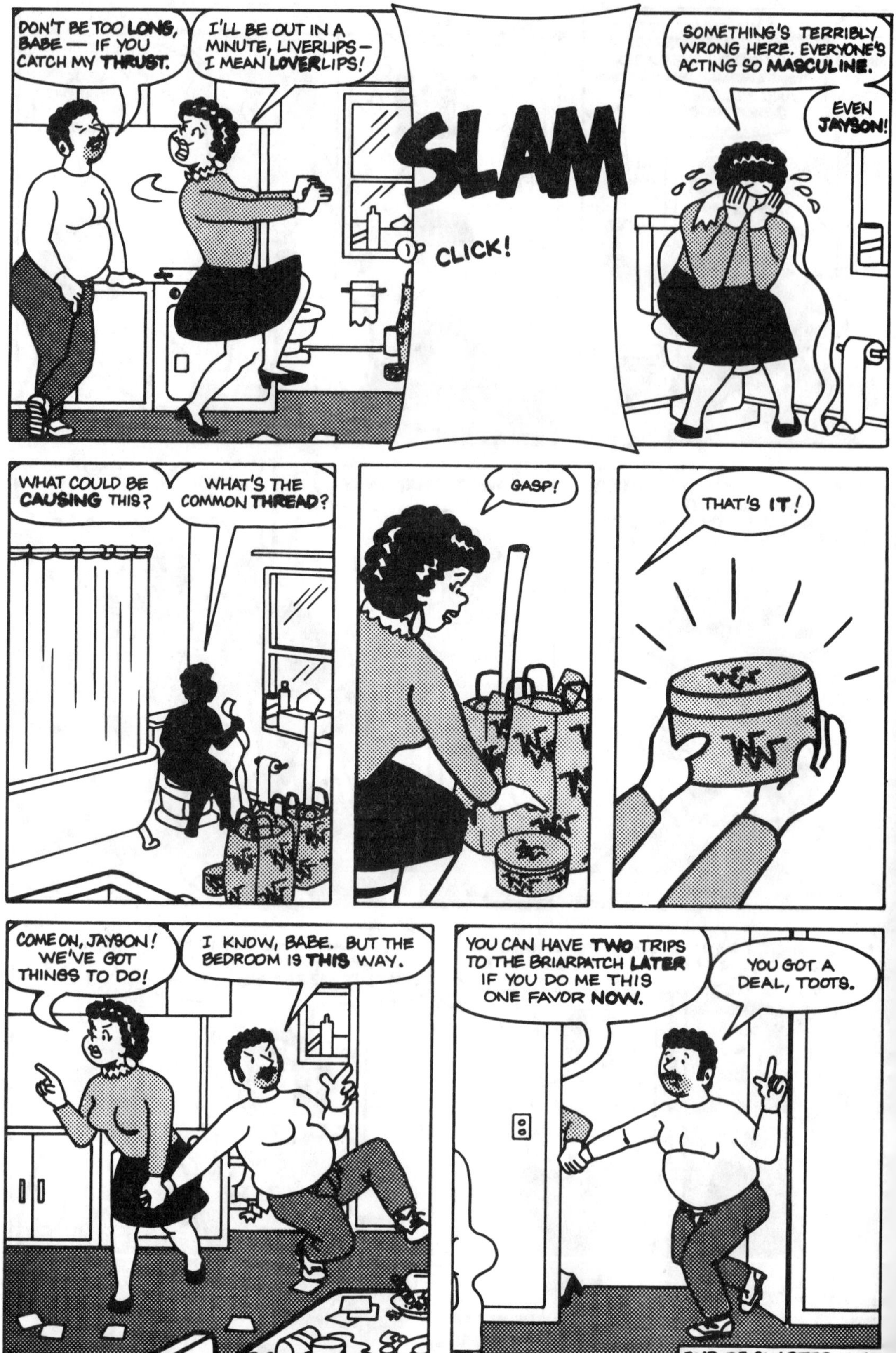
DON'T BE TOO LONG, BABE — IF YOU CATCH MY THRUST.
I'LL BE OUT IN A MINUTE, LIVERLIPS — I MEAN LOVERLIPS!
SLAM
CLICK!
SOMETHING'S TERRIBLY WRONG HERE. EVERYONE'S ACTING SO MASCULINE.
EVEN JAYSON!
WHAT COULD BE CAUSING THIS?
WHAT'S THE COMMON THREAD?
GASP!
THAT'S IT!
COME ON, JAYSON! WE'VE GOT THINGS TO DO!
I KNOW, BABE. BUT THE BEDROOM IS THIS WAY.
YOU CAN HAVE TWO TRIPS TO THE BRIARPATCH LATER IF YOU DO ME THIS ONE FAVOR NOW.
YOU GOT A DEAL, TOOTS.
END OF CHAPTER TWO

Jayson™ becomes a man CHAPTER THREE

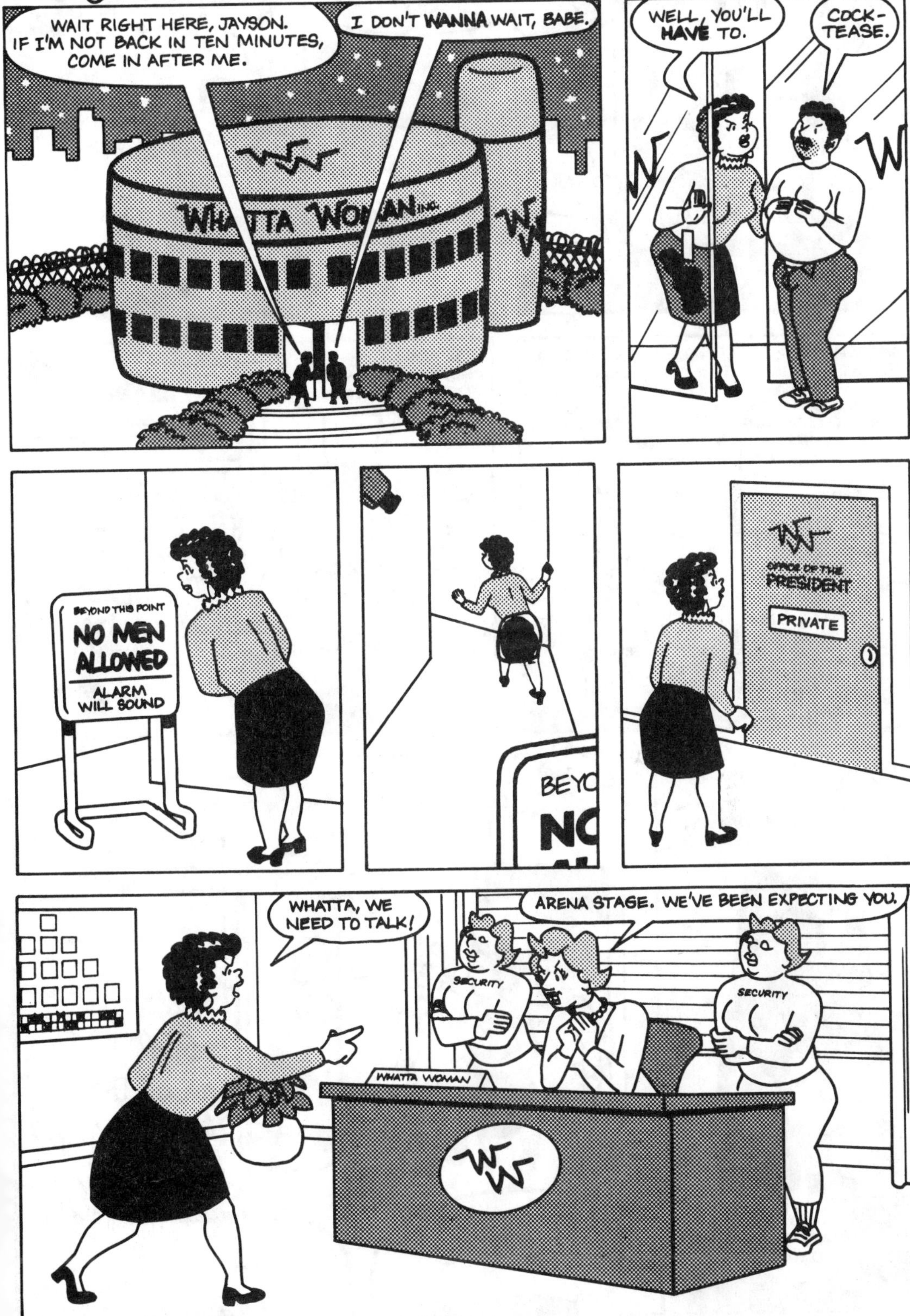
WAIT RIGHT HERE, JAYSON. IF I'M NOT BACK IN TEN MINUTES, COME IN AFTER ME.
I DON'T WANNA WAIT, BABE.
WHATTA WOMAN INC.
WELL, YOU'LL HAVE TO.
COCK-TEASE.
BEYOND THIS POINT
NO MEN ALLOWED
ALARM WILL SOUND
OFFICE OF THE PRESIDENT
PRIVATE
WHATTA, WE NEED TO TALK!
ARENA STAGE. WE'VE BEEN EXPECTING YOU.
SECURITY
SECURITY
WHATTA WOMAN

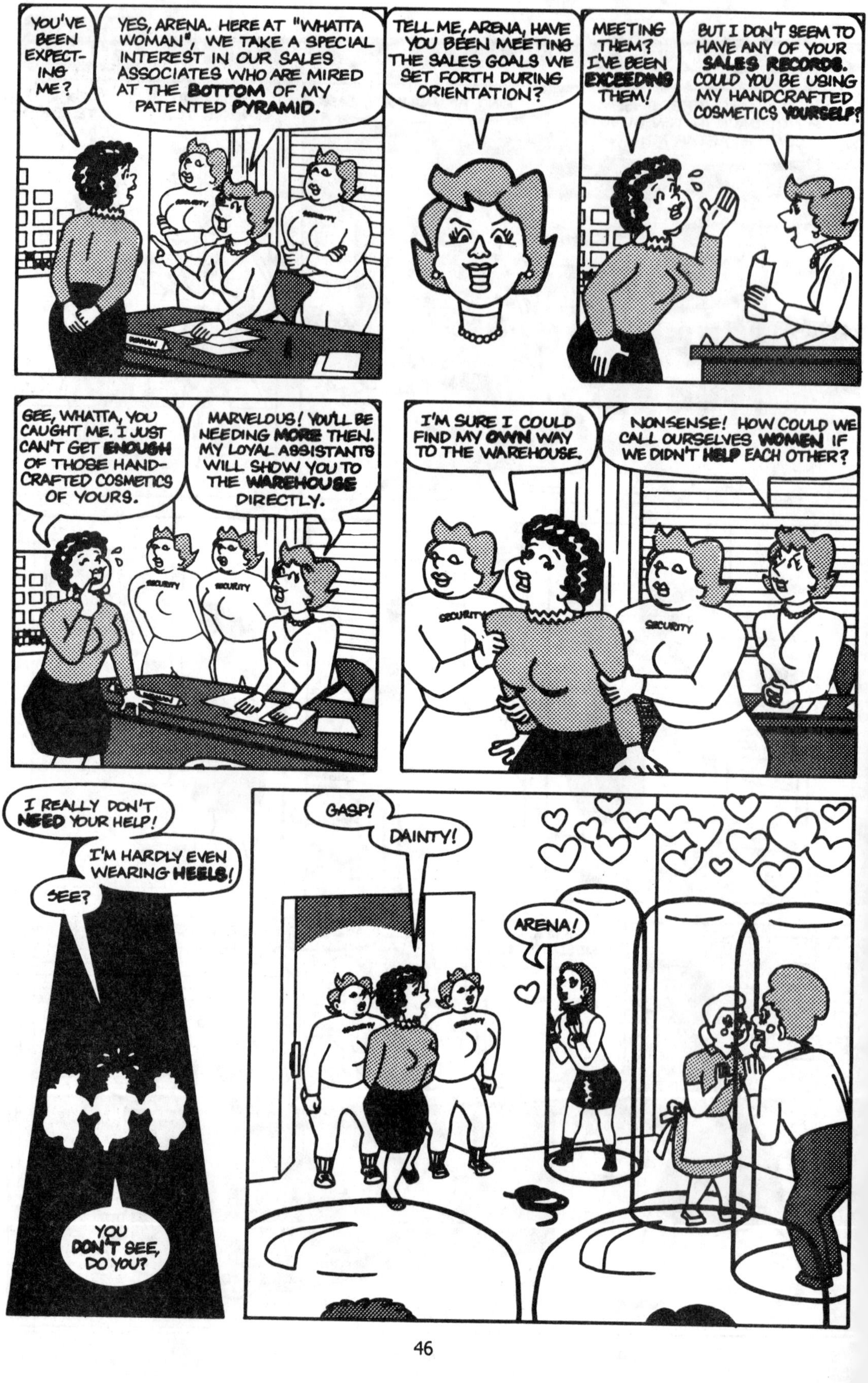
YOU'VE BEEN EXPECTING ME?
YES, ARENA. HERE AT "WHATTA WOMAN", WE TAKE A SPECIAL INTEREST IN OUR SALES ASSOCIATES WHO ARE MIRED AT THE BOTTOM OF MY PATENTED PYRAMID.
SECURITY
SECURITY
TELL ME, ARENA, HAVE YOU BEEN MEETING THE SALES GOALS WE SET FORTH DURING ORIENTATION?
MEETING THEM? I'VE BEEN EXCEEDING THEM!
BUT I DON'T SEEM TO HAVE ANY OF YOUR SALES RECORDS. COULD YOU BE USING MY HANDCRAFTED COSMETICS YOURSELF?
SEE, WHATTA, YOU CAUGHT ME. I JUST CAN'T GET ENOUGH OF THOSE HAND-CRAFTED COSMETICS OF YOURS.
MARVELOUS! YOU'LL BE NEEDING MORE THEN. MY LOYAL ASSISTANTS WILL SHOW YOU TO THE WAREHOUSE DIRECTLY.
SECURITY
SECURITY
I'M SURE I COULD FIND MY OWN WAY TO THE WAREHOUSE.
NONSENSE! HOW COULD WE CALL OURSELVES WOMEN IF WE DIDN'T HELP EACH OTHER?
SECURITY
SECURITY
I REALLY DON'T NEED YOUR HELP!
I'M HARDLY EVEN WEARING HEELS!
SEE?
YOU DON'T SEE, DO YOU?
GASP!
DAINTY!
ARENA!
SECURITY
SECURITY

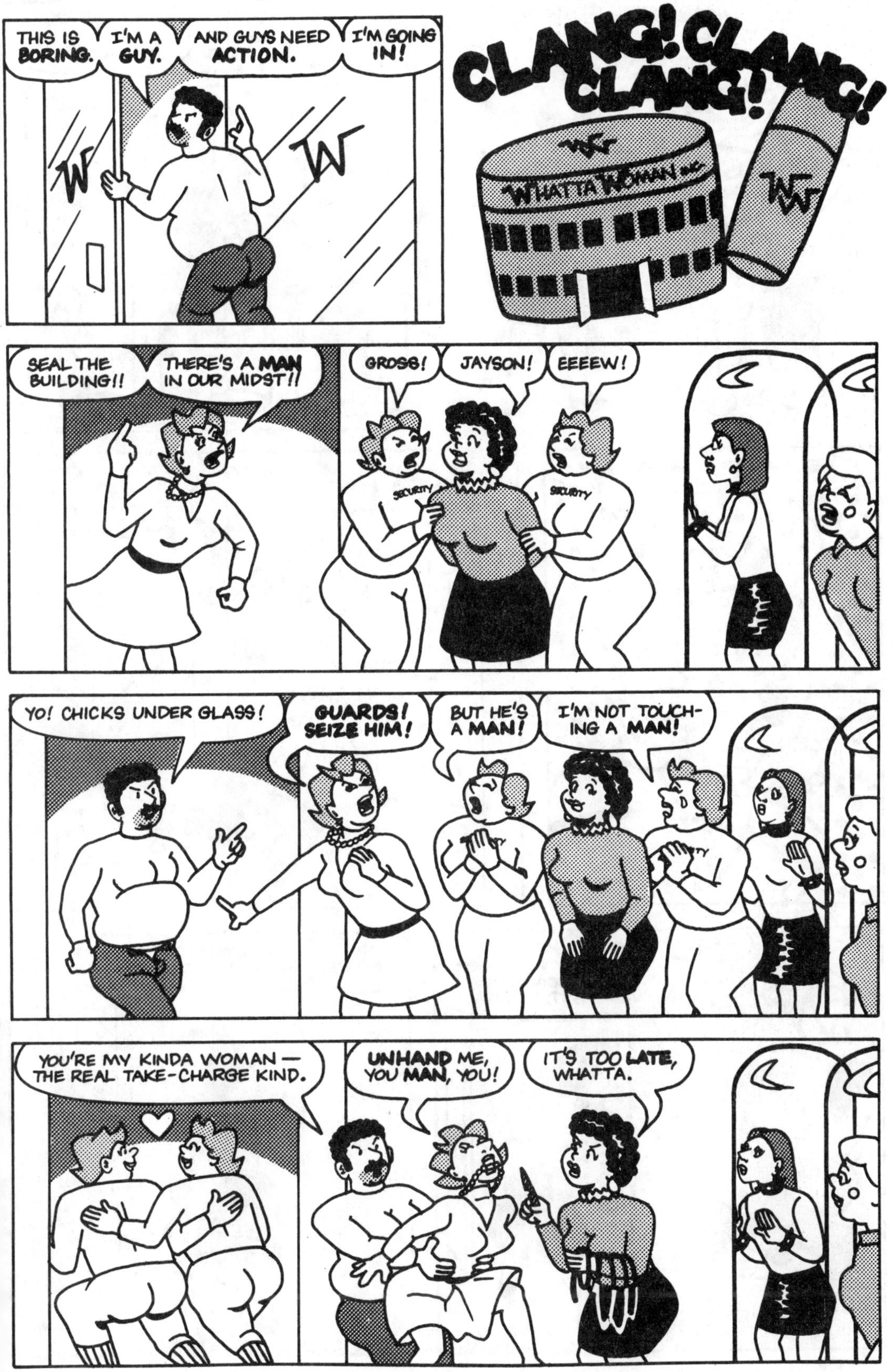
THIS IS BORING.
I'M A GUY.
AND GUYS NEED ACTION.
I'M GOING IN!
CLANG! CLANG! CLANG!
WHATTA WOMAN INC.
SEAL THE BUILDING!!
THERE'S A MAN IN OUR MIDST!!
GROSS!
JAYSON!
EEEEW!
SECURITY
SECURITY
YO! CHICKS UNDER GLASS!
GUARDS! SEIZE HIM!
BUT HE'S A MAN!
I'M NOT TOUCHING A MAN!
YOU'RE MY KINDA WOMAN — THE REAL TAKE-CHARGE KIND.
UNHAND ME, YOU MAN, YOU!
IT'S TOO LATE, WHATTA.

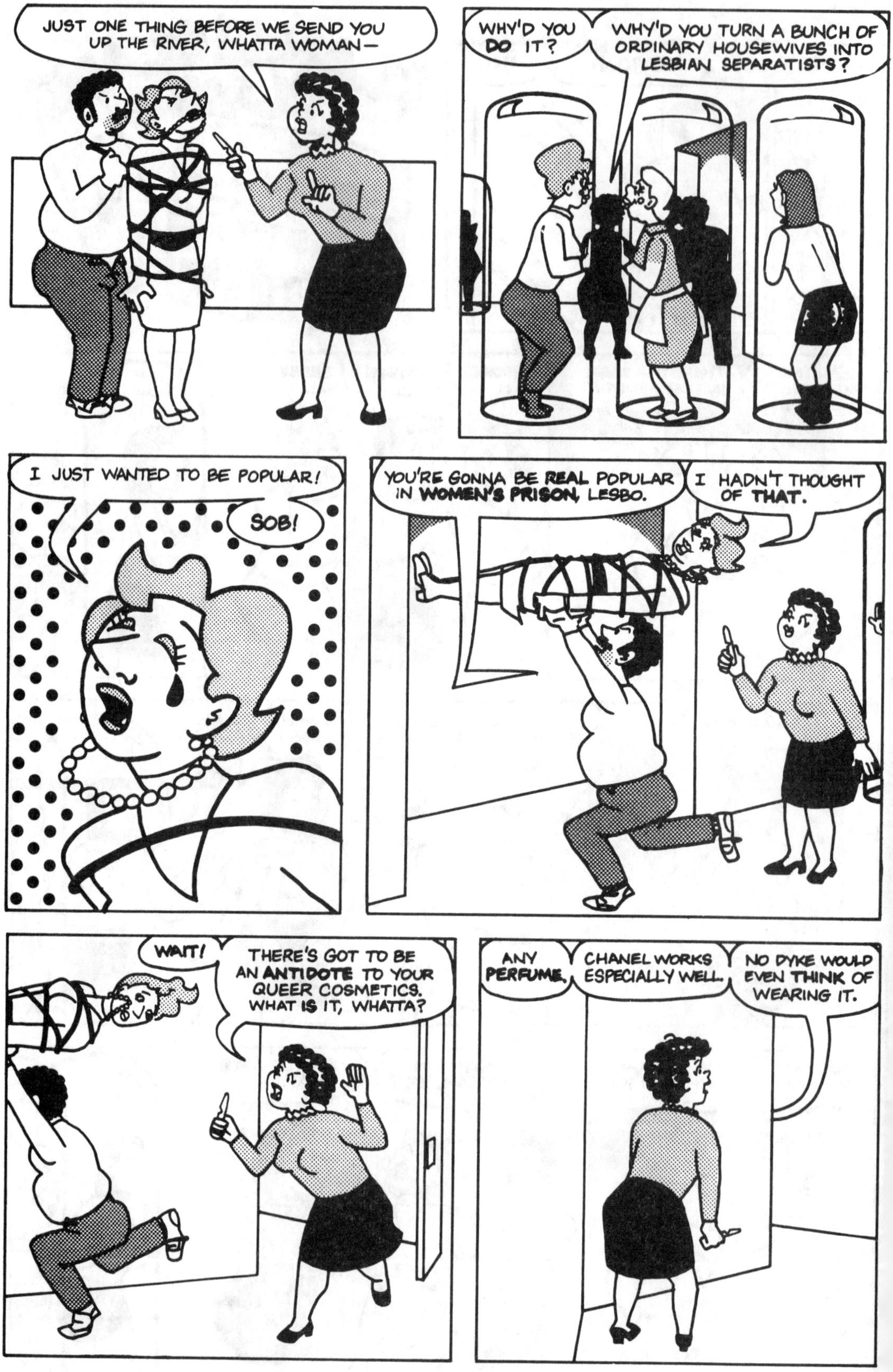
JUST ONE THING BEFORE WE SEND YOU UP THE RIVER, WHATTA WOMAN—
WHY'D YOU DO IT?
WHY'D YOU TURN A BUNCH OF ORDINARY HOUSEWIVES INTO LESBIAN SEPARATISTS?
I JUST WANTED TO BE POPULAR!
SOB!
YOU'RE GONNA BE REAL POPULAR IN WOMEN'S PRISON, LESBO.
I HADN'T THOUGHT OF THAT.
WAIT!
THERE'S GOT TO BE AN ANTIDOTE TO YOUR QUEER COSMETICS. WHAT IS IT, WHATTA?
ANY PERFUME.
CHANEL WORKS ESPECIALLY WELL.
NO DYKE WOULD EVEN THINK OF WEARING IT.

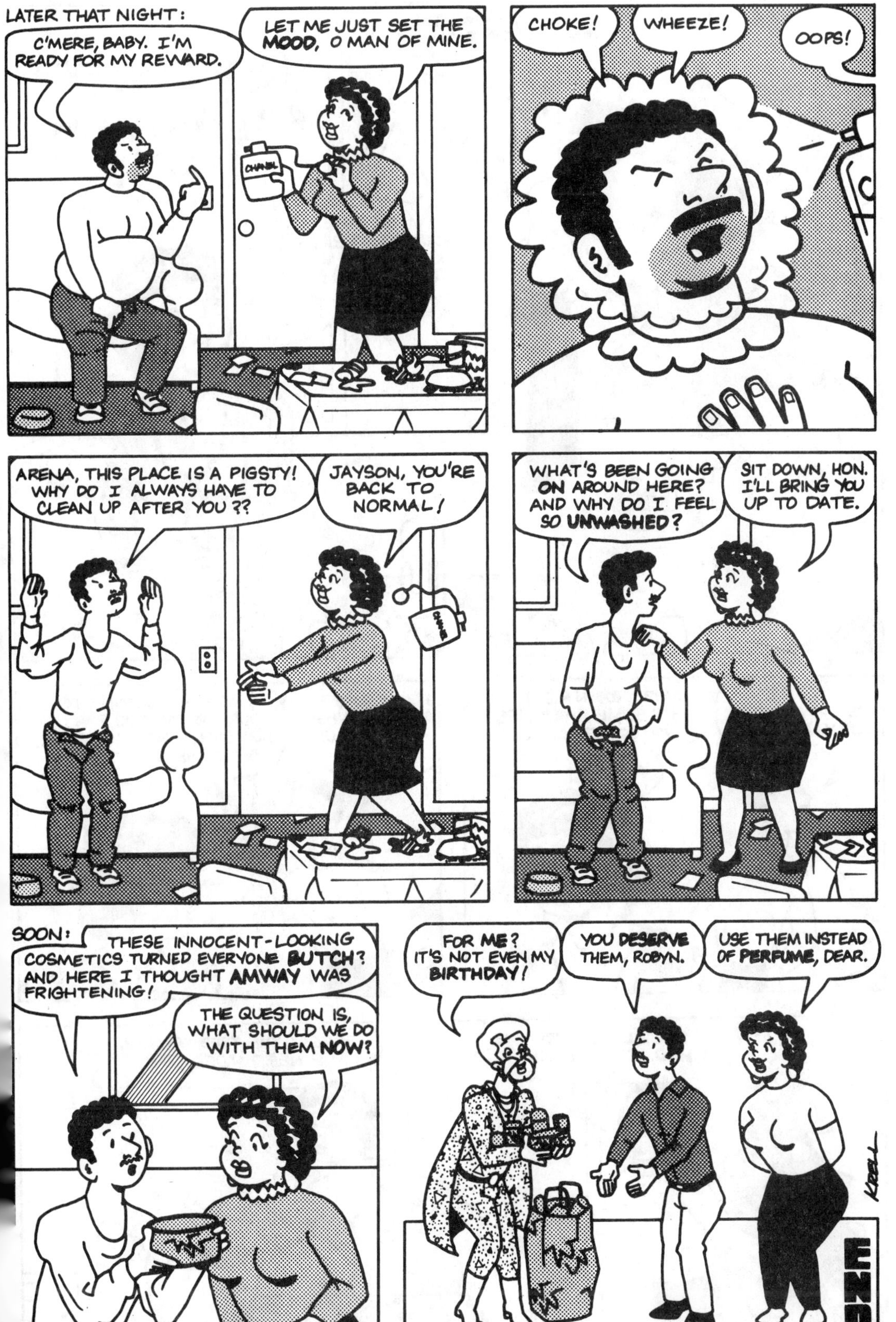
LATER THAT NIGHT:
C'MERE, BABY. I'M READY FOR MY REWARD.
LET ME JUST SET THE MOOD, O MAN OF MINE.
CHANEL
CHOKE!
WHEEZE!
OOPS!
ARENA, THIS PLACE IS A PIGSTY! WHY DO I ALWAYS HAVE TO CLEAN UP AFTER YOU??
JAYSON, YOU'RE BACK TO NORMAL!
WHAT'S BEEN GOING ON AROUND HERE? AND WHY DO I FEEL SO UNWASHED?
SIT DOWN, HON. I'LL BRING YOU UP TO DATE.
SOON:
THESE INNOCENT-LOOKING COSMETICS TURNED EVERYONE BUTCH? AND HERE I THOUGHT AMWAY WAS FRIGHTENING!
THE QUESTION IS, WHAT SHOULD WE DO WITH THEM NOW?
FOR ME? IT'S NOT EVEN MY BIRTHDAY!
YOU DESERVE THEM, ROBYN.
USE THEM INSTEAD OF PERFUME, DEAR.
KRELL
END

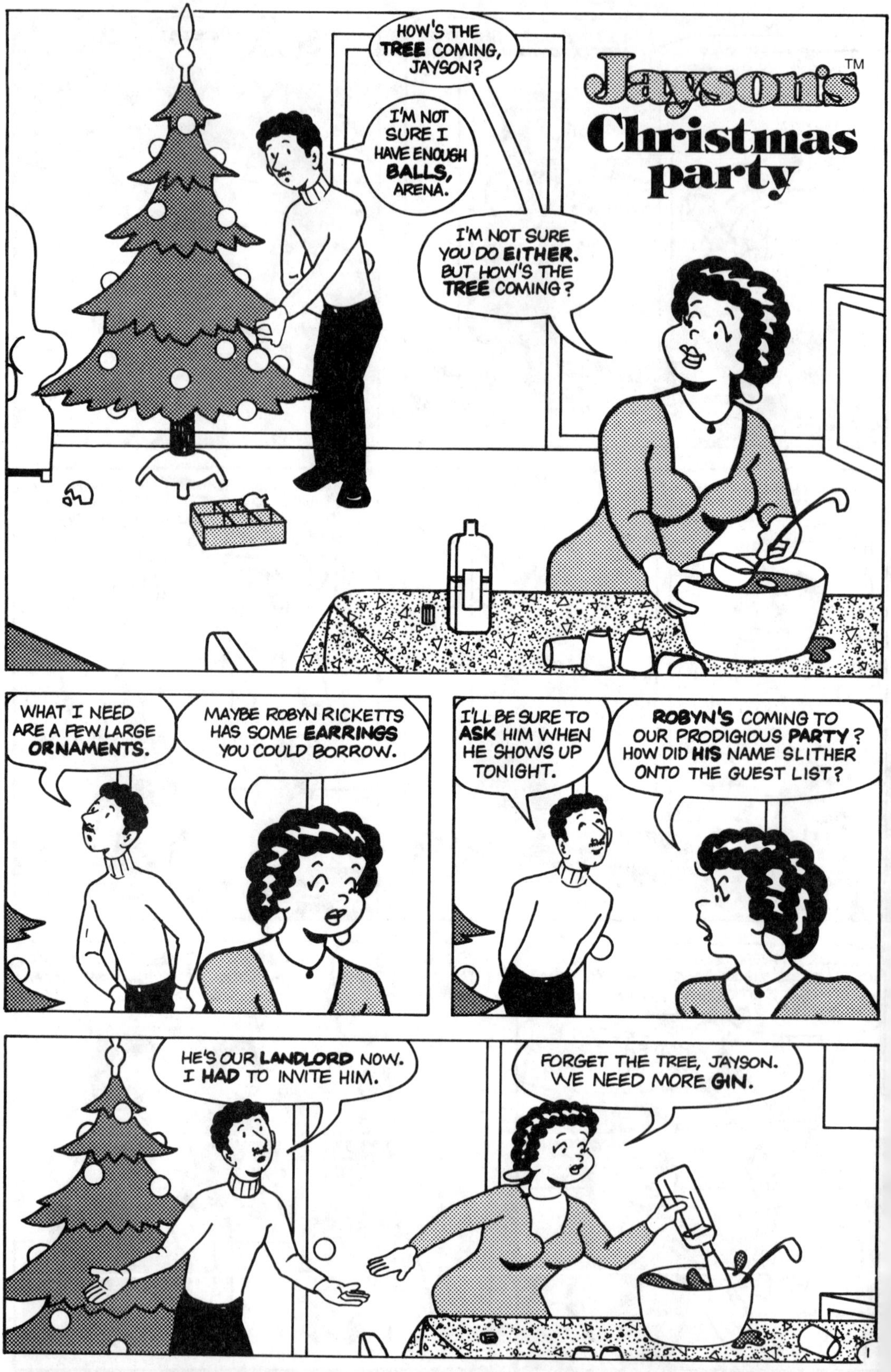

Jayson's™ Christmas party
HOW'S THE TREE COMING, JAYSON?
I'M NOT SURE I HAVE ENOUGH BALLS, ARENA.
I'M NOT SURE YOU DO EITHER. BUT HOW'S THE TREE COMING?
WHAT I NEED ARE A FEW LARGE ORNAMENTS.
MAYBE ROBYN RICKETTS HAS SOME EARRINGS YOU COULD BORROW.
I'LL BE SURE TO ASK HIM WHEN HE SHOWS UP TONIGHT.
ROBYN'S COMING TO OUR PRODIGIOUS PARTY? HOW DID HIS NAME SLITHER ONTO THE GUEST LIST?
HE'S OUR LANDLORD NOW. I HAD TO INVITE HIM.
FORGET THE TREE, JAYSON. WE NEED MORE GIN.
1

ORIGINALLY PRESENTED IN JAYSON: A NEW COLLECTION, 1997

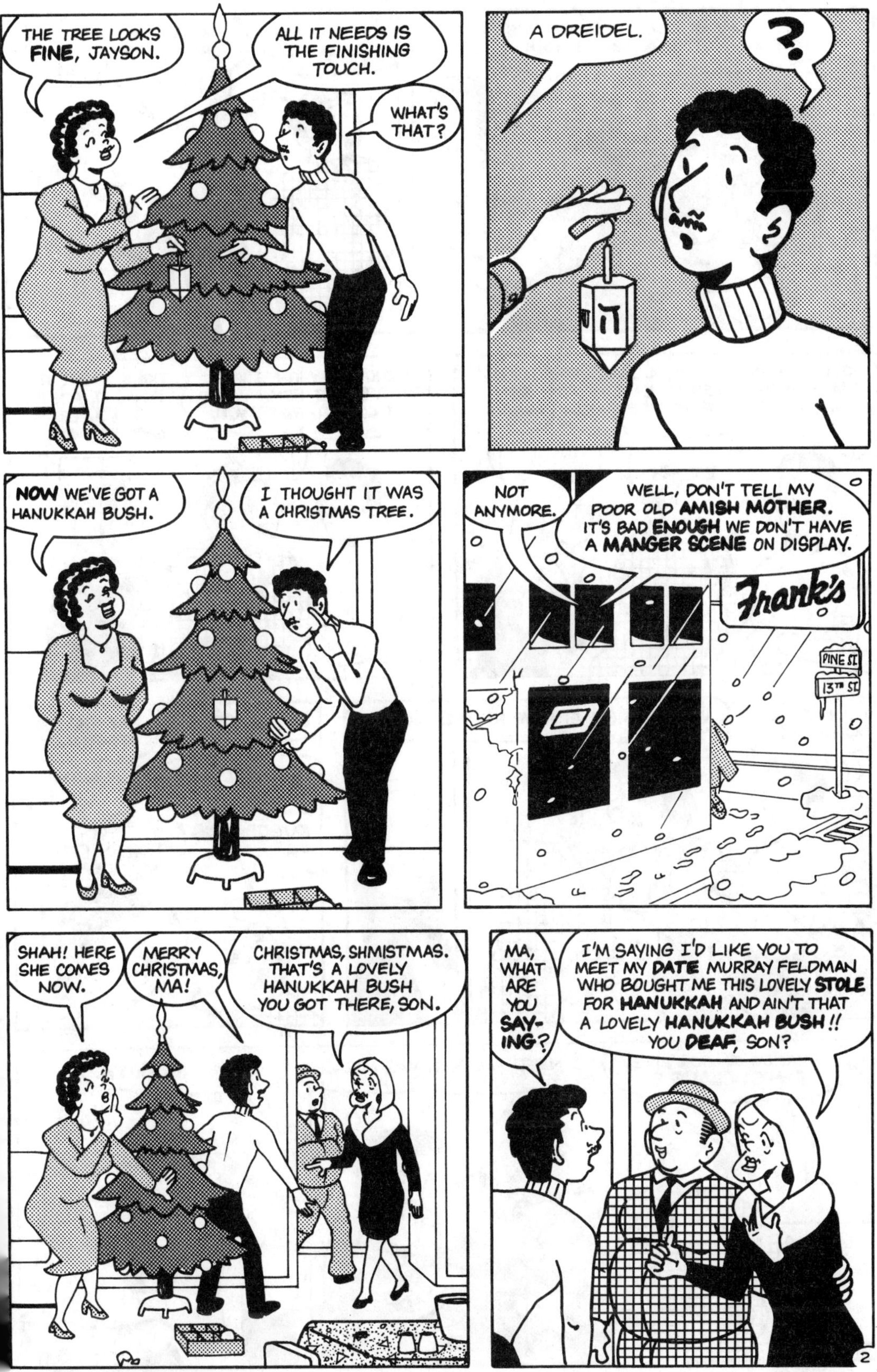
THE TREE LOOKS FINE, JAYSON.
ALL IT NEEDS IS THE FINISHING TOUCH.
WHAT'S THAT?
A DREIDEL.
?
NOW WE'VE GOT A HANUKKAH BUSH.
I THOUGHT IT WAS A CHRISTMAS TREE.
NOT ANYMORE.
WELL, DON'T TELL MY POOR OLD AMISH MOTHER. IT'S BAD ENOUGH WE DON'T HAVE A MANGER SCENE ON DISPLAY.
Frank's
PINE ST.
13TH ST.
SHAH! HERE SHE COMES NOW.
MERRY CHRISTMAS, MA!
CHRISTMAS, SHMISTMAS. THAT'S A LOVELY HANUKKAH BUSH YOU GOT THERE, SON.
MA, WHAT ARE YOU SAYING?
I'M SAYING I'D LIKE YOU TO MEET MY DATE MURRAY FELDMAN WHO BOUGHT ME THIS LOVELY STOLE FOR HANUKKAH AND AIN'T THAT A LOVELY HANUKKAH BUSH!! YOU DEAF, SON?
2

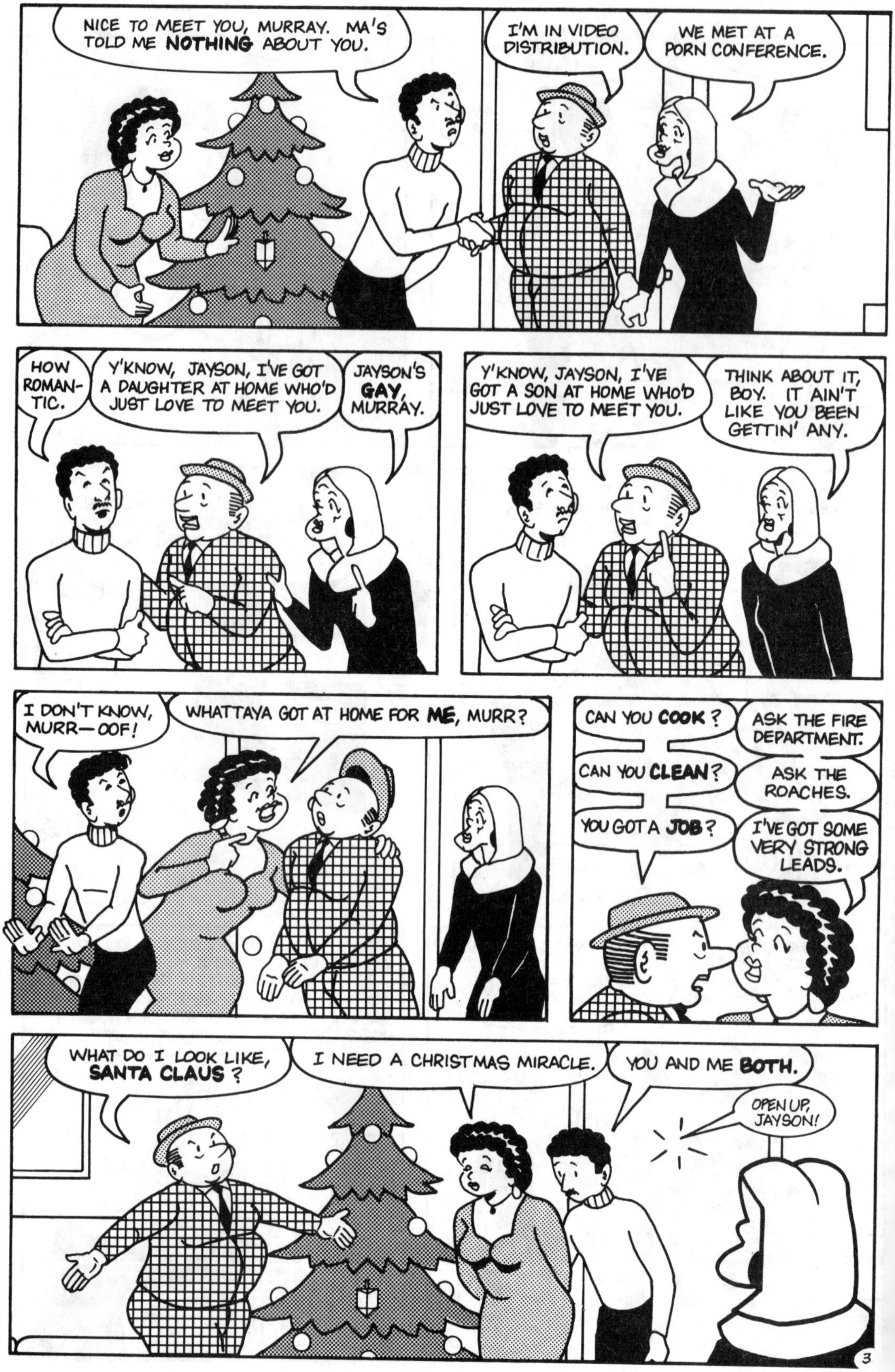
NICE TO MEET YOU, MURRAY. MA'S TOLD ME **NOTHING** ABOUT YOU.
I'M IN VIDEO DISTRIBUTION.
WE MET AT A PORN CONFERENCE.
HOW ROMAN-TIC.
Y'KNOW, JAYSON, I'VE GOT A DAUGHTER AT HOME WHO'D JUST LOVE TO MEET YOU.
JAYSON'S **GAY**, MURRAY.
Y'KNOW, JAYSON, I'VE GOT A SON AT HOME WHO'D JUST LOVE TO MEET YOU.
THINK ABOUT IT, BOY. IT AIN'T LIKE YOU BEEN GETTIN' ANY.
I DON'T KNOW, MURR—OOF!
WHATTAYA GOT AT HOME FOR **ME**, MURR?
CAN YOU **COOK**?
ASK THE FIRE DEPARTMENT.
CAN YOU **CLEAN**?
ASK THE ROACHES.
YOU GOT A **JOB**?
I'VE GOT SOME VERY STRONG LEADS.
WHAT DO I LOOK LIKE, **SANTA CLAUS**?
I NEED A CHRISTMAS MIRACLE.
YOU AND ME **BOTH**.
OPEN UP, JAYSON!
3

MERRY CHRISTMAS, EVERYBODY!
ROBYN!
KISS ME, KIDS. I'VE GOT MISTLETOE.
I DON'T CARE IF YOU'VE GOT HAMMERTOES.
KRELL
IS THAT ANY WAY TO TREAT ME AFTER THE LOVELY PRESENT I'VE BROUGHT YOU?
WHAT PRESENT? I DON'T SEE ANY PRESENT.
KIDS, MEET HILL AND DALE. YOU CAN HOLD THEM BUT YOU CAN'T UNWRAP THEM TILL MIDNIGHT.
WHAT A THOUGHTFUL AND TIMELY GIFT!
CAN I AT LEAST SHAKE THE PACKAGE?
THIS IS EVEN BETTER THAN HANUKKAH!
ARE YOU ONE OF THOSE GIFTS THAT KEEP ON GIVING?
NICE TREE — EXCEPT FOR THAT HUNK OF CLAY IN THE MIDDLE.
A COCKTAIL RING WOULD SURE GO NICE WITH THIS STOLE.
WHEN'S YOUR BIRTHDAY, BERTHA?
end

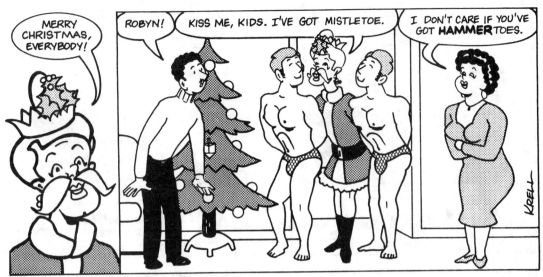

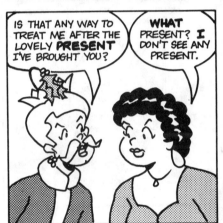

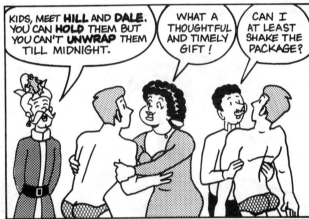

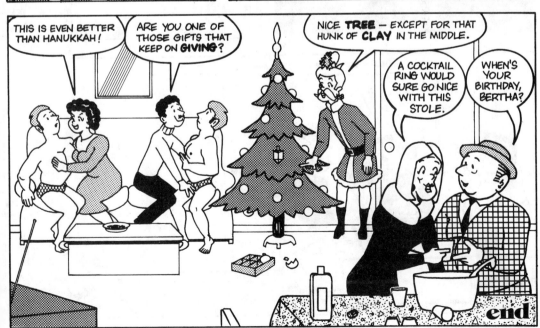

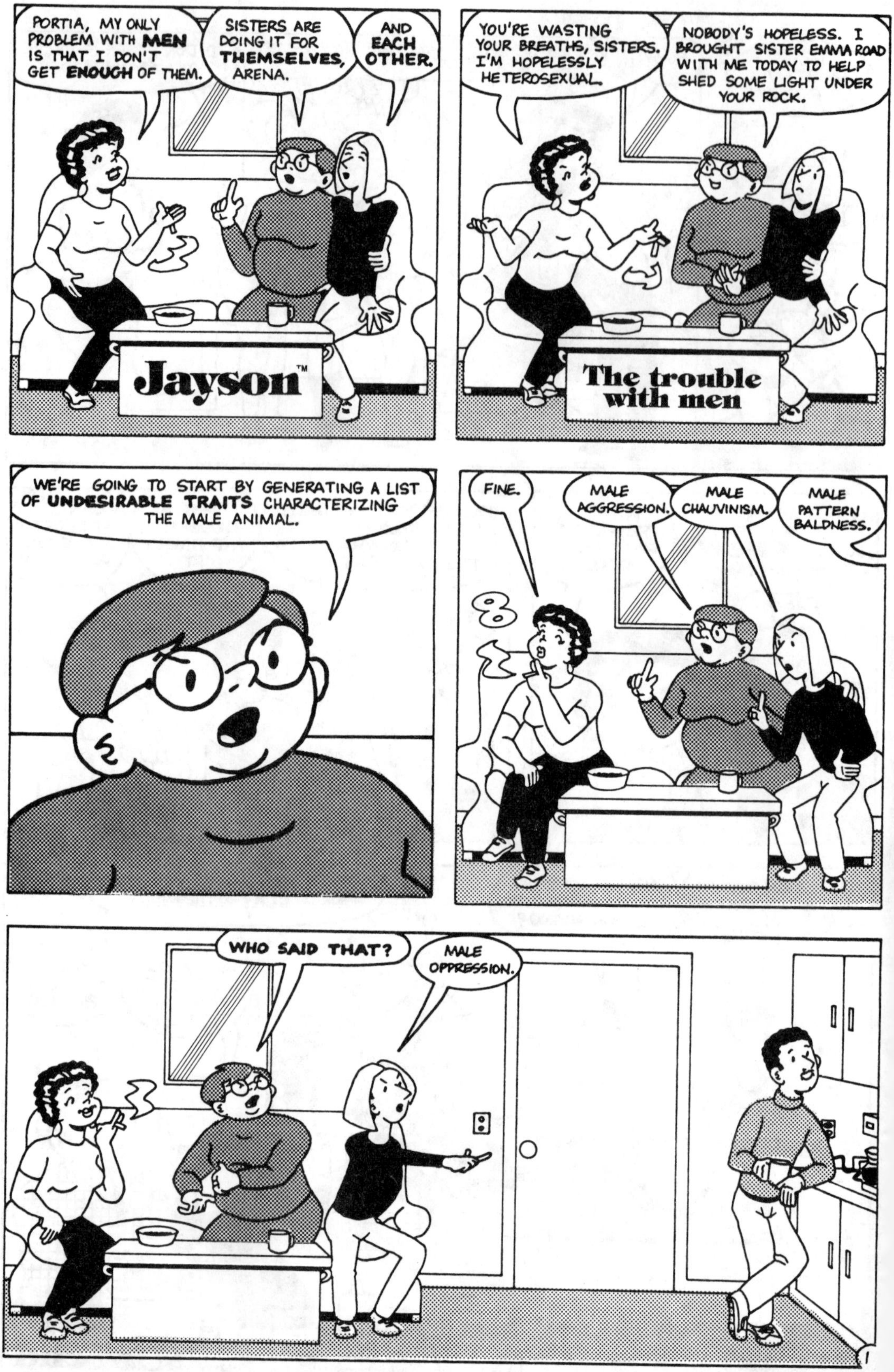
PORTIA, MY ONLY PROBLEM WITH MEN IS THAT I DON'T GET ENOUGH OF THEM.
SISTERS ARE DOING IT FOR THEMSELVES, ARENA.
AND EACH OTHER.
Jayson™
YOU'RE WASTING YOUR BREATHS, SISTERS. I'M HOPELESSLY HETEROSEXUAL.
NOBODY'S HOPELESS. I BROUGHT SISTER EMMA ROAD WITH ME TODAY TO HELP SHED SOME LIGHT UNDER YOUR ROCK.
The trouble with men
WE'RE GOING TO START BY GENERATING A LIST OF UNDESIRABLE TRAITS CHARACTERIZING THE MALE ANIMAL.
FINE.
MALE AGGRESSION.
MALE CHAUVINISM.
MALE PATTERN BALDNESS.
WHO SAID THAT?
MALE OPPRESSION.

ORIGINALLY PRESENTED IN JAYSON: A NEW COLLECTION, 1997

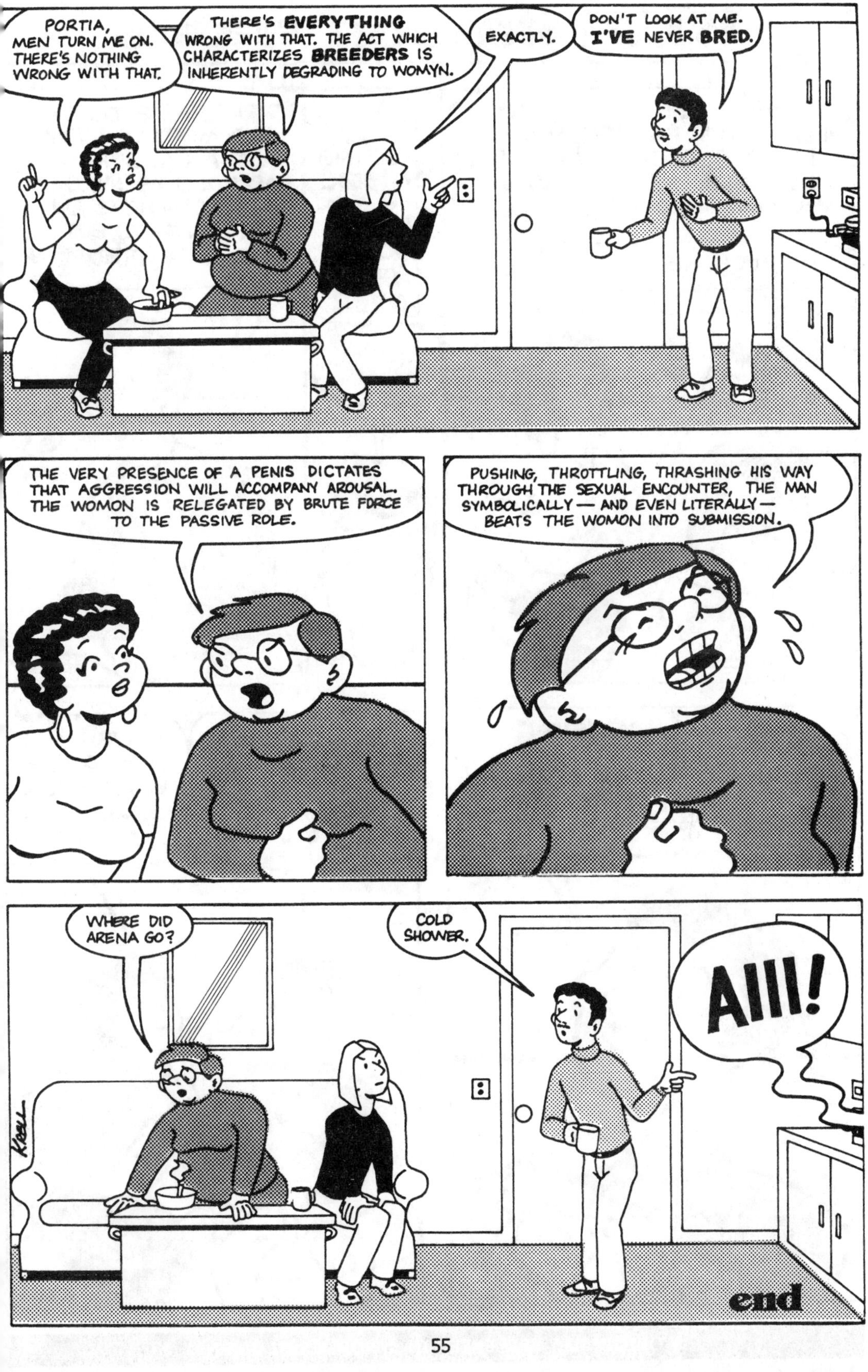
PORTIA, MEN TURN ME ON. THERE'S NOTHING WRONG WITH THAT.
THERE'S **EVERYTHING** WRONG WITH THAT. THE ACT WHICH CHARACTERIZES **BREEDERS** IS INHERENTLY DEGRADING TO WOMYN.
EXACTLY.
DON'T LOOK AT ME. **I'VE** NEVER **BRED.**
THE VERY PRESENCE OF A PENIS DICTATES THAT AGGRESSION WILL ACCOMPANY AROUSAL. THE WOMON IS RELEGATED BY BRUTE FORCE TO THE PASSIVE ROLE.
PUSHING, THROTTLING, THRASHING HIS WAY THROUGH THE SEXUAL ENCOUNTER, THE MAN SYMBOLICALLY — AND EVEN LITERALLY — BEATS THE WOMON INTO SUBMISSION.
WHERE DID ARENA GO?
COLD SHOWER.
AIII!
KROLL
end

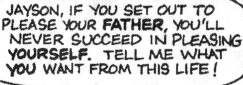

What Jayson™ wants

JAYSON, IF YOU SET OUT TO PLEASE YOUR **FATHER**, YOU'LL NEVER SUCCEED IN PLEASING **YOURSELF**. TELL ME WHAT YOU WANT FROM THIS LIFE!

NOT MUCH, REALLY.

I'D LIKE AN EXCITING CAREER.

AND I'D LIKE A DASHING LOVER.

NAMED "DIRK."

"DIRK" HAS GOOD SKIN AND A GREAT BODY AND A CAREER AS FABULOUS AS MY OWN. "DIRK" CAN HAVE ANY MAN HE WANTS, BUT HE'S UTTERLY DEVOTED TO ME.

WE OWN A MANSION ON THE MAIN LINE! A CHALET IN SWITZERLAND! A PONY FARM!! A MOVIE STUDIO!!!

BETTE MIDLER WORKS FOR US AND MAKES **GOOD** FILMS FOR A CHANGE!

MAYBE WE SHOULD SEE WHAT YOUR **FATHER** WANTS.

KRELL

end

ORIGINALLY PRESENTED IN SYNDICATION, 1995

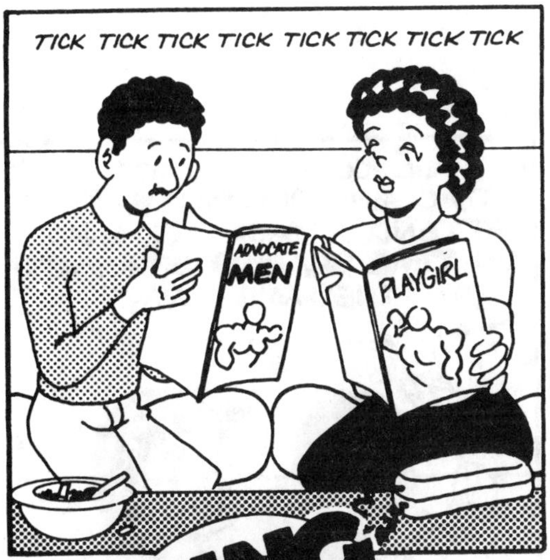
TICK TICK TICK TICK TICK TICK TICK TICK
ADVOCATE MEN
PLAYGIRL

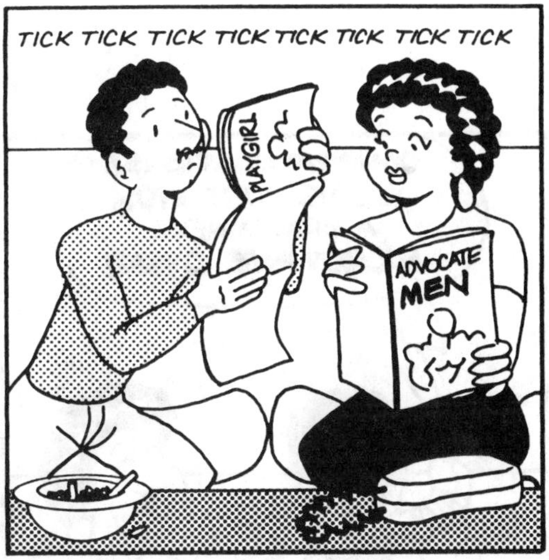
TICK TICK TICK TICK TICK TICK TICK TICK
PLAYGIRL
ADVOCATE MEN

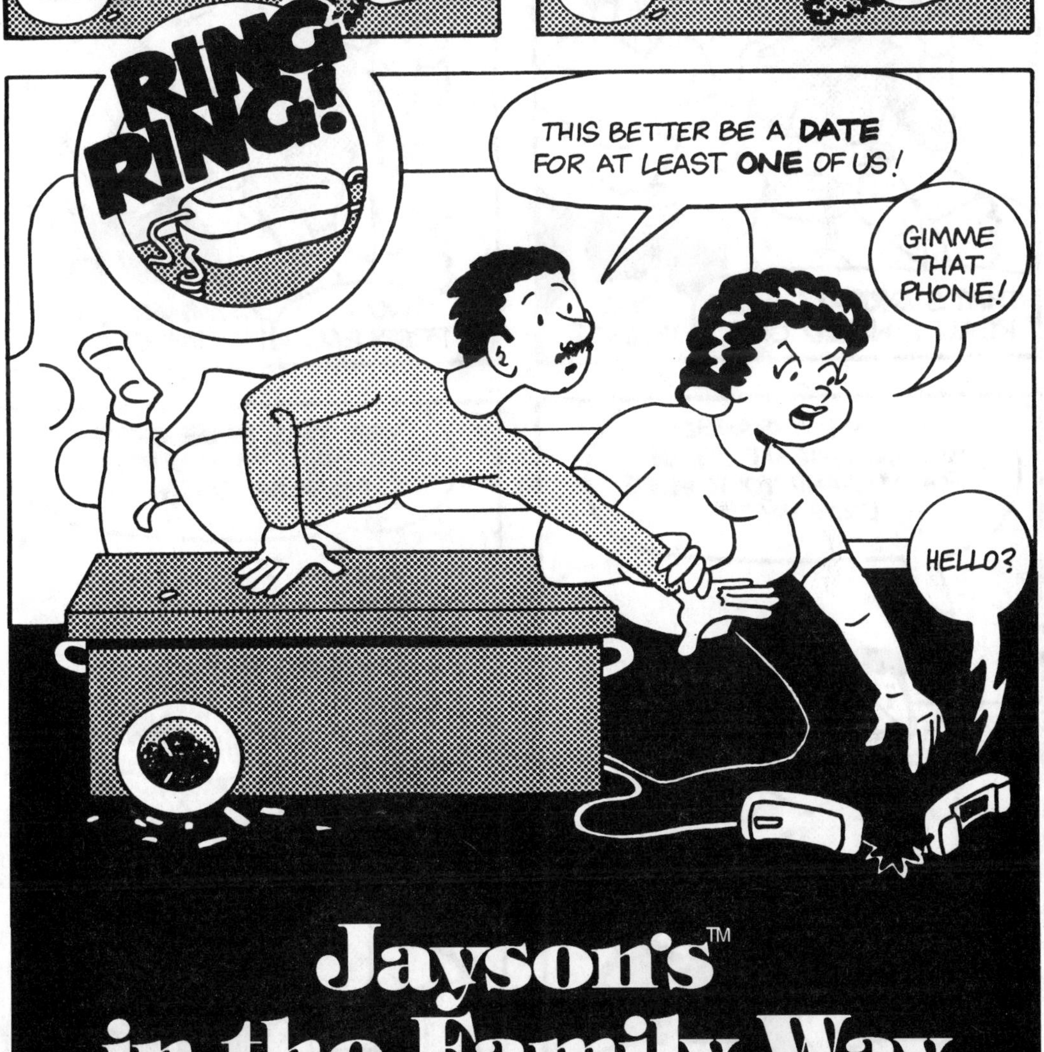
RING! RING!
THIS BETTER BE A DATE FOR AT LEAST ONE OF US!
GIMME THAT PHONE!
HELLO?
Jayson's™
in the Family Way

ORIGINALLY PRESENTED IN MEATMEN VOL. 10, 1991

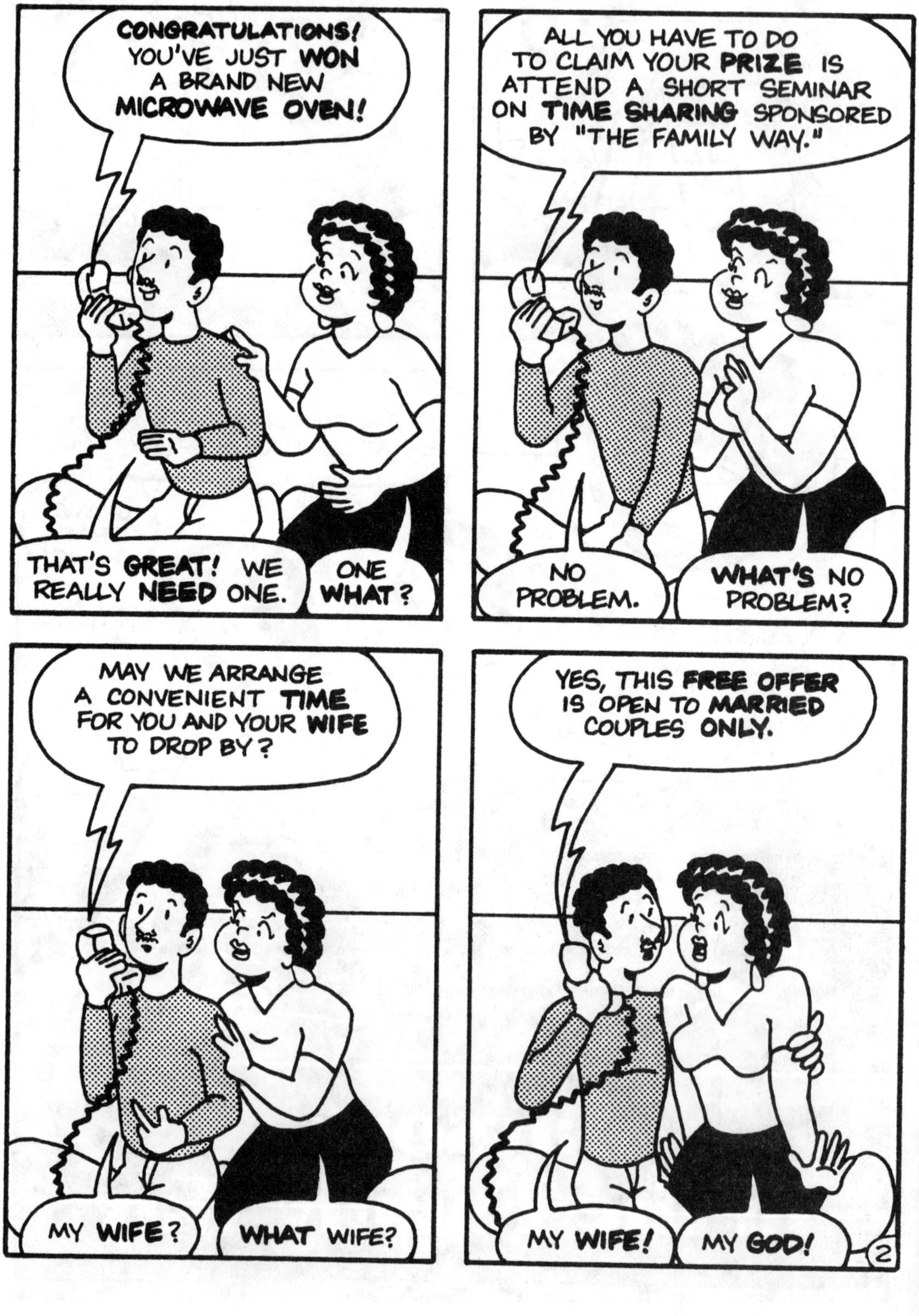
CONGRATULATIONS! YOU'VE JUST WON A BRAND NEW MICROWAVE OVEN!
THAT'S GREAT! WE REALLY NEED ONE.
ONE WHAT?
ALL YOU HAVE TO DO TO CLAIM YOUR PRIZE IS ATTEND A SHORT SEMINAR ON TIME SHARING SPONSORED BY "THE FAMILY WAY."
NO PROBLEM.
WHAT'S NO PROBLEM?
MAY WE ARRANGE A CONVENIENT TIME FOR YOU AND YOUR WIFE TO DROP BY?
MY WIFE?
WHAT WIFE?
YES, THIS FREE OFFER IS OPEN TO MARRIED COUPLES ONLY.
MY WIFE!
MY GOD!
2

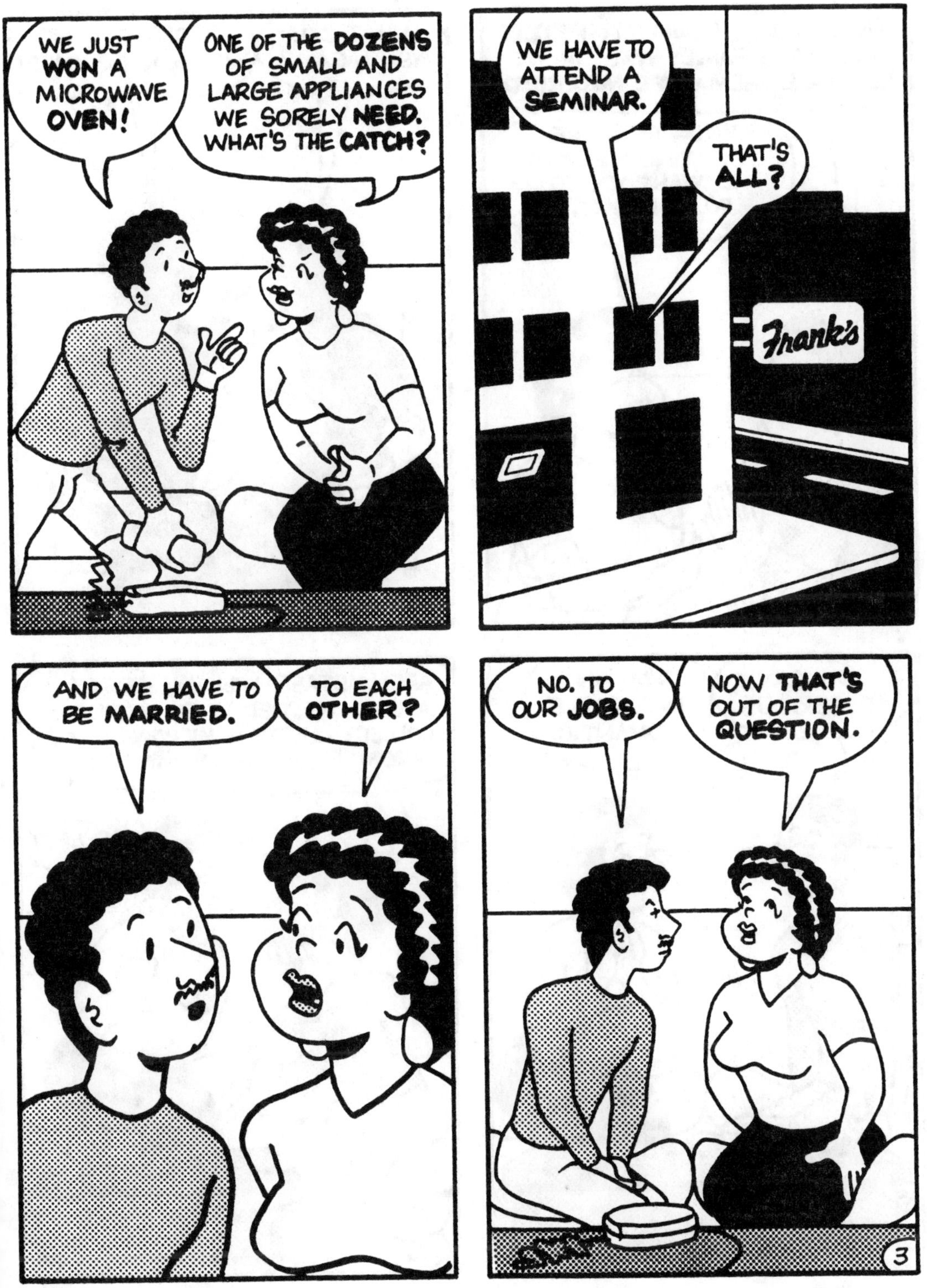
WE JUST WON A MICROWAVE OVEN!
ONE OF THE DOZENS OF SMALL AND LARGE APPLIANCES WE SORELY NEED. WHAT'S THE CATCH?
WE HAVE TO ATTEND A SEMINAR.
THAT'S ALL?
Frank's
AND WE HAVE TO BE MARRIED.
TO EACH OTHER?
NO. TO OUR JOBS.
NOW THAT'S OUT OF THE QUESTION.
3

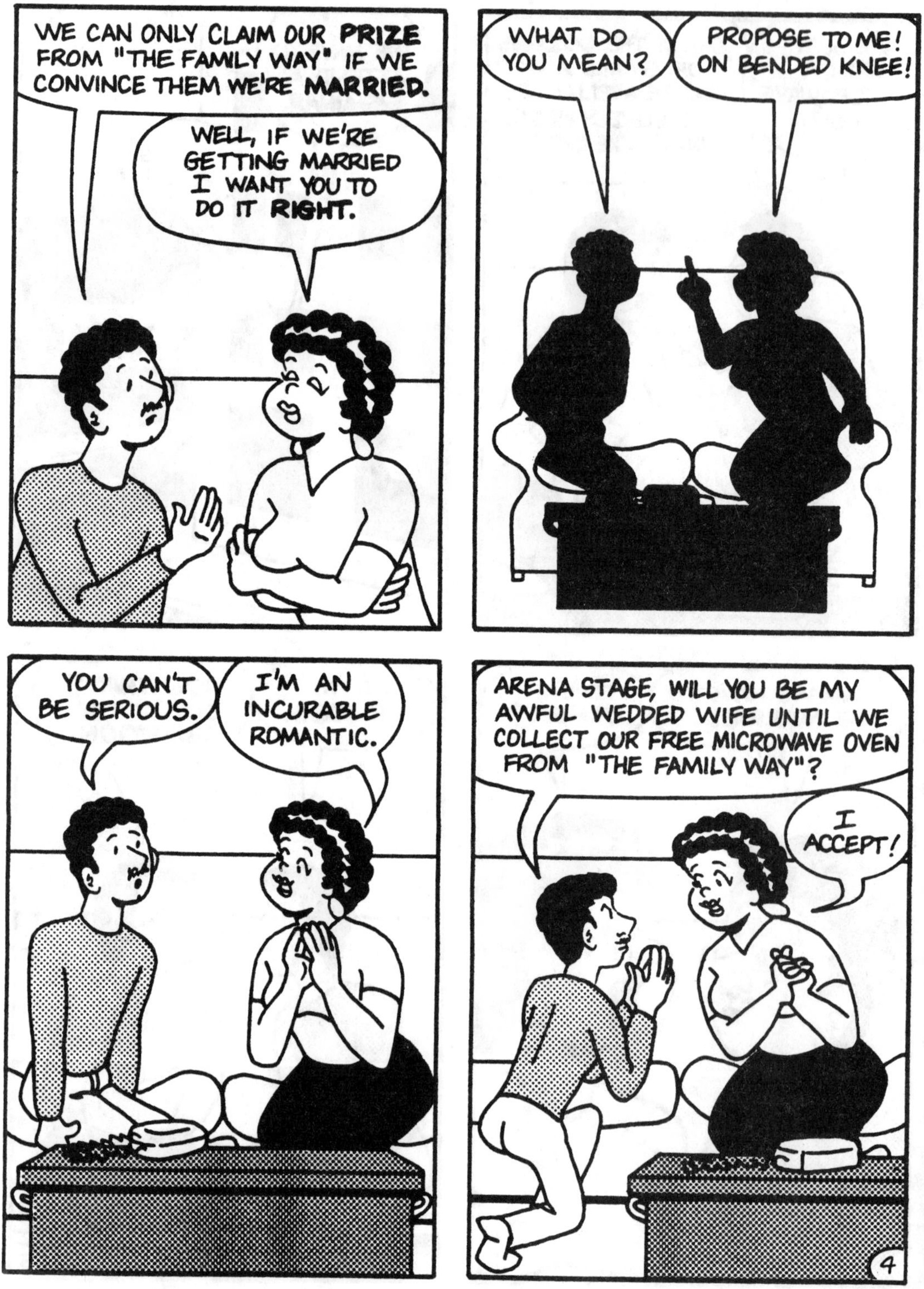
WE CAN ONLY CLAIM OUR PRIZE FROM "THE FAMILY WAY" IF WE CONVINCE THEM WE'RE MARRIED.
WELL, IF WE'RE GETTING MARRIED I WANT YOU TO DO IT RIGHT.
WHAT DO YOU MEAN?
PROPOSE TO ME! ON BENDED KNEE!
YOU CAN'T BE SERIOUS.
I'M AN INCURABLE ROMANTIC.
ARENA STAGE, WILL YOU BE MY AWFUL WEDDED WIFE UNTIL WE COLLECT OUR FREE MICROWAVE OVEN FROM "THE FAMILY WAY"?
I ACCEPT!
4

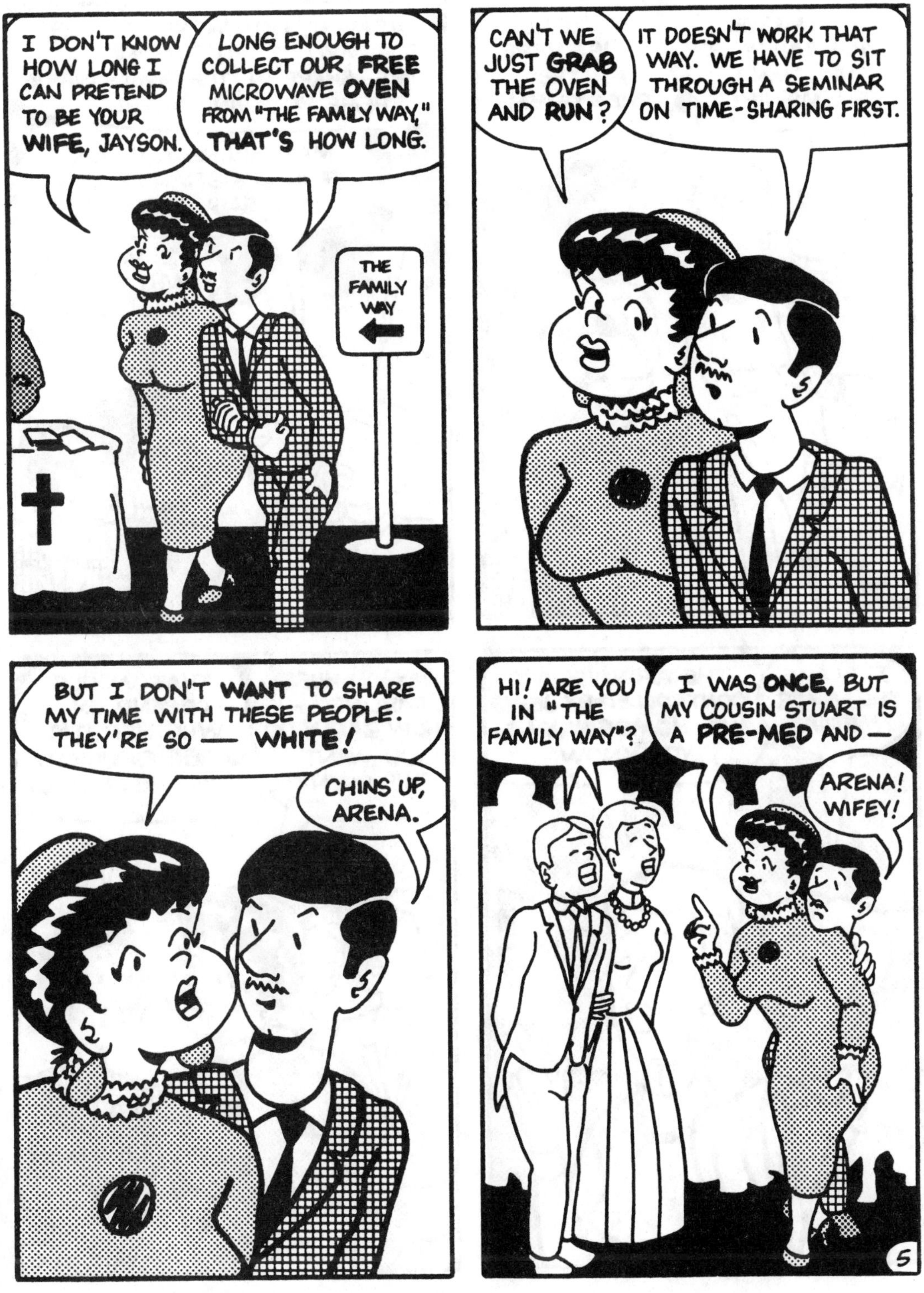
I DON'T KNOW HOW LONG I CAN PRETEND TO BE YOUR WIFE, JAYSON.
LONG ENOUGH TO COLLECT OUR FREE MICROWAVE OVEN FROM "THE FAMILY WAY," THAT'S HOW LONG.
THE FAMILY WAY
CAN'T WE JUST GRAB THE OVEN AND RUN?
IT DOESN'T WORK THAT WAY. WE HAVE TO SIT THROUGH A SEMINAR ON TIME-SHARING FIRST.
BUT I DON'T WANT TO SHARE MY TIME WITH THESE PEOPLE. THEY'RE SO — WHITE!
CHINS UP, ARENA.
HI! ARE YOU IN "THE FAMILY WAY"?
I WAS ONCE, BUT MY COUSIN STUART IS A PRE-MED AND —
ARENA! WIFEY!
5

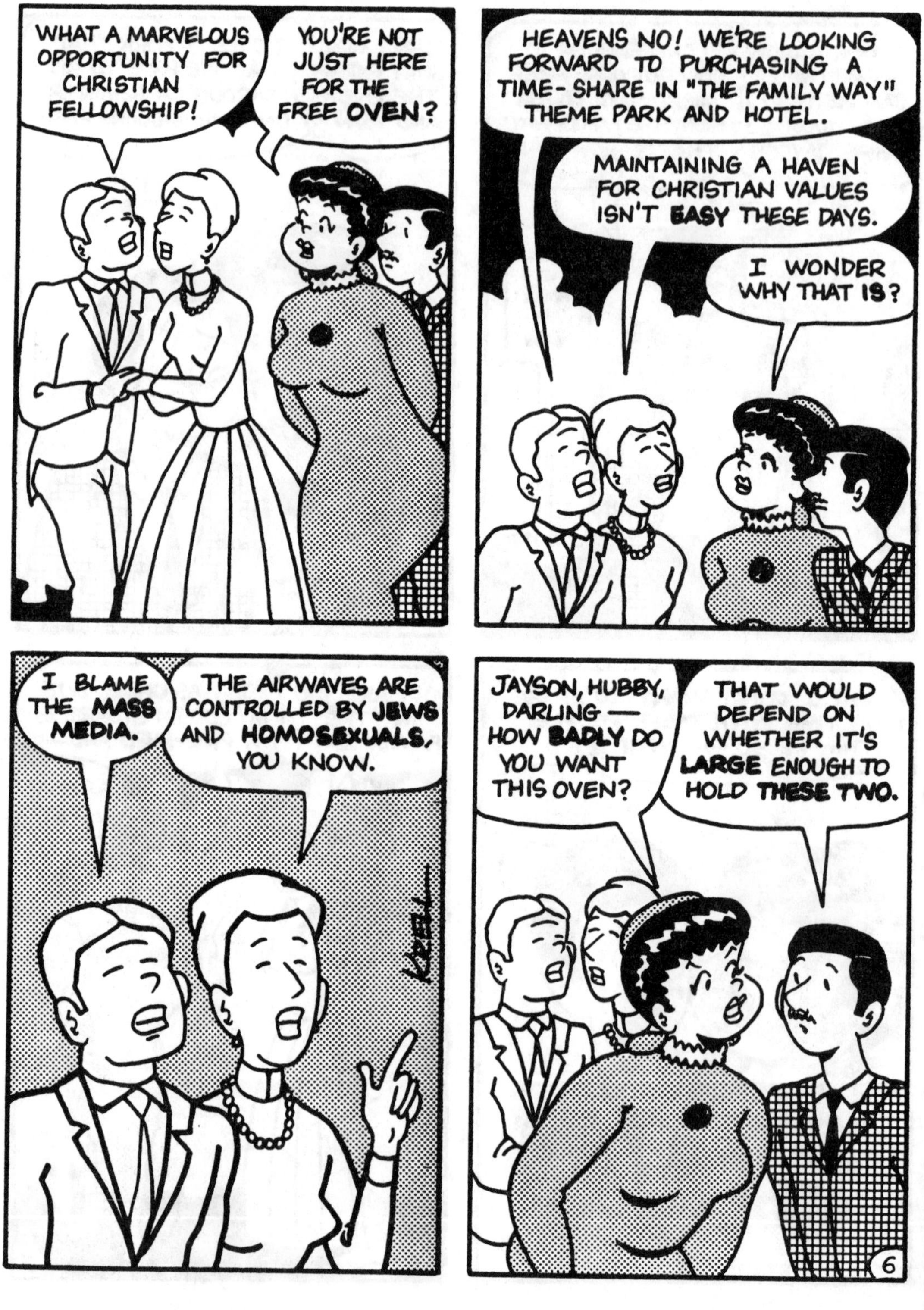
WHAT A MARVELOUS OPPORTUNITY FOR CHRISTIAN FELLOWSHIP!
YOU'RE NOT JUST HERE FOR THE FREE OVEN?
HEAVENS NO! WE'RE LOOKING FORWARD TO PURCHASING A TIME-SHARE IN "THE FAMILY WAY" THEME PARK AND HOTEL.
MAINTAINING A HAVEN FOR CHRISTIAN VALUES ISN'T EASY THESE DAYS.
I WONDER WHY THAT IS?
I BLAME THE MASS MEDIA.
THE AIRWAVES ARE CONTROLLED BY JEWS AND HOMOSEXUALS, YOU KNOW.
JAYSON, HUBBY, DARLING — HOW BADLY DO YOU WANT THIS OVEN?
THAT WOULD DEPEND ON WHETHER IT'S LARGE ENOUGH TO HOLD THESE TWO.
6

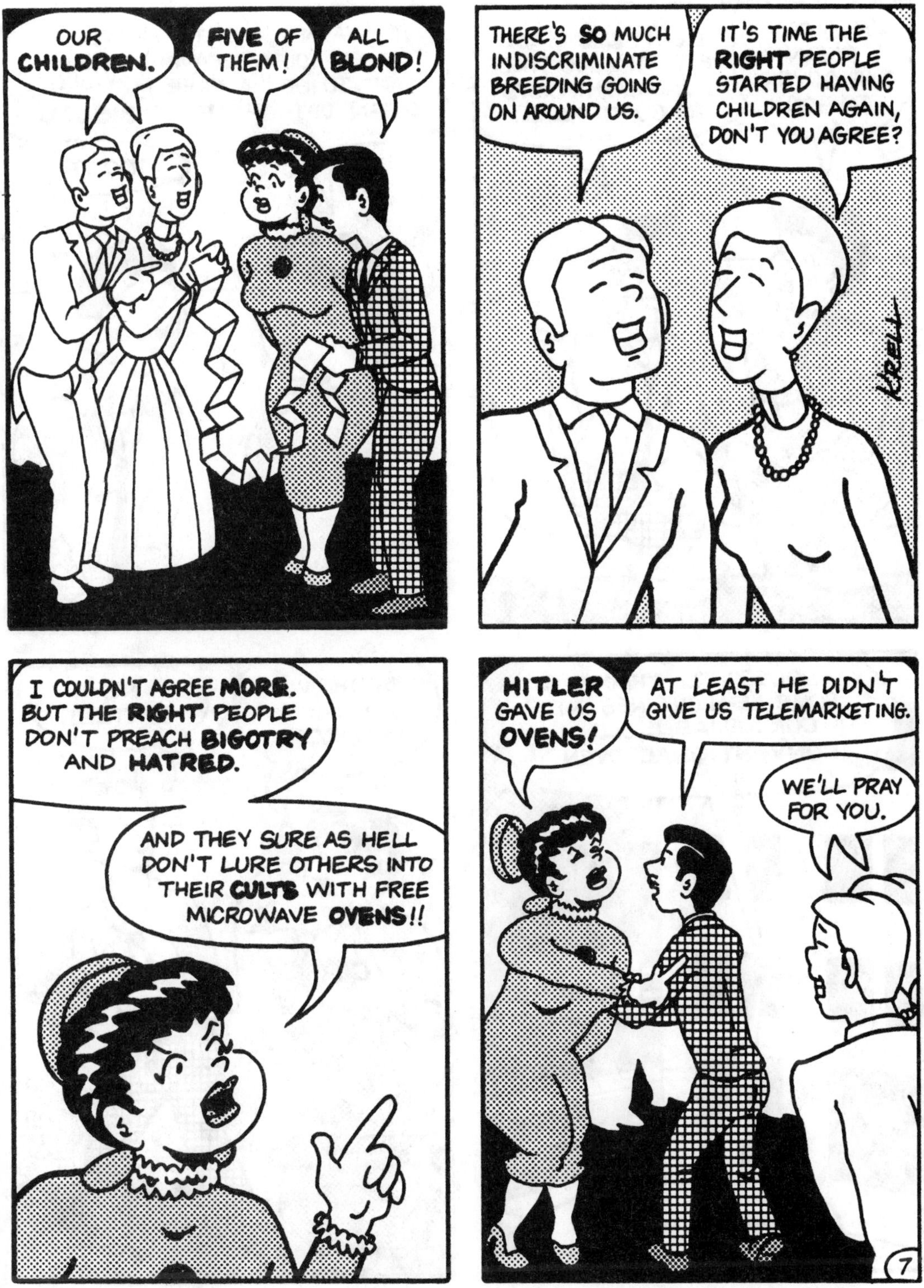
OUR CHILDREN.
FIVE OF THEM!
ALL BLOND!
THERE'S SO MUCH INDISCRIMINATE BREEDING GOING ON AROUND US.
IT'S TIME THE RIGHT PEOPLE STARTED HAVING CHILDREN AGAIN, DON'T YOU AGREE?
KRELL
I COULDN'T AGREE MORE. BUT THE RIGHT PEOPLE DON'T PREACH BIGOTRY AND HATRED.
AND THEY SURE AS HELL DON'T LURE OTHERS INTO THEIR CULTS WITH FREE MICROWAVE OVENS!!
HITLER GAVE US OVENS!
AT LEAST HE DIDN'T GIVE US TELEMARKETING.
WE'LL PRAY FOR YOU.
7

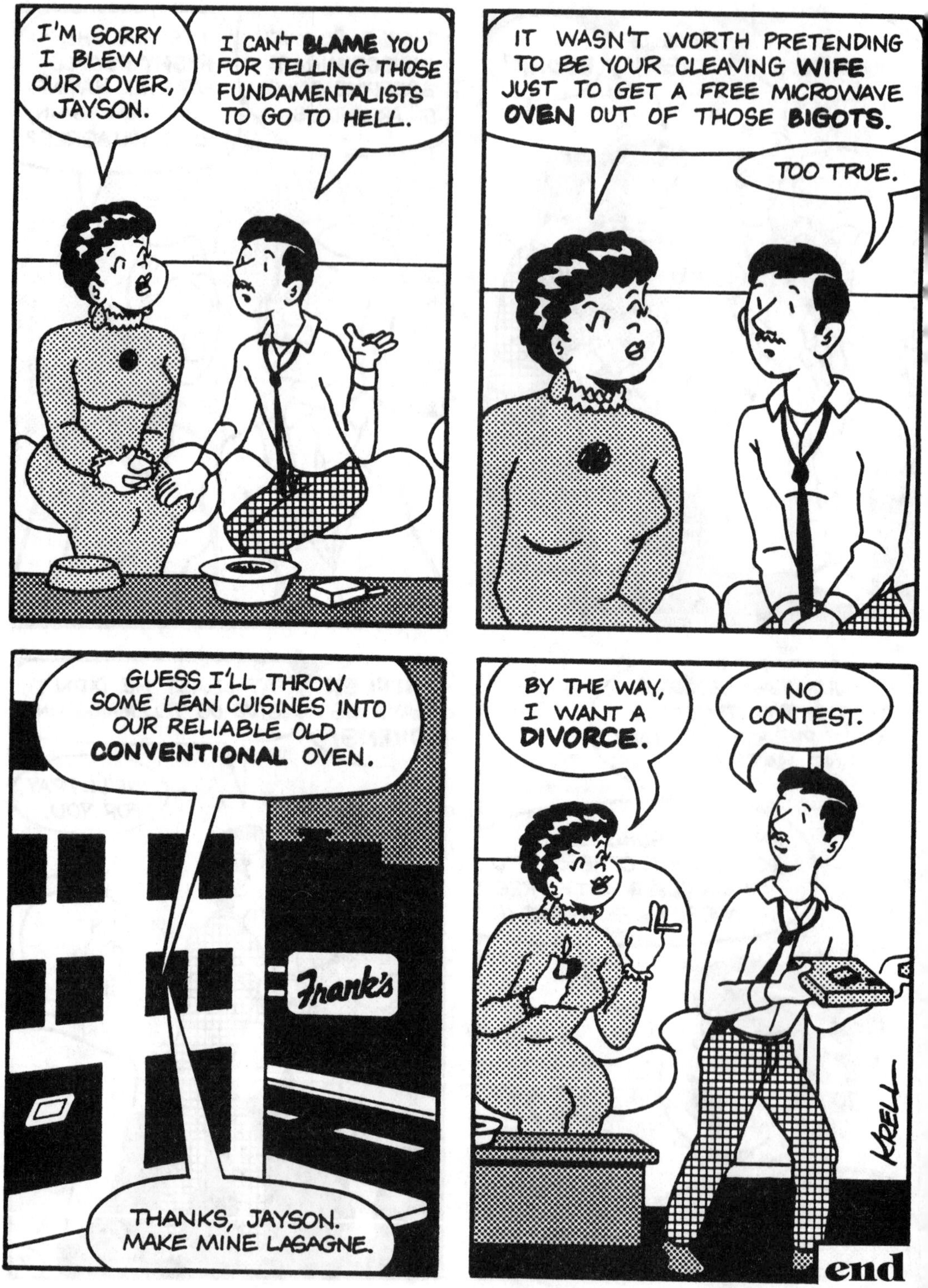

I'M SORRY I BLEW OUR COVER, JAYSON.
I CAN'T BLAME YOU FOR TELLING THOSE FUNDAMENTALISTS TO GO TO HELL.
IT WASN'T WORTH PRETENDING TO BE YOUR CLEAVING WIFE JUST TO GET A FREE MICROWAVE OVEN OUT OF THOSE BIGOTS.
TOO TRUE.
GUESS I'LL THROW SOME LEAN CUISINES INTO OUR RELIABLE OLD CONVENTIONAL OVEN.
Frank's
THANKS, JAYSON. MAKE MINE LASAGNE.
BY THE WAY, I WANT A DIVORCE.
NO CONTEST.
KRELL
end

Jayson's™ dream man

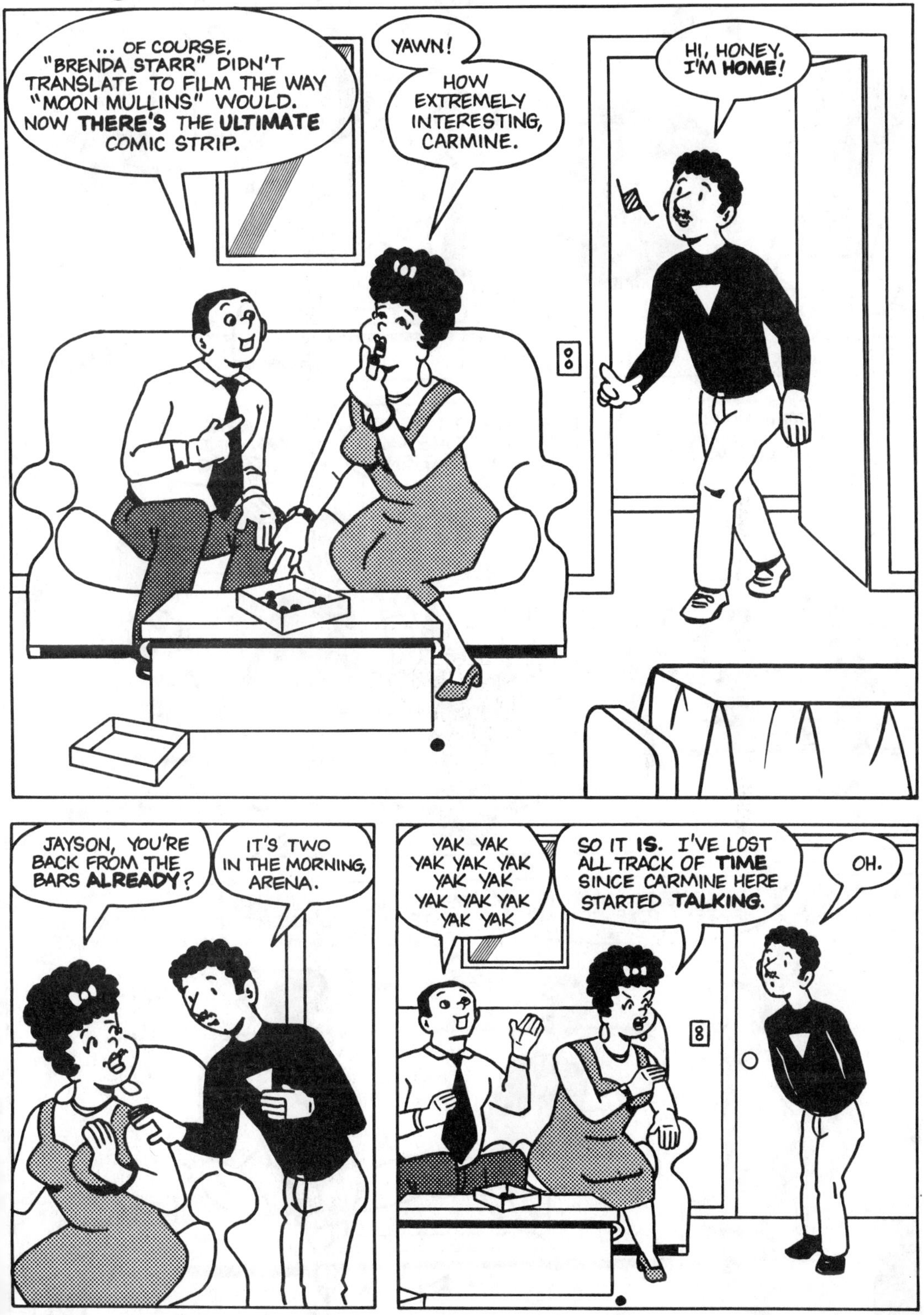

... OF COURSE, "BRENDA STARR" DIDN'T TRANSLATE TO FILM THE WAY "MOON MULLINS" WOULD. NOW THERE'S THE ULTIMATE COMIC STRIP.
YAWN! HOW EXTREMELY INTERESTING, CARMINE.
HI, HONEY. I'M HOME!
JAYSON, YOU'RE BACK FROM THE BARS ALREADY?
IT'S TWO IN THE MORNING, ARENA.
YAK YAK YAK YAK YAK YAK YAK YAK YAK YAK YAK YAK
SO IT IS. I'VE LOST ALL TRACK OF TIME SINCE CARMINE HERE STARTED TALKING.
OH.

ORIGINALLY PRESENTED IN MEATMEN VOL. 16, 1994

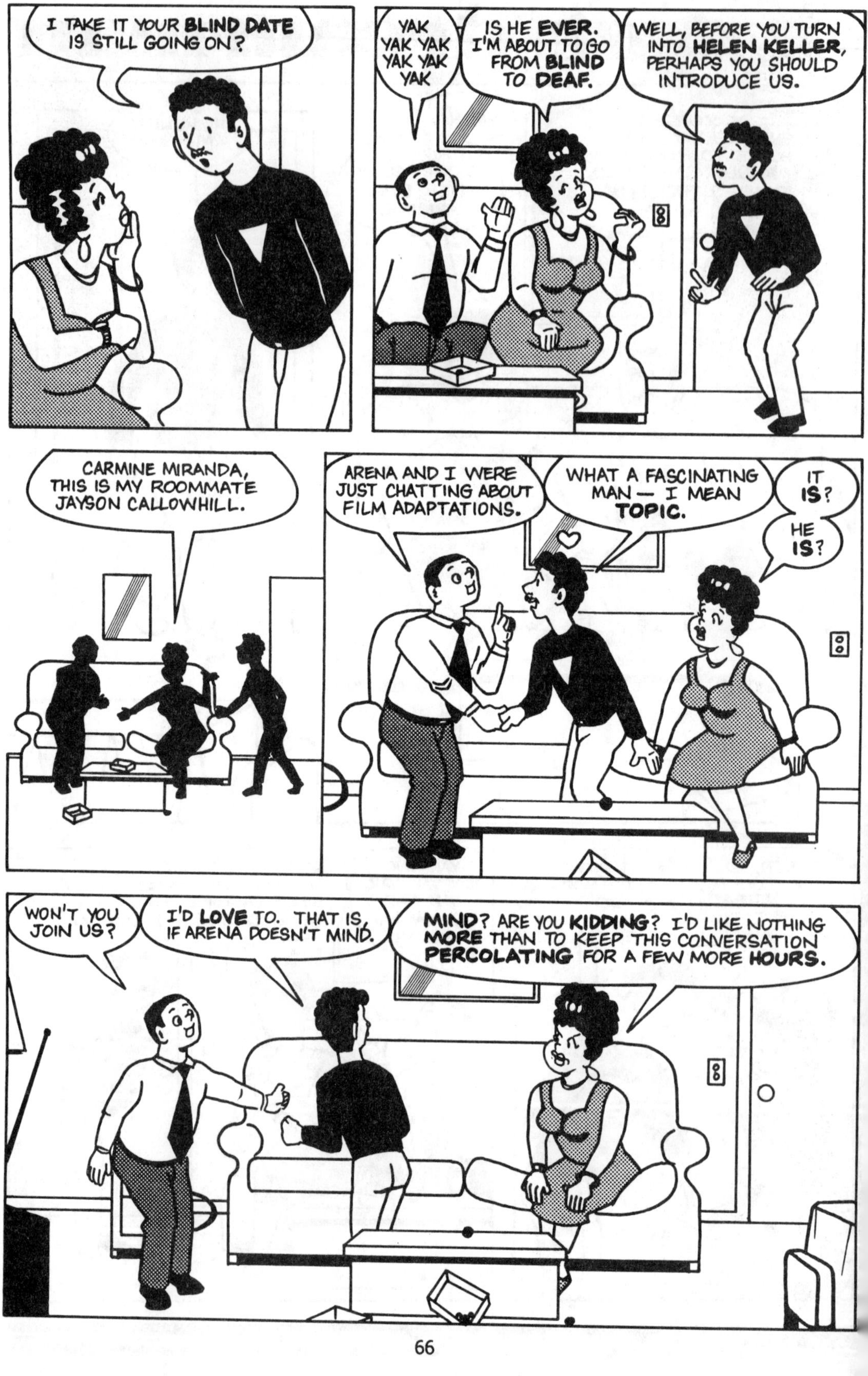
I TAKE IT YOUR BLIND DATE IS STILL GOING ON?
YAK YAK YAK YAK YAK YAK
IS HE EVER. I'M ABOUT TO GO FROM BLIND TO DEAF.
WELL, BEFORE YOU TURN INTO HELEN KELLER, PERHAPS YOU SHOULD INTRODUCE US.
CARMINE MIRANDA, THIS IS MY ROOMMATE JAYSON CALLOWHILL.
ARENA AND I WERE JUST CHATTING ABOUT FILM ADAPTATIONS.
WHAT A FASCINATING MAN — I MEAN TOPIC.
IT IS?
HE IS?
WON'T YOU JOIN US?
I'D LOVE TO. THAT IS, IF ARENA DOESN'T MIND.
MIND? ARE YOU KIDDING? I'D LIKE NOTHING MORE THAN TO KEEP THIS CONVERSATION PERCOLATING FOR A FEW MORE HOURS.

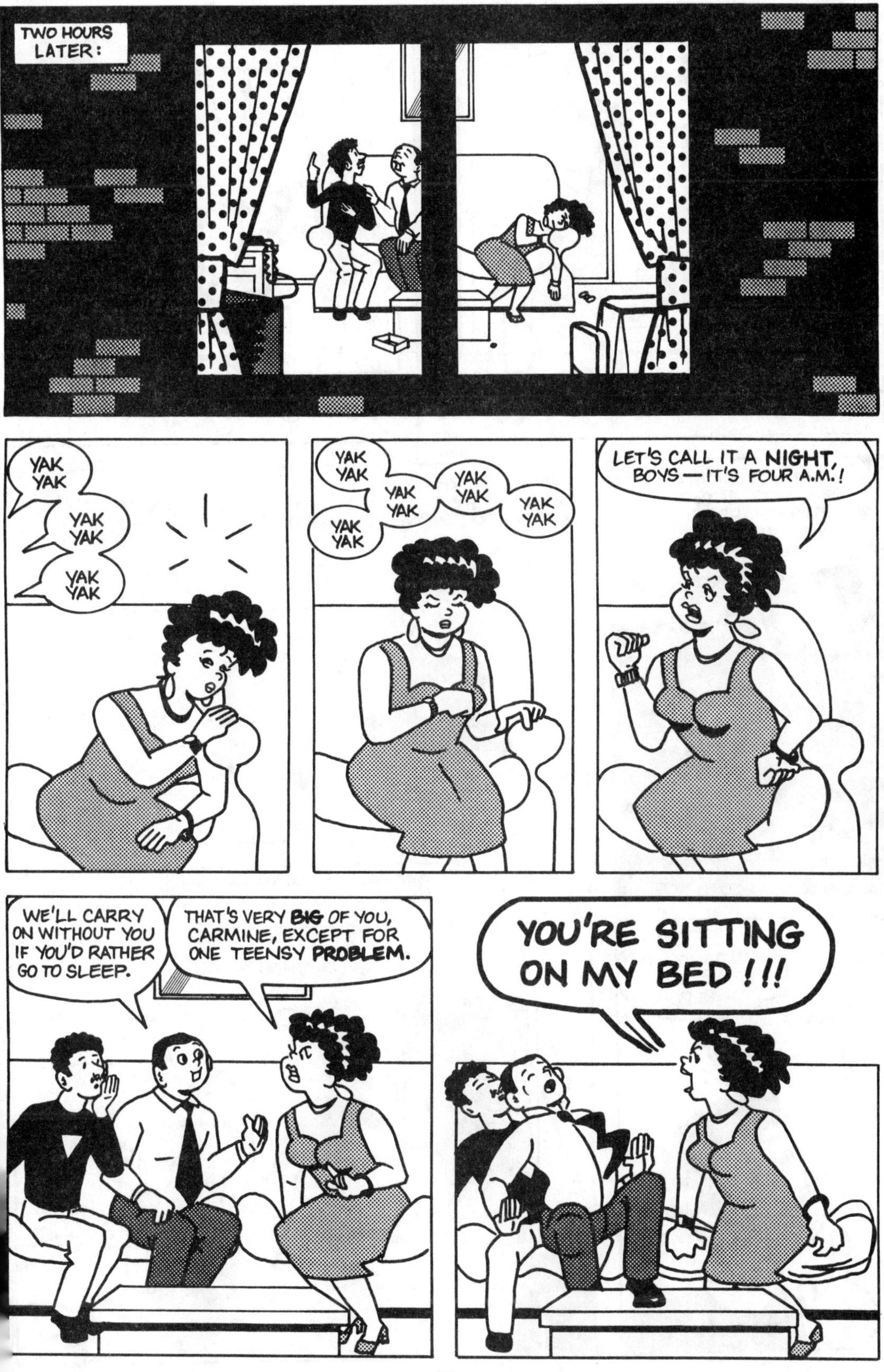
TWO HOURS LATER:
YAK YAK
YAK YAK
YAK YAK
YAK YAK
YAK YAK
YAK YAK
YAK YAK
YAK YAK
LET'S CALL IT A **NIGHT**, BOYS — IT'S FOUR A.M.!
WE'LL CARRY ON WITHOUT YOU IF YOU'D RATHER GO TO SLEEP.
THAT'S VERY **BIG** OF YOU, CARMINE, EXCEPT FOR ONE TEENSY **PROBLEM**.
YOU'RE SITTING ON MY BED!!!

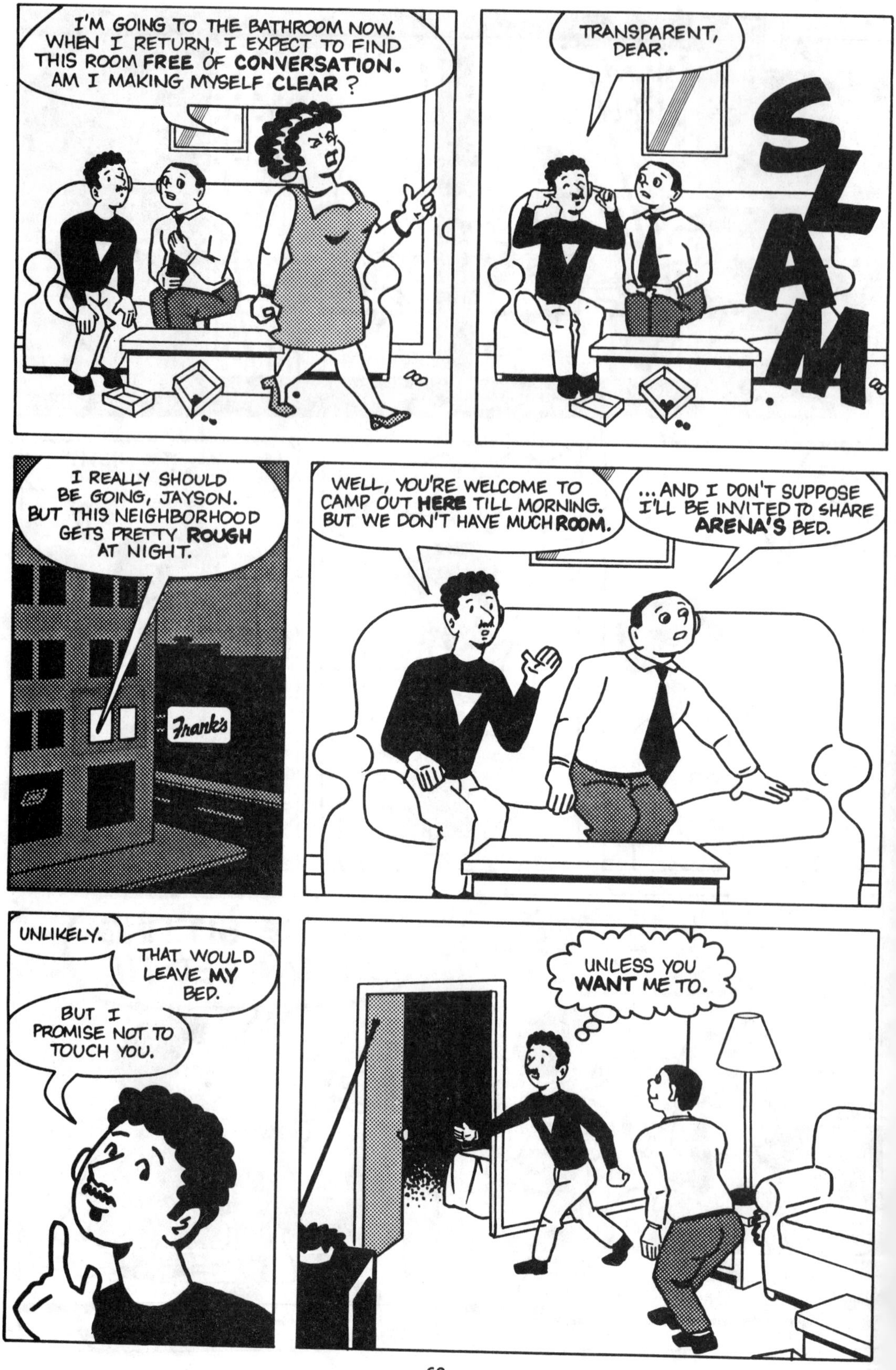
I'M GOING TO THE BATHROOM NOW. WHEN I RETURN, I EXPECT TO FIND THIS ROOM FREE OF CONVERSATION. AM I MAKING MYSELF CLEAR ?
TRANSPARENT, DEAR.
SLAM
I REALLY SHOULD BE GOING, JAYSON. BUT THIS NEIGHBORHOOD GETS PRETTY ROUGH AT NIGHT.
Frank's
WELL, YOU'RE WELCOME TO CAMP OUT HERE TILL MORNING. BUT WE DON'T HAVE MUCH ROOM.
...AND I DON'T SUPPOSE I'LL BE INVITED TO SHARE ARENA'S BED.
UNLIKELY.
THAT WOULD LEAVE MY BED.
BUT I PROMISE NOT TO TOUCH YOU.
UNLESS YOU WANT ME TO.

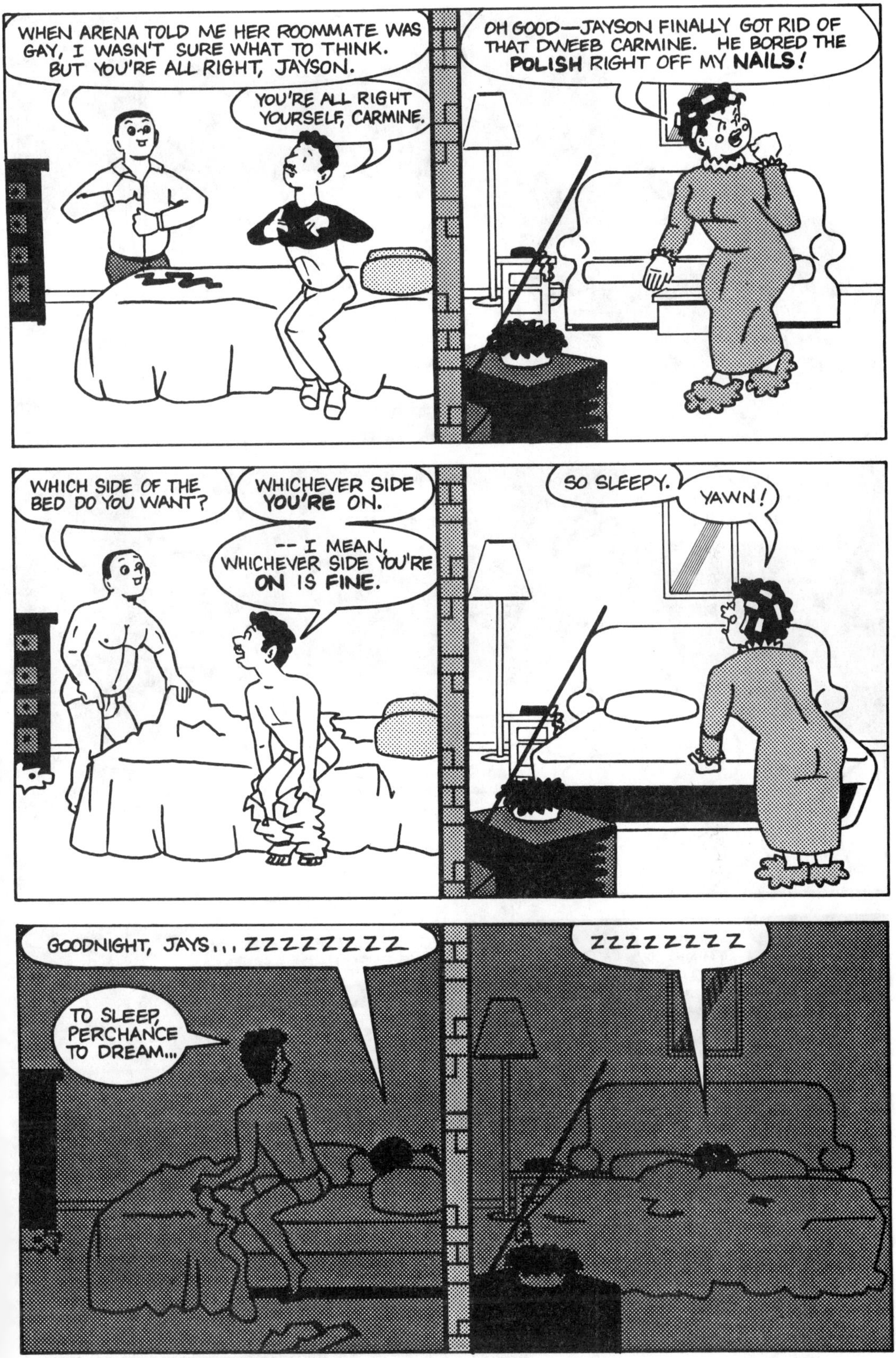
WHEN ARENA TOLD ME HER ROOMMATE WAS GAY, I WASN'T SURE WHAT TO THINK. BUT YOU'RE ALL RIGHT, JAYSON.
YOU'RE ALL RIGHT YOURSELF, CARMINE.
OH GOOD—JAYSON FINALLY GOT RID OF THAT DWEEB CARMINE. HE BORED THE **POLISH** RIGHT OFF MY **NAILS**!
WHICH SIDE OF THE BED DO YOU WANT?
WHICHEVER SIDE **YOU'RE** ON.
-- I MEAN, WHICHEVER SIDE YOU'RE **ON** IS **FINE**.
SO SLEEPY.
YAWN!
GOODNIGHT, JAYS... ZZZZZZZZ
TO SLEEP, PERCHANCE TO DREAM...
ZZZZZZZZ

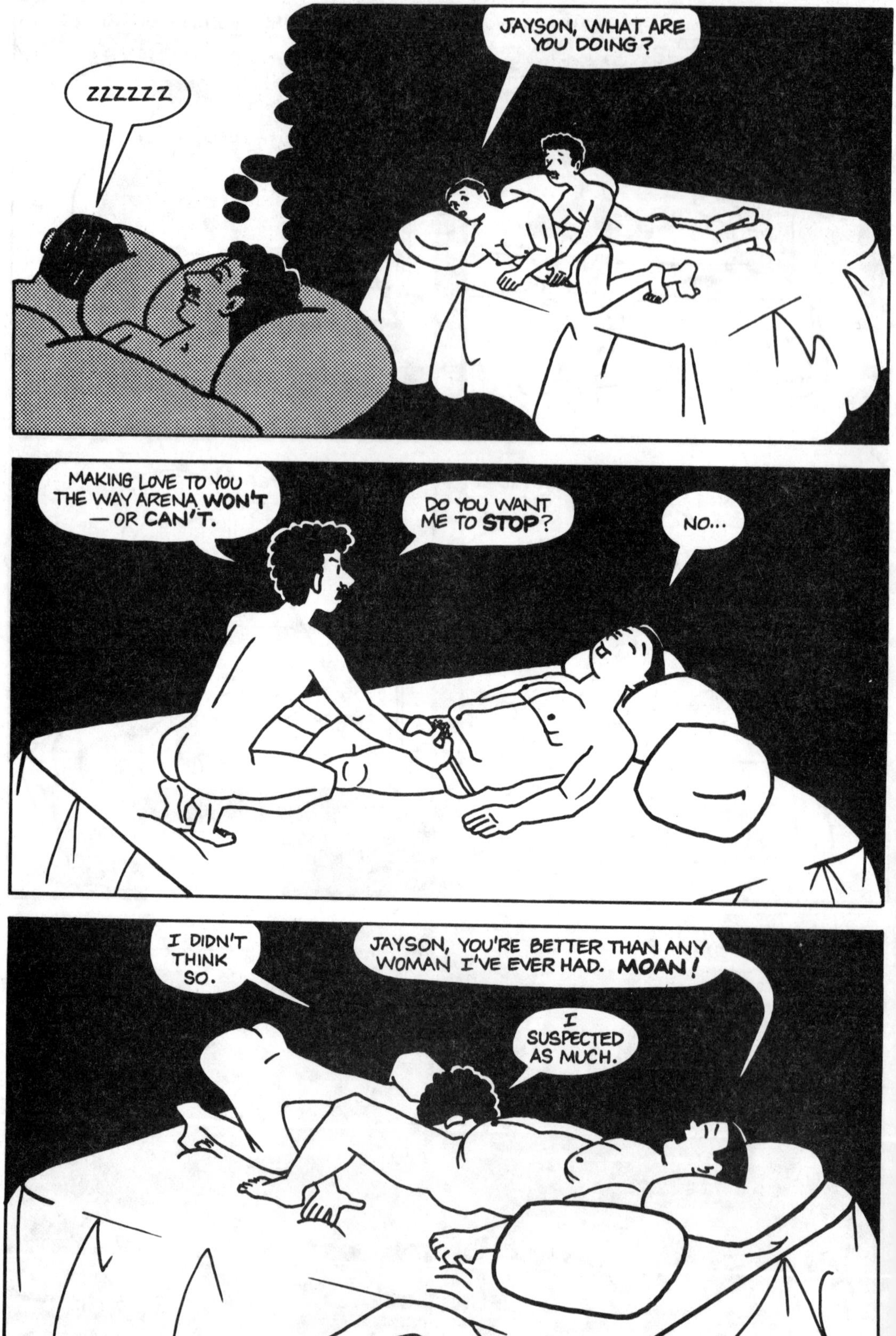
ZZZZZZ
JAYSON, WHAT ARE YOU DOING?
MAKING LOVE TO YOU THE WAY ARENA **WON'T** — OR **CAN'T**.
DO YOU WANT ME TO **STOP**?
NO...
I DIDN'T THINK SO.
JAYSON, YOU'RE BETTER THAN ANY WOMAN I'VE EVER HAD. **MOAN**!
I SUSPECTED AS MUCH.

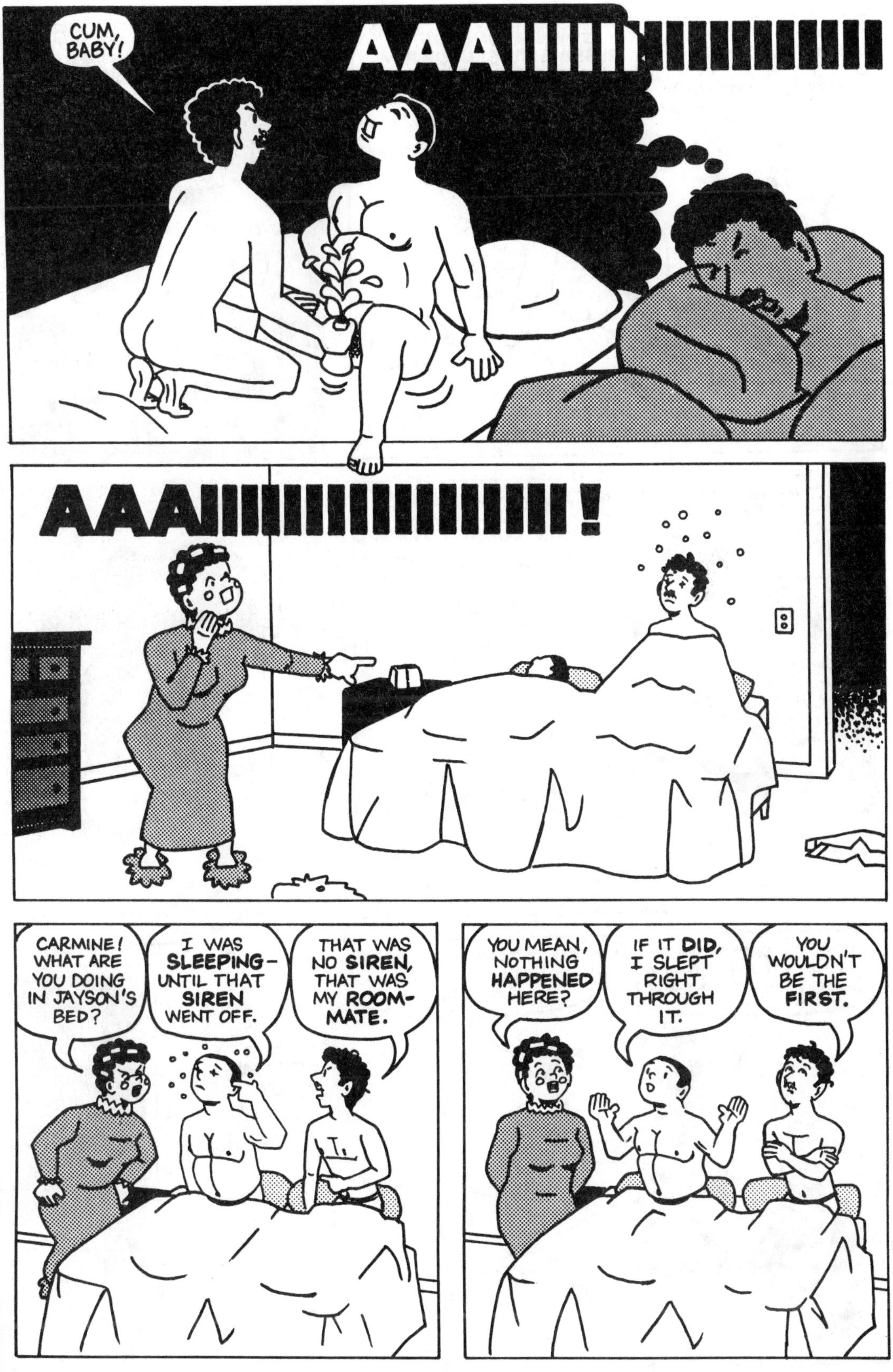
CUM, BABY!
AAAIIIIIIIIIIIIIIIIIII
AAAIIIIIIIIIIIIIIIIIIIIII!
CARMINE! WHAT ARE YOU DOING IN JAYSON'S BED?
I WAS SLEEPING– UNTIL THAT SIREN WENT OFF.
THAT WAS NO SIREN, THAT WAS MY ROOMMATE.
YOU MEAN, NOTHING HAPPENED HERE?
IF IT DID, I SLEPT RIGHT THROUGH IT.
YOU WOULDN'T BE THE FIRST.

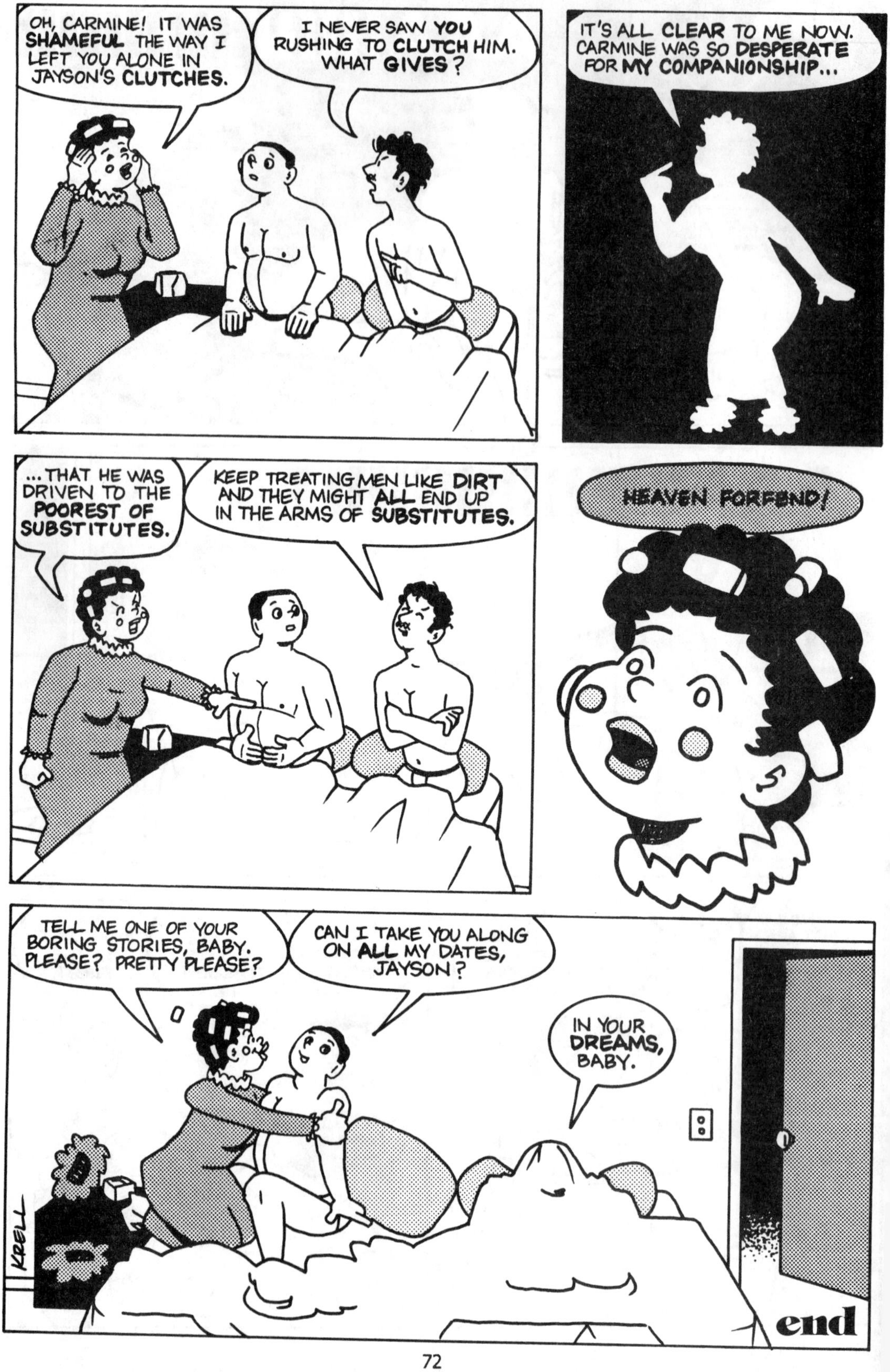
OH, CARMINE! IT WAS SHAMEFUL THE WAY I LEFT YOU ALONE IN JAYSON'S CLUTCHES.
I NEVER SAW YOU RUSHING TO CLUTCH HIM. WHAT GIVES?
IT'S ALL CLEAR TO ME NOW. CARMINE WAS SO DESPERATE FOR MY COMPANIONSHIP...
...THAT HE WAS DRIVEN TO THE POOREST OF SUBSTITUTES.
KEEP TREATING MEN LIKE DIRT AND THEY MIGHT ALL END UP IN THE ARMS OF SUBSTITUTES.
HEAVEN FORFEND!
TELL ME ONE OF YOUR BORING STORIES, BABY. PLEASE? PRETTY PLEASE?
CAN I TAKE YOU ALONG ON ALL MY DATES, JAYSON?
IN YOUR DREAMS, BABY.
KRELL
end

Jayson™ works out

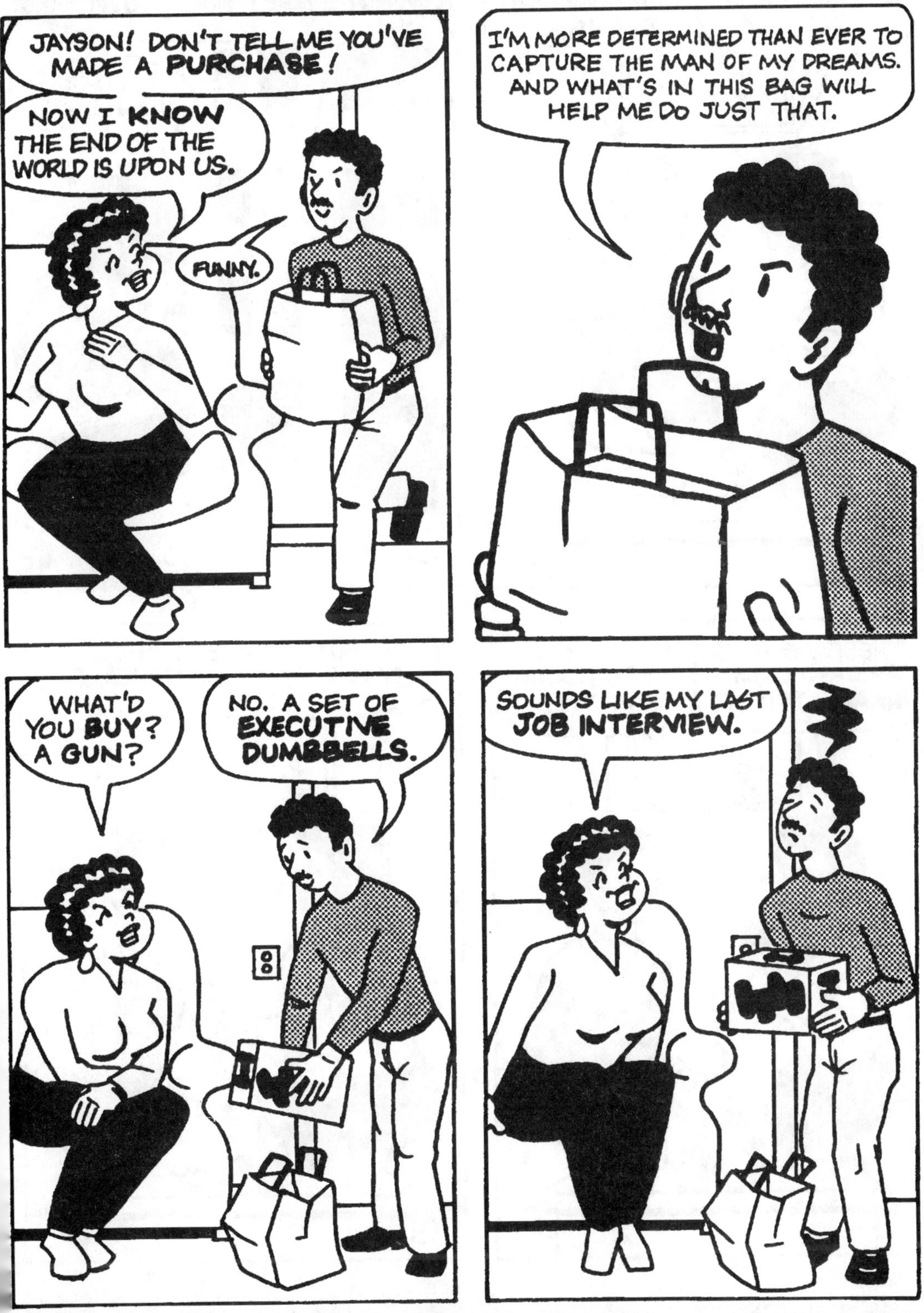

JAYSON! DON'T TELL ME YOU'VE MADE A PURCHASE!
NOW I KNOW THE END OF THE WORLD IS UPON US.
FUNNY.
I'M MORE DETERMINED THAN EVER TO CAPTURE THE MAN OF MY DREAMS. AND WHAT'S IN THIS BAG WILL HELP ME DO JUST THAT.
WHAT'D YOU BUY? A GUN?
NO. A SET OF EXECUTIVE DUMBBELLS.
SOUNDS LIKE MY LAST JOB INTERVIEW.

ORIGINALLY PRESENTED IN MEATMEN VOL. 19, 1997

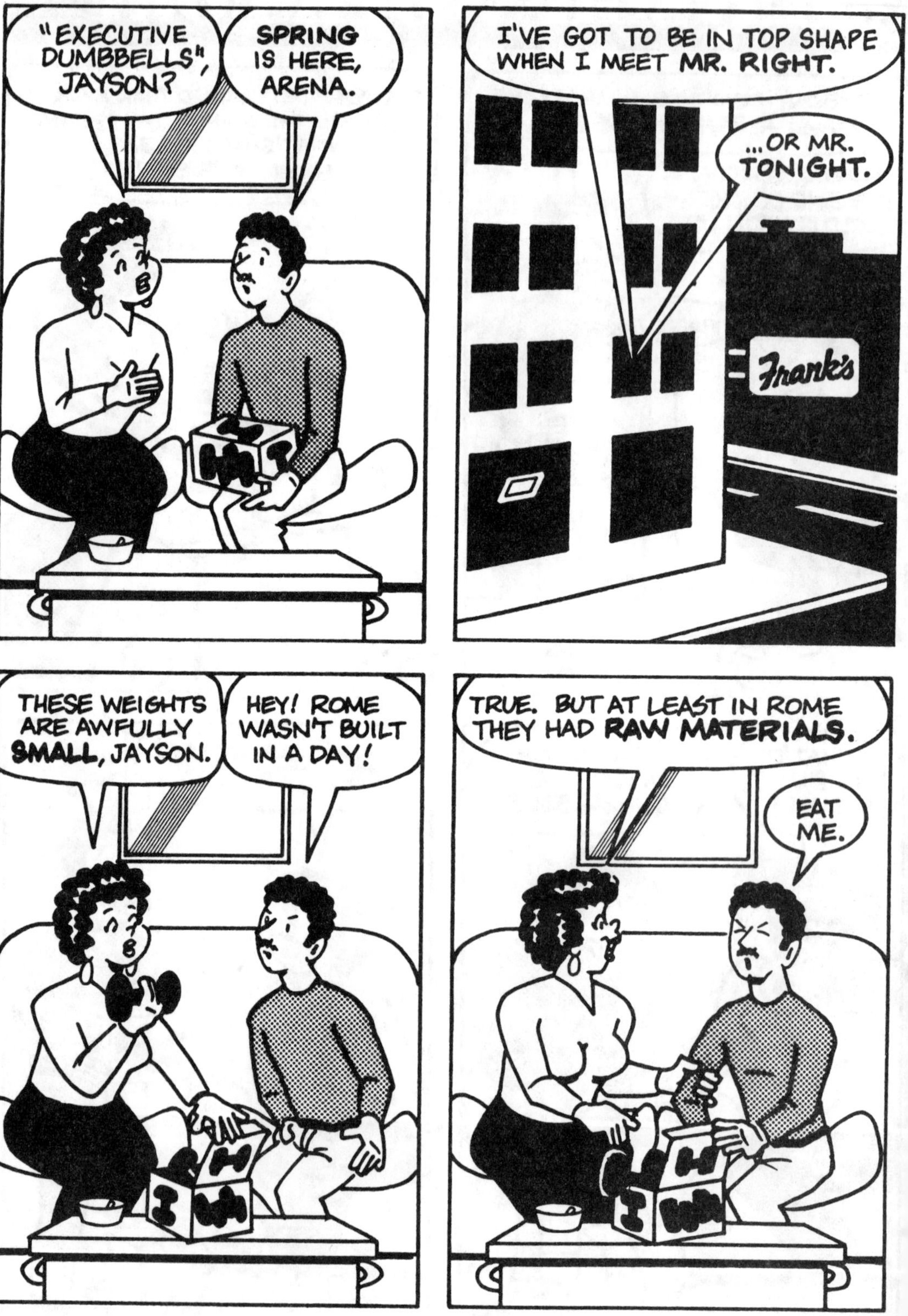
"EXECUTIVE DUMBBELLS", JAYSON?
SPRING IS HERE, ARENA.
I'VE GOT TO BE IN TOP SHAPE WHEN I MEET MR. RIGHT.
...OR MR. TONIGHT.
Frank's
THESE WEIGHTS ARE AWFULLY SMALL, JAYSON.
HEY! ROME WASN'T BUILT IN A DAY!
TRUE. BUT AT LEAST IN ROME THEY HAD RAW MATERIALS.
EAT ME.

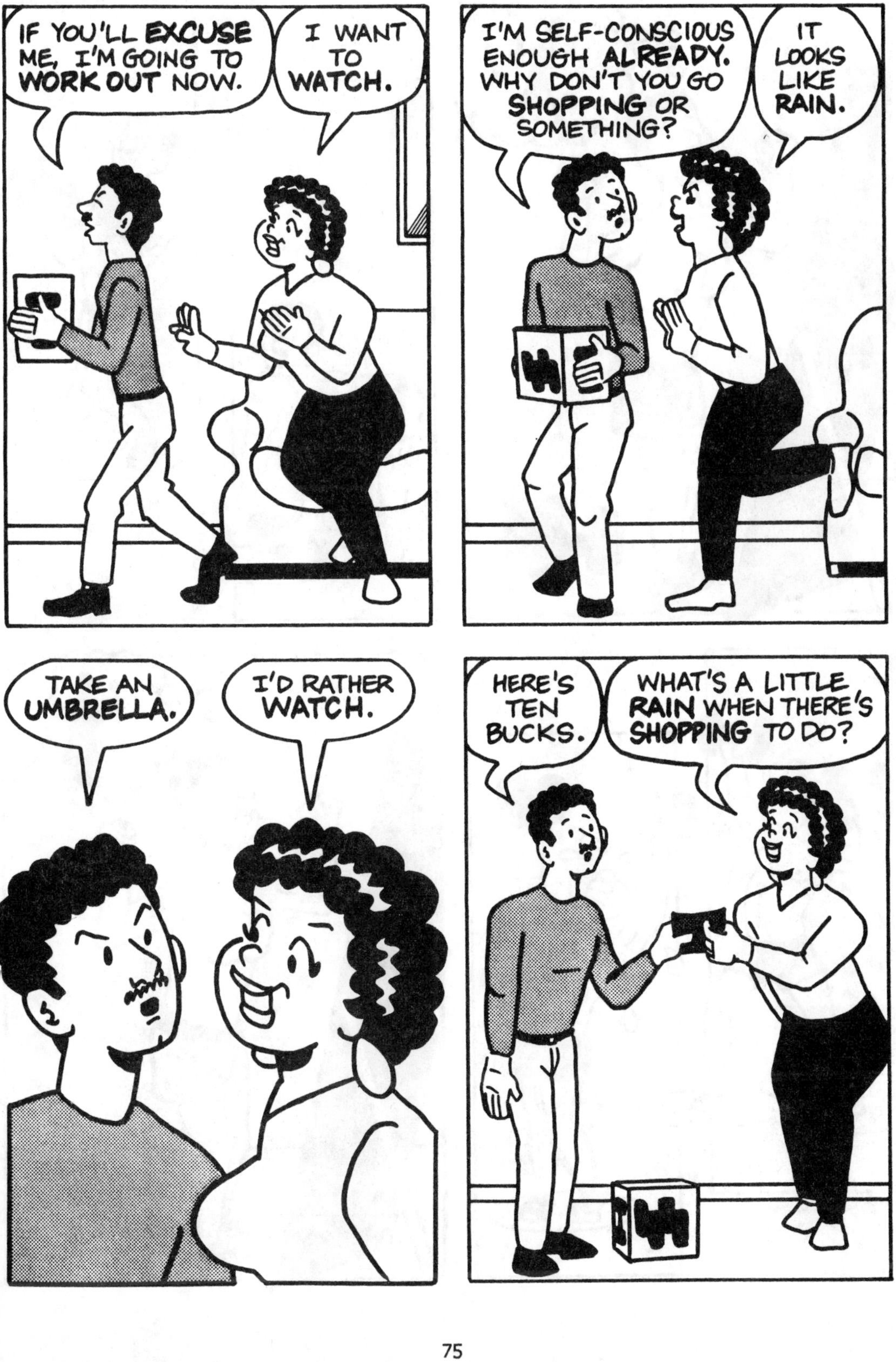
IF YOU'LL EXCUSE ME, I'M GOING TO WORK OUT NOW.
I WANT TO WATCH.
I'M SELF-CONSCIOUS ENOUGH ALREADY. WHY DON'T YOU GO SHOPPING OR SOMETHING?
IT LOOKS LIKE RAIN.
TAKE AN UMBRELLA.
I'D RATHER WATCH.
HERE'S TEN BUCKS.
WHAT'S A LITTLE RAIN WHEN THERE'S SHOPPING TO DO?

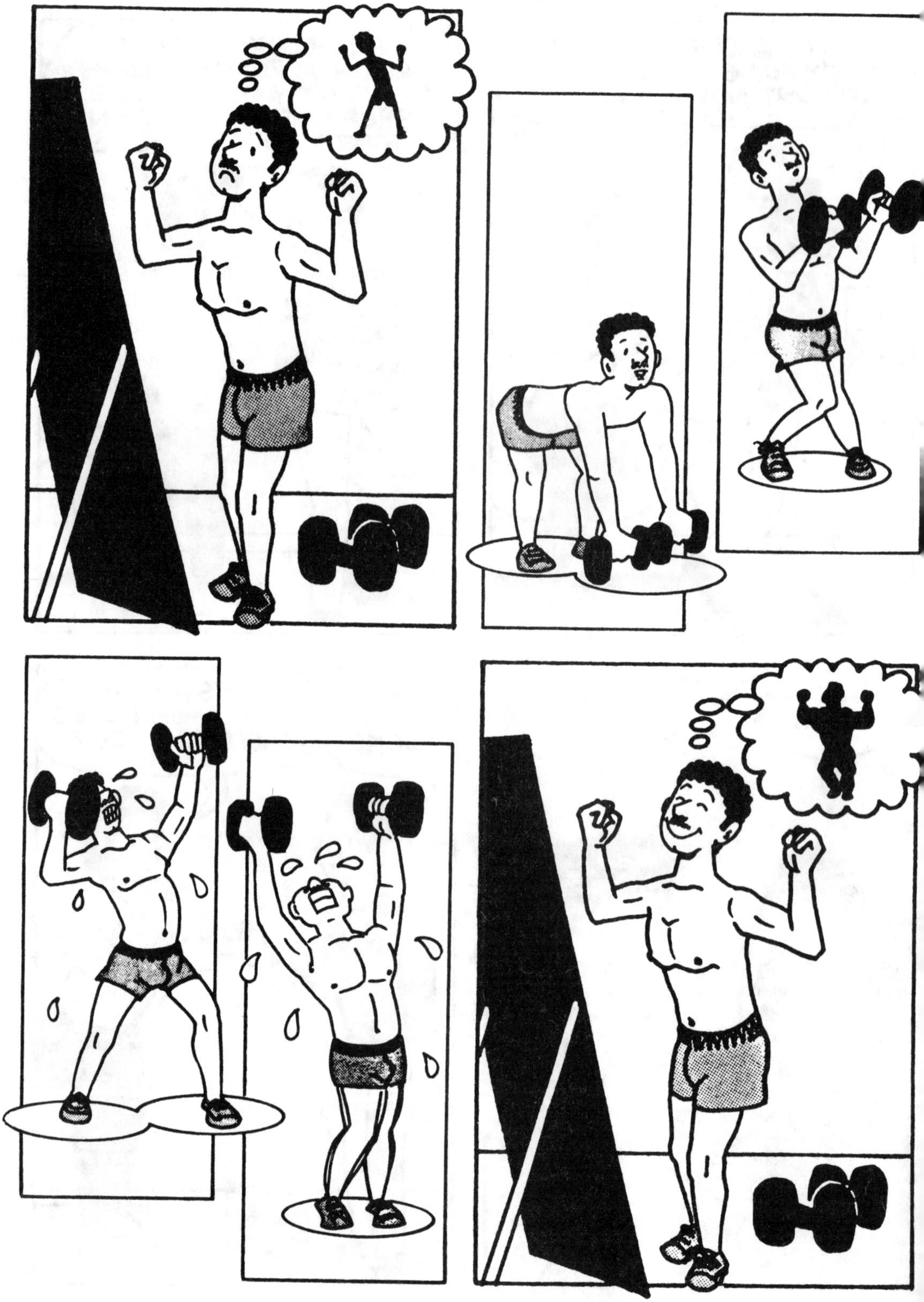

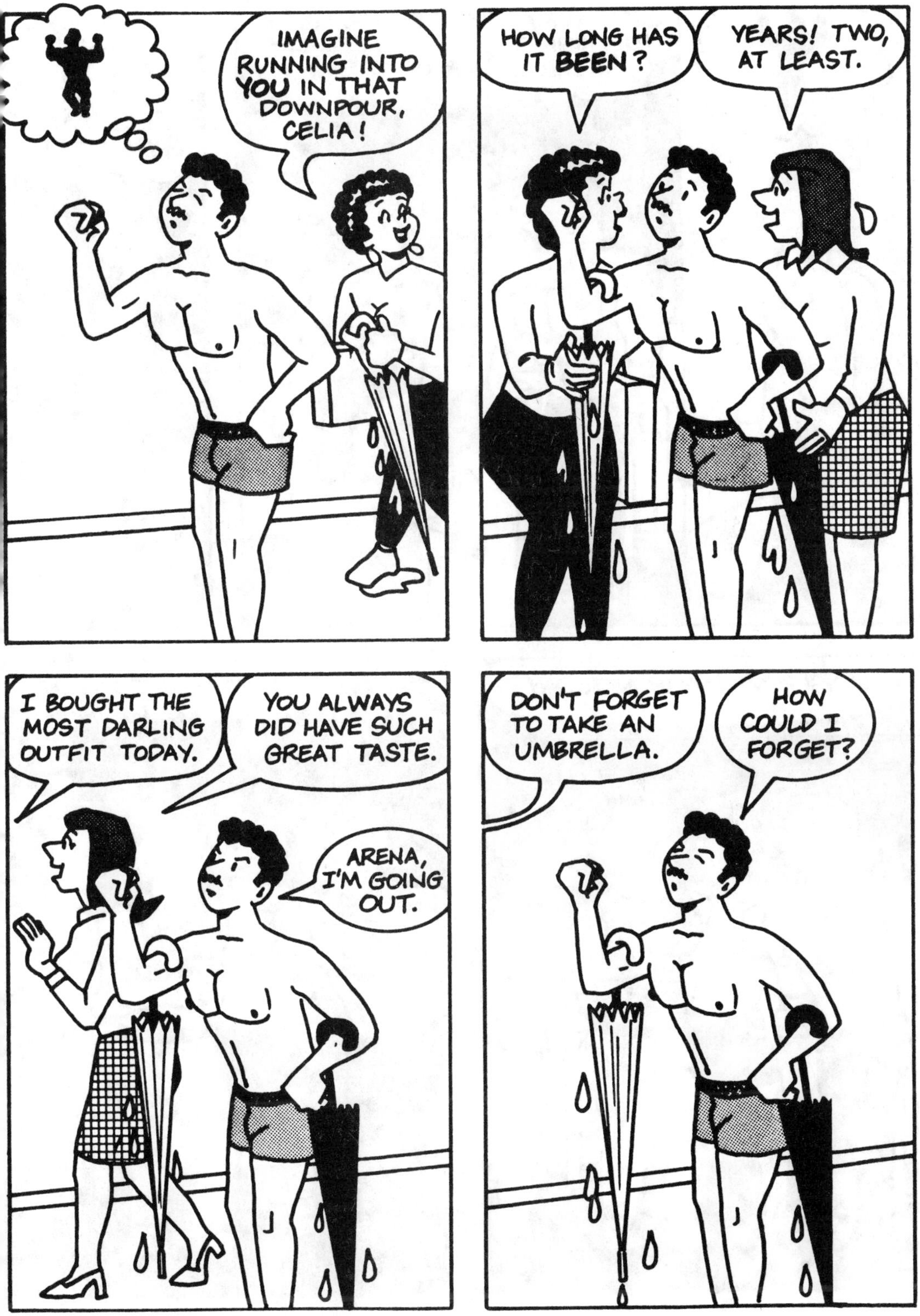
IMAGINE RUNNING INTO YOU IN THAT DOWNPOUR, CELIA!
HOW LONG HAS IT BEEN?
YEARS! TWO, AT LEAST.
I BOUGHT THE MOST DARLING OUTFIT TODAY.
YOU ALWAYS DID HAVE SUCH GREAT TASTE.
ARENA, I'M GOING OUT.
DON'T FORGET TO TAKE AN UMBRELLA.
HOW COULD I FORGET?

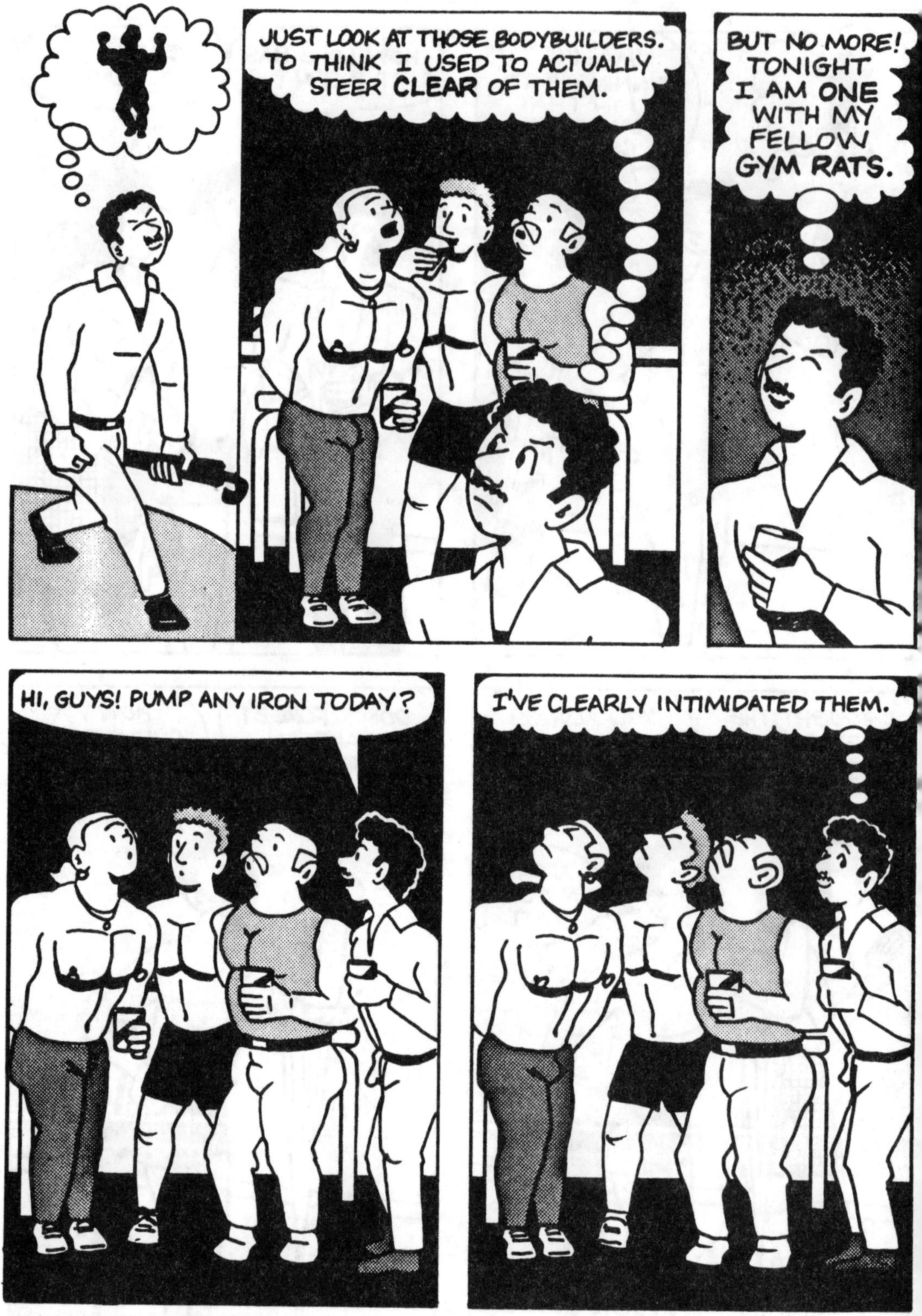
JUST LOOK AT THOSE BODYBUILDERS. TO THINK I USED TO ACTUALLY STEER CLEAR OF THEM.
BUT NO MORE! TONIGHT I AM ONE WITH MY FELLOW GYM RATS.
HI, GUYS! PUMP ANY IRON TODAY?
I'VE CLEARLY INTIMIDATED THEM.

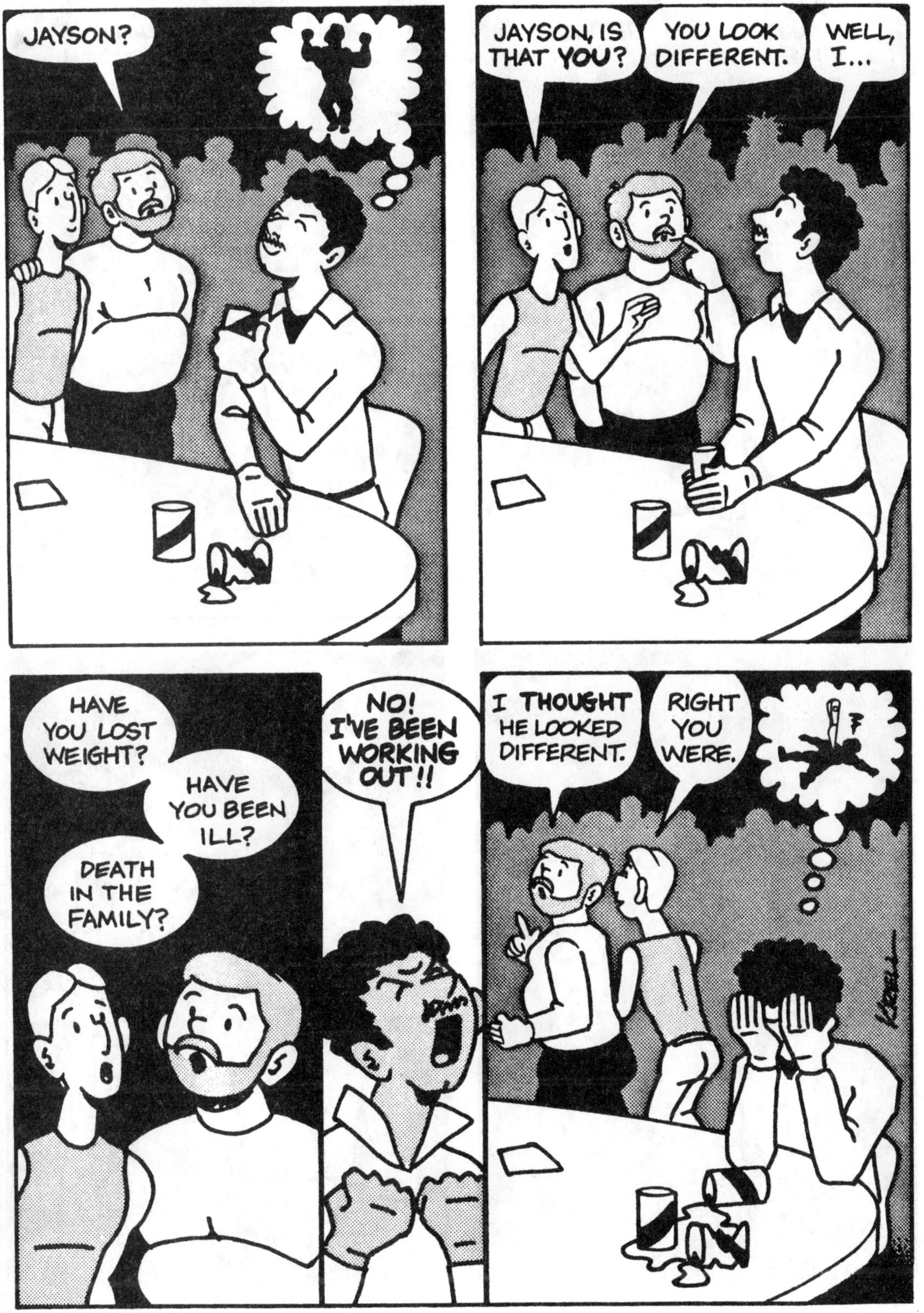
JAYSON?
JAYSON, IS THAT YOU?
YOU LOOK DIFFERENT.
WELL, I...
HAVE YOU LOST WEIGHT?
HAVE YOU BEEN ILL?
DEATH IN THE FAMILY?
NO! I'VE BEEN WORKING OUT!!
I THOUGHT HE LOOKED DIFFERENT.
RIGHT YOU WERE.

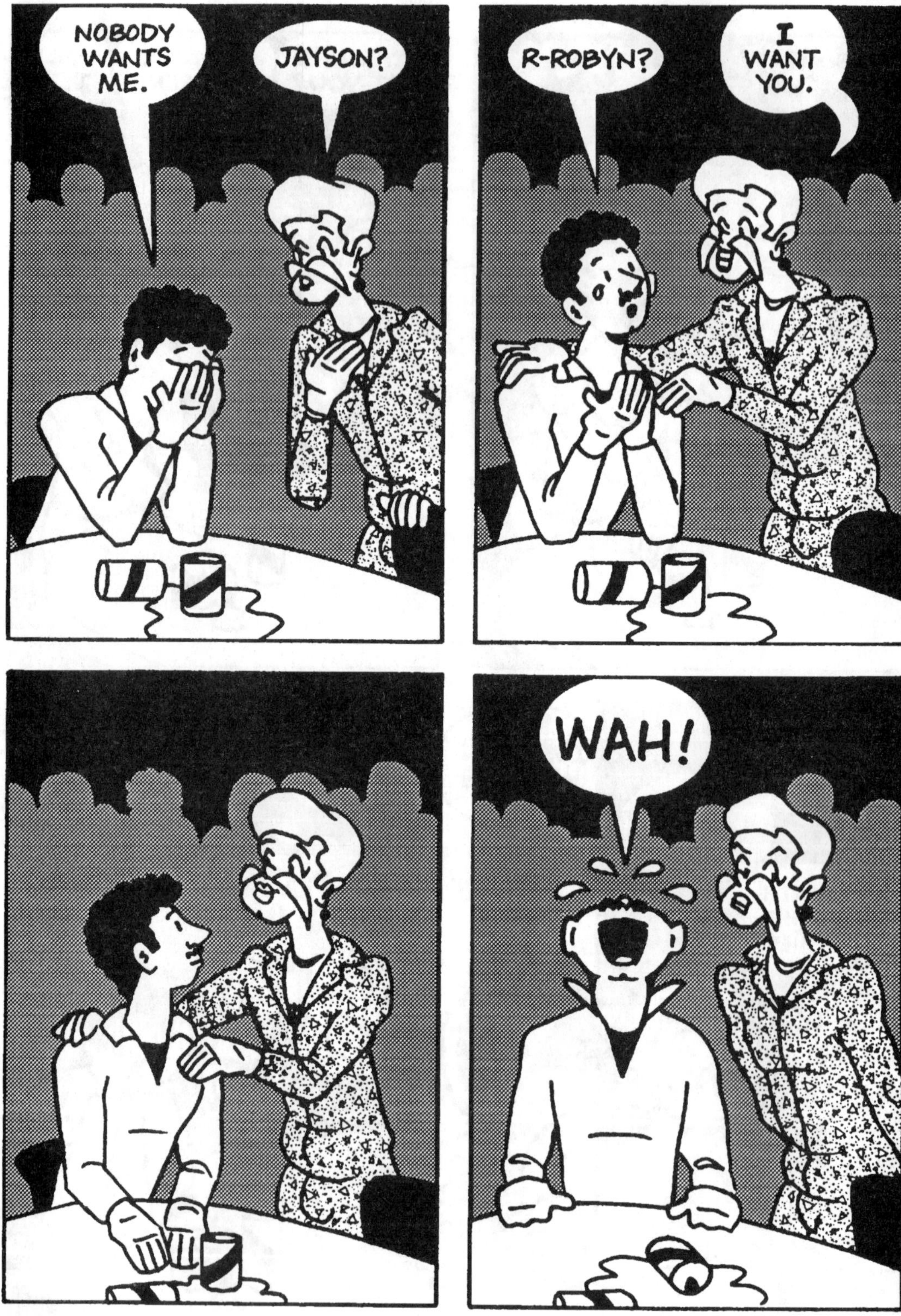
NOBODY WANTS ME.
JAYSON?
R-ROBYN?
I WANT YOU.
WAH!

MY WORKOUT PROGRAM IS A COMPLETE FAILURE.
JAYSON, LIFTING WEIGHTS ISN'T THE ANSWER.
IT'S NOT?
NO. LOOK AT ME! I NEVER WORK OUT.
THE ONLY THING I EVER LIFT IS MY LEGS.
...AND I'M NEVER WITHOUT A MAN.
WHY?
BECAUSE, DAHLING, IT'S WHAT'S INSIDE THAT COUNTS.
RIGHT. INSIDE YOUR WALLET.
MY PLACE.
YES SIR!

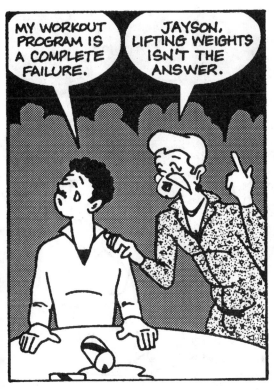

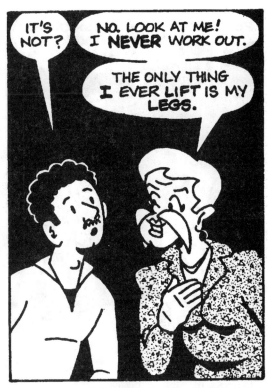

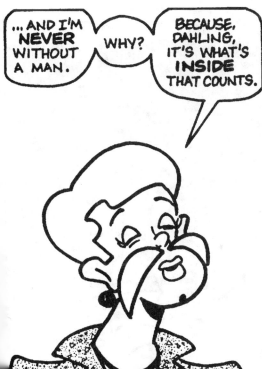

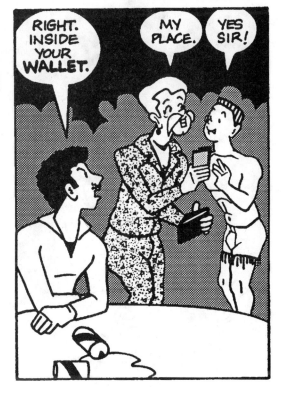

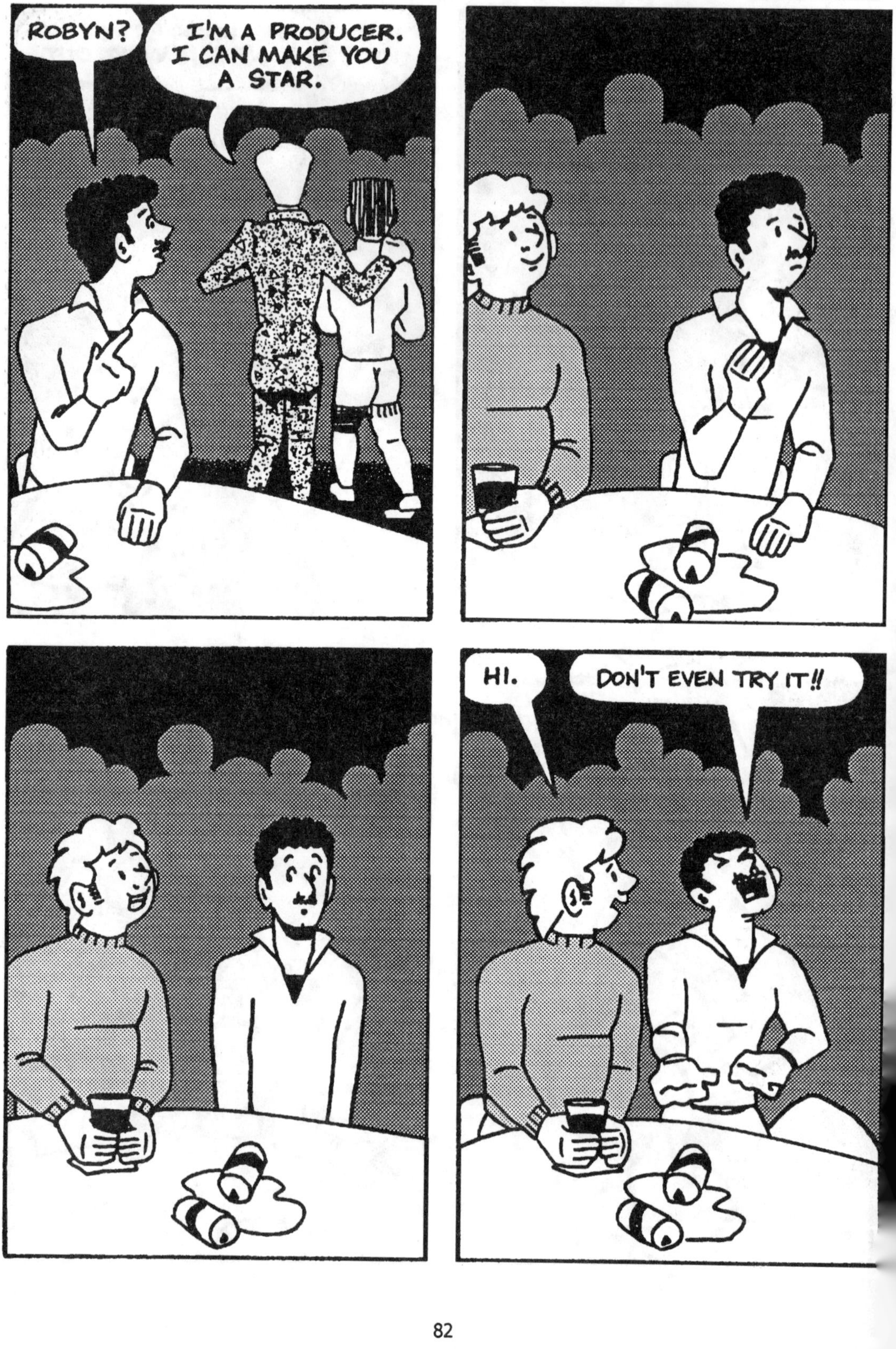
ROBYN?
I'M A PRODUCER. I CAN MAKE YOU A STAR.
HI.
DON'T EVEN TRY IT!!

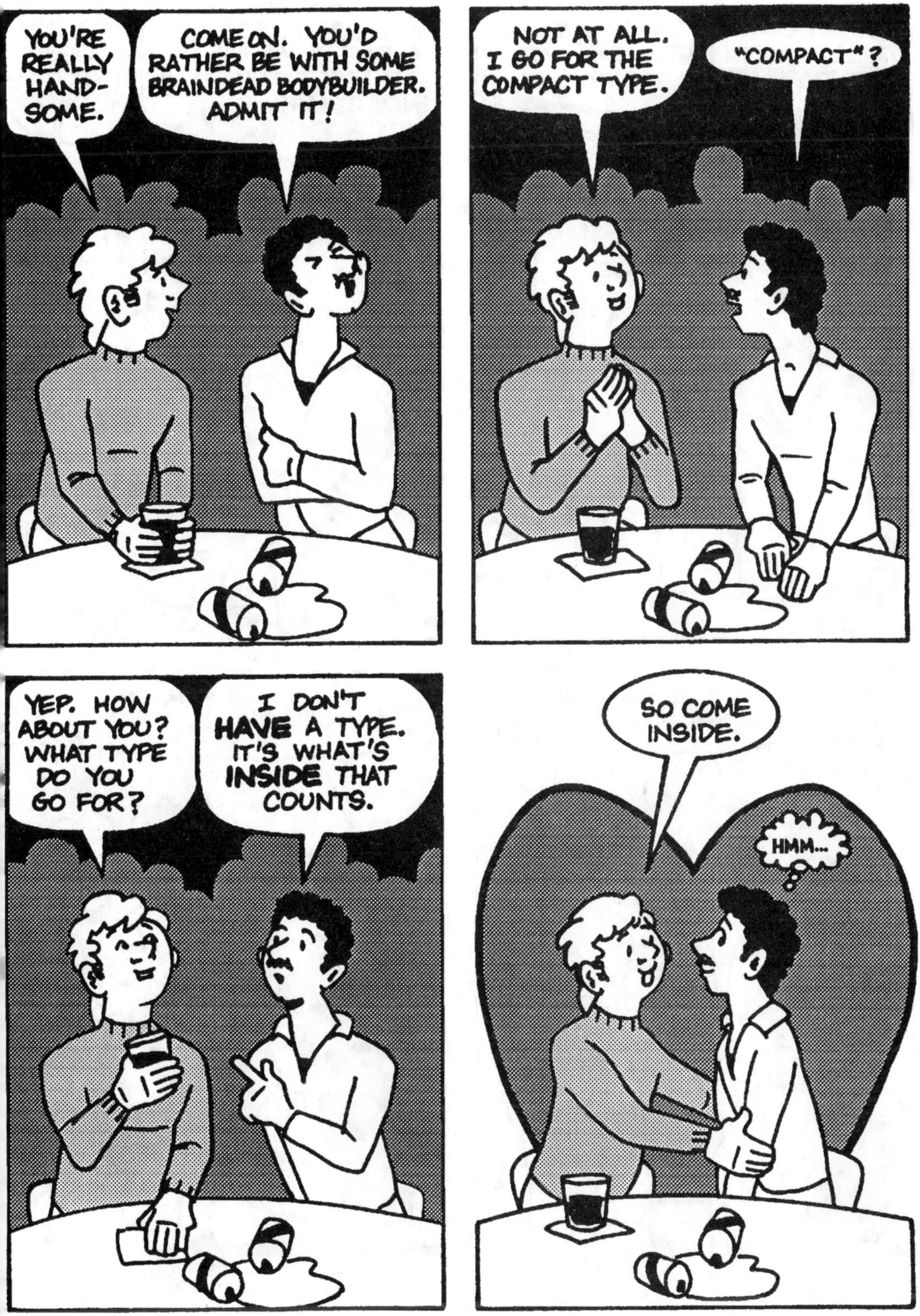
YOU'RE REALLY HAND-SOME.
COME ON. YOU'D RATHER BE WITH SOME BRAINDEAD BODYBUILDER. ADMIT IT!
NOT AT ALL. I GO FOR THE COMPACT TYPE.
"COMPACT"?
YEP. HOW ABOUT YOU? WHAT TYPE DO YOU GO FOR?
I DON'T HAVE A TYPE. IT'S WHAT'S INSIDE THAT COUNTS.
SO COME INSIDE.
HMM...

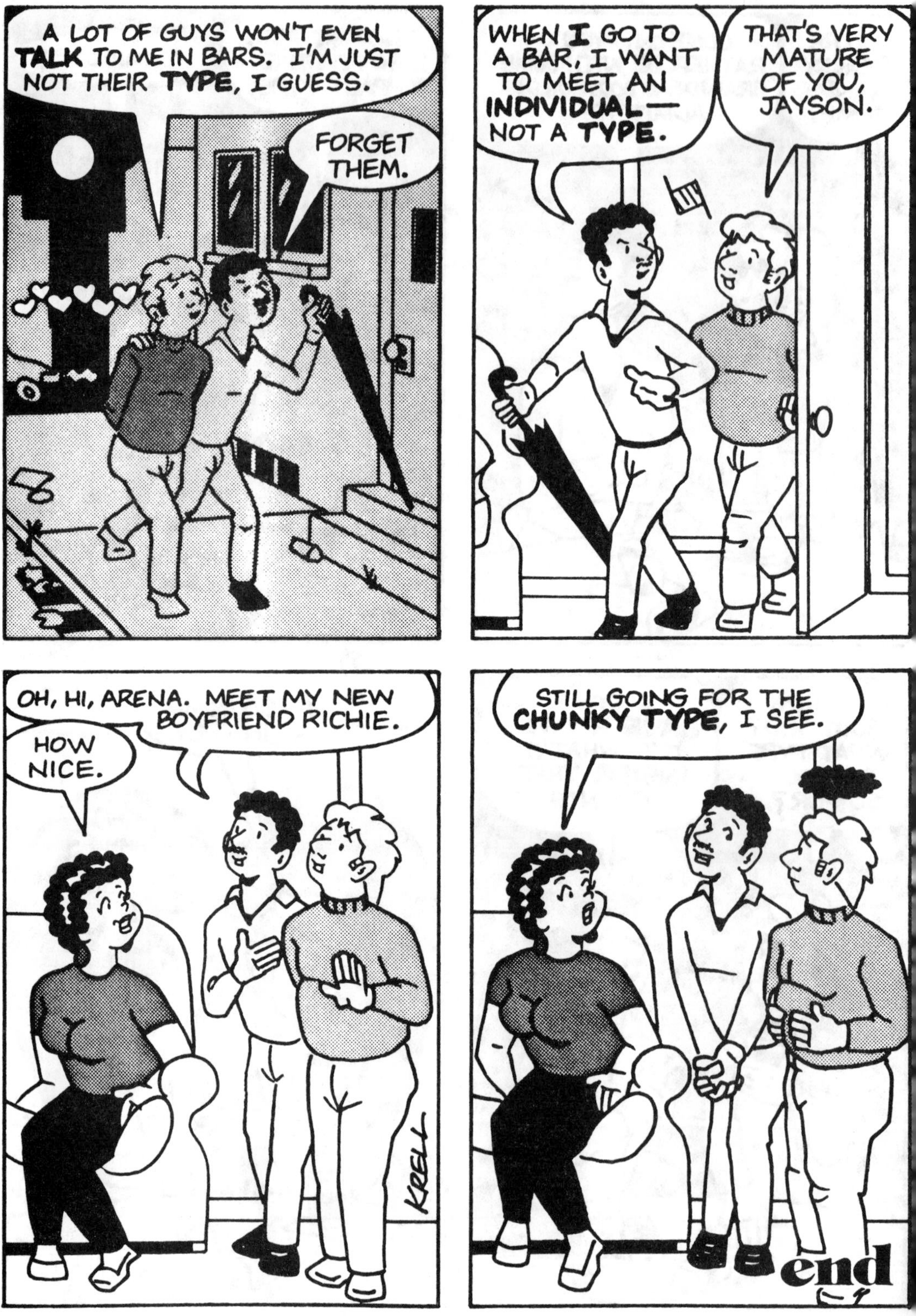
A LOT OF GUYS WON'T EVEN TALK TO ME IN BARS. I'M JUST NOT THEIR TYPE, I GUESS.
FORGET THEM.
WHEN I GO TO A BAR, I WANT TO MEET AN INDIVIDUAL— NOT A TYPE.
THAT'S VERY MATURE OF YOU, JAYSON.
OH, HI, ARENA. MEET MY NEW BOYFRIEND RICHIE.
HOW NICE.
KRELL
STILL GOING FOR THE CHUNKY TYPE, I SEE.
end

Jayson™ visits Planet 69

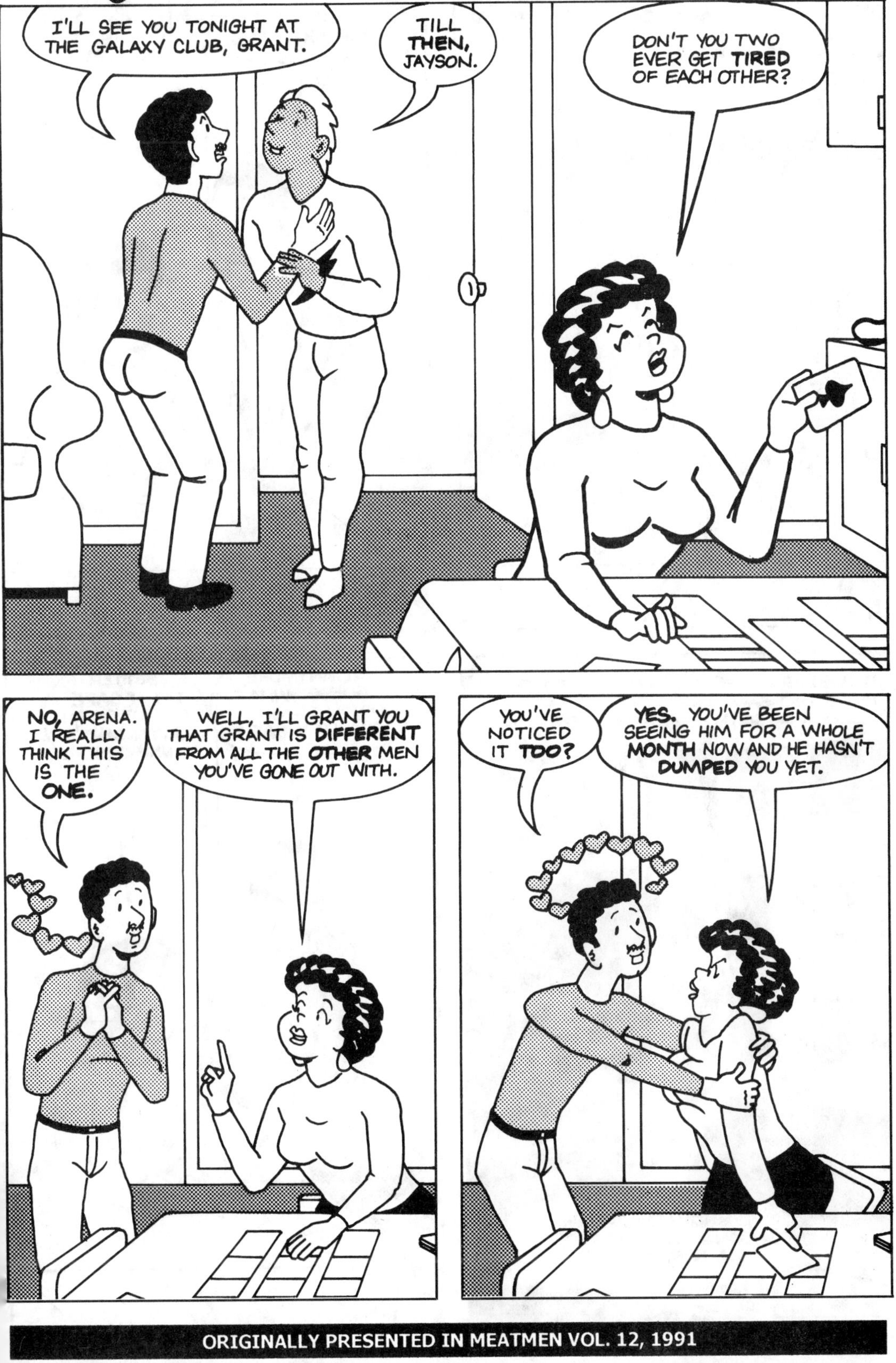

I'LL SEE YOU TONIGHT AT THE GALAXY CLUB, GRANT.
TILL THEN, JAYSON.
DON'T YOU TWO EVER GET TIRED OF EACH OTHER?
NO, ARENA. I REALLY THINK THIS IS THE ONE.
WELL, I'LL GRANT YOU THAT GRANT IS DIFFERENT FROM ALL THE OTHER MEN YOU'VE GONE OUT WITH.
YOU'VE NOTICED IT TOO?
YES. YOU'VE BEEN SEEING HIM FOR A WHOLE MONTH NOW AND HE HASN'T DUMPED YOU YET.

ORIGINALLY PRESENTED IN MEATMEN VOL. 12, 1991

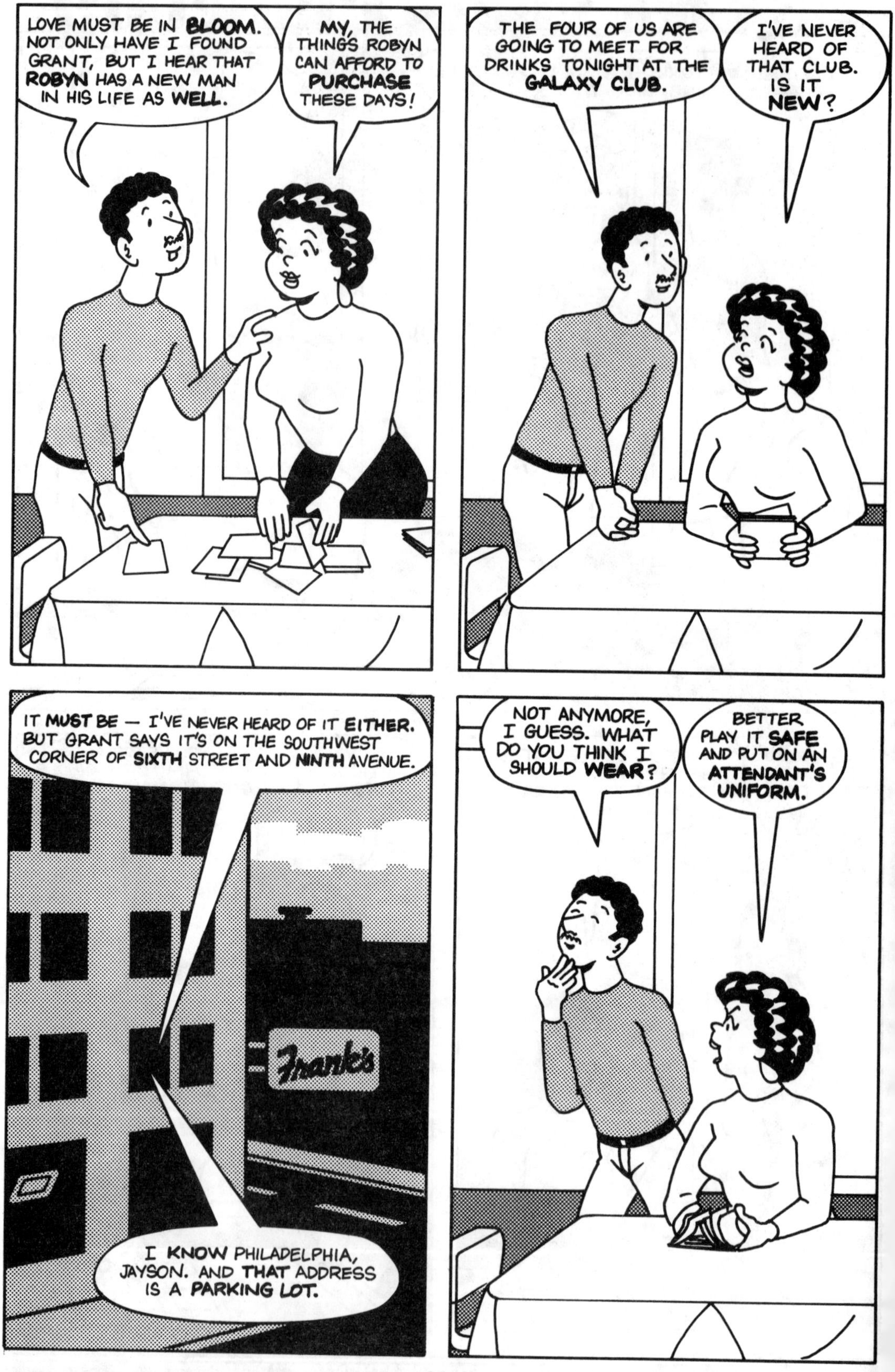
LOVE MUST BE IN BLOOM. NOT ONLY HAVE I FOUND GRANT, BUT I HEAR THAT ROBYN HAS A NEW MAN IN HIS LIFE AS WELL.
MY, THE THINGS ROBYN CAN AFFORD TO PURCHASE THESE DAYS!
THE FOUR OF US ARE GOING TO MEET FOR DRINKS TONIGHT AT THE GALAXY CLUB.
I'VE NEVER HEARD OF THAT CLUB. IS IT NEW?
IT MUST BE — I'VE NEVER HEARD OF IT EITHER. BUT GRANT SAYS IT'S ON THE SOUTHWEST CORNER OF SIXTH STREET AND NINTH AVENUE.
Frank's
I KNOW PHILADELPHIA, JAYSON. AND THAT ADDRESS IS A PARKING LOT.
NOT ANYMORE, I GUESS. WHAT DO YOU THINK I SHOULD WEAR?
BETTER PLAY IT SAFE AND PUT ON AN ATTENDANT'S UNIFORM.

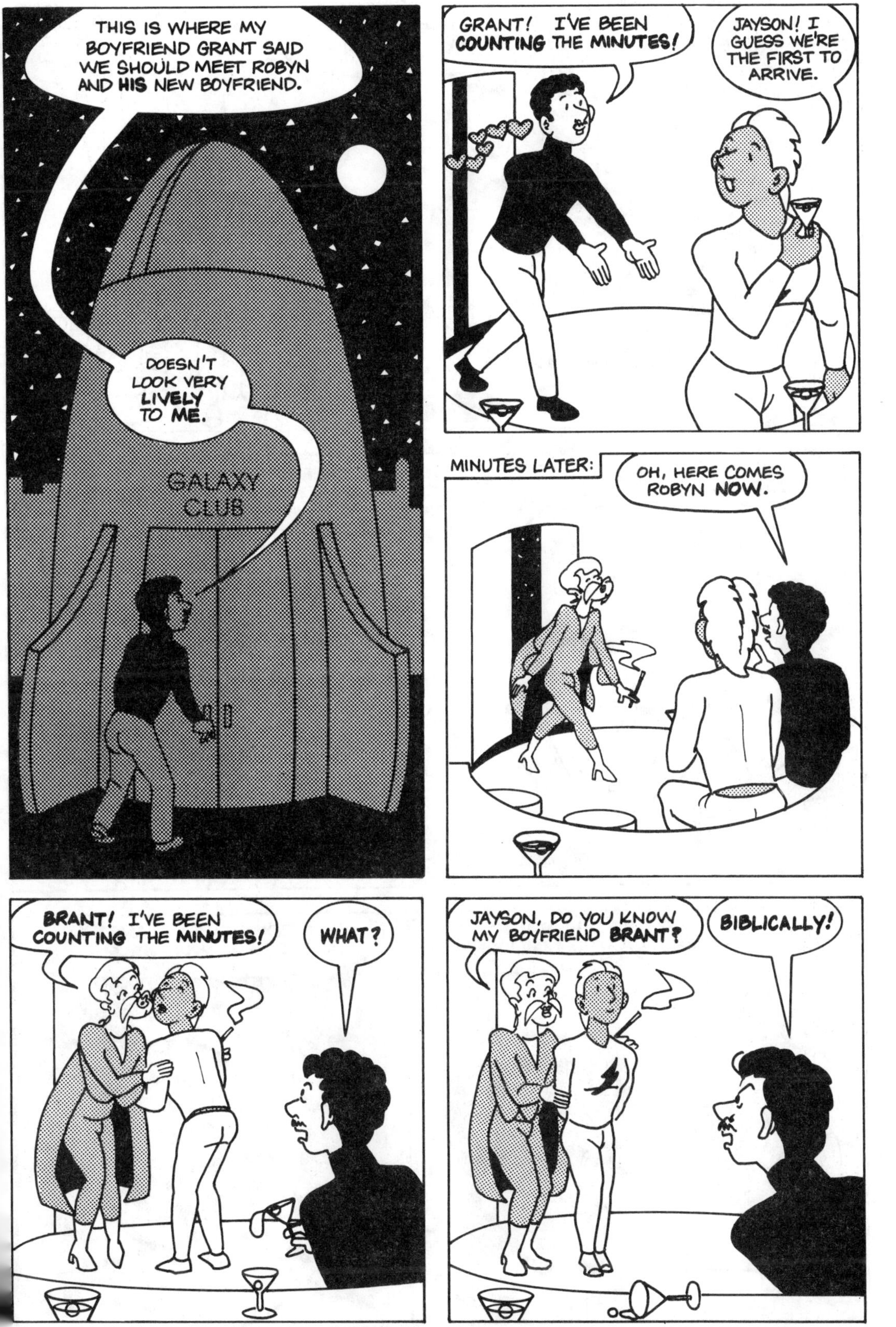

THIS IS WHERE MY BOYFRIEND GRANT SAID WE SHOULD MEET ROBYN AND HIS NEW BOYFRIEND.
DOESN'T LOOK VERY LIVELY TO ME.
GALAXY CLUB
GRANT! I'VE BEEN COUNTING THE MINUTES!
JAYSON! I GUESS WE'RE THE FIRST TO ARRIVE.
MINUTES LATER:
OH, HERE COMES ROBYN NOW.
BRANT! I'VE BEEN COUNTING THE MINUTES!
WHAT?
JAYSON, DO YOU KNOW MY BOYFRIEND BRANT?
BIBLICALLY!

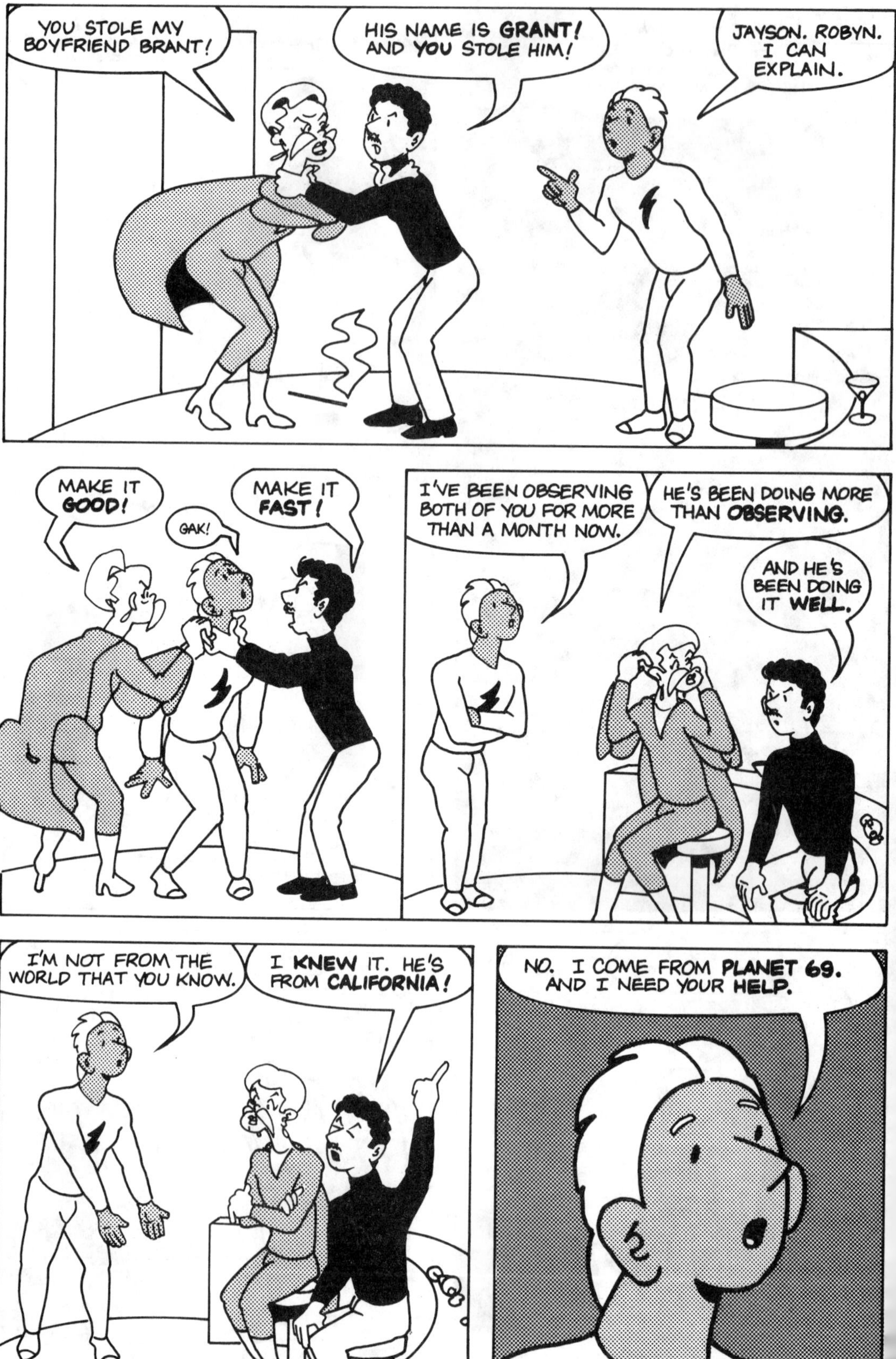
YOU STOLE MY BOYFRIEND BRANT!
HIS NAME IS GRANT! AND YOU STOLE HIM!
JAYSON. ROBYN. I CAN EXPLAIN.
MAKE IT GOOD!
GAK!
MAKE IT FAST!
I'VE BEEN OBSERVING BOTH OF YOU FOR MORE THAN A MONTH NOW.
HE'S BEEN DOING MORE THAN OBSERVING.
AND HE'S BEEN DOING IT WELL.
I'M NOT FROM THE WORLD THAT YOU KNOW.
I KNEW IT. HE'S FROM CALIFORNIA!
NO. I COME FROM PLANET 69. AND I NEED YOUR HELP.

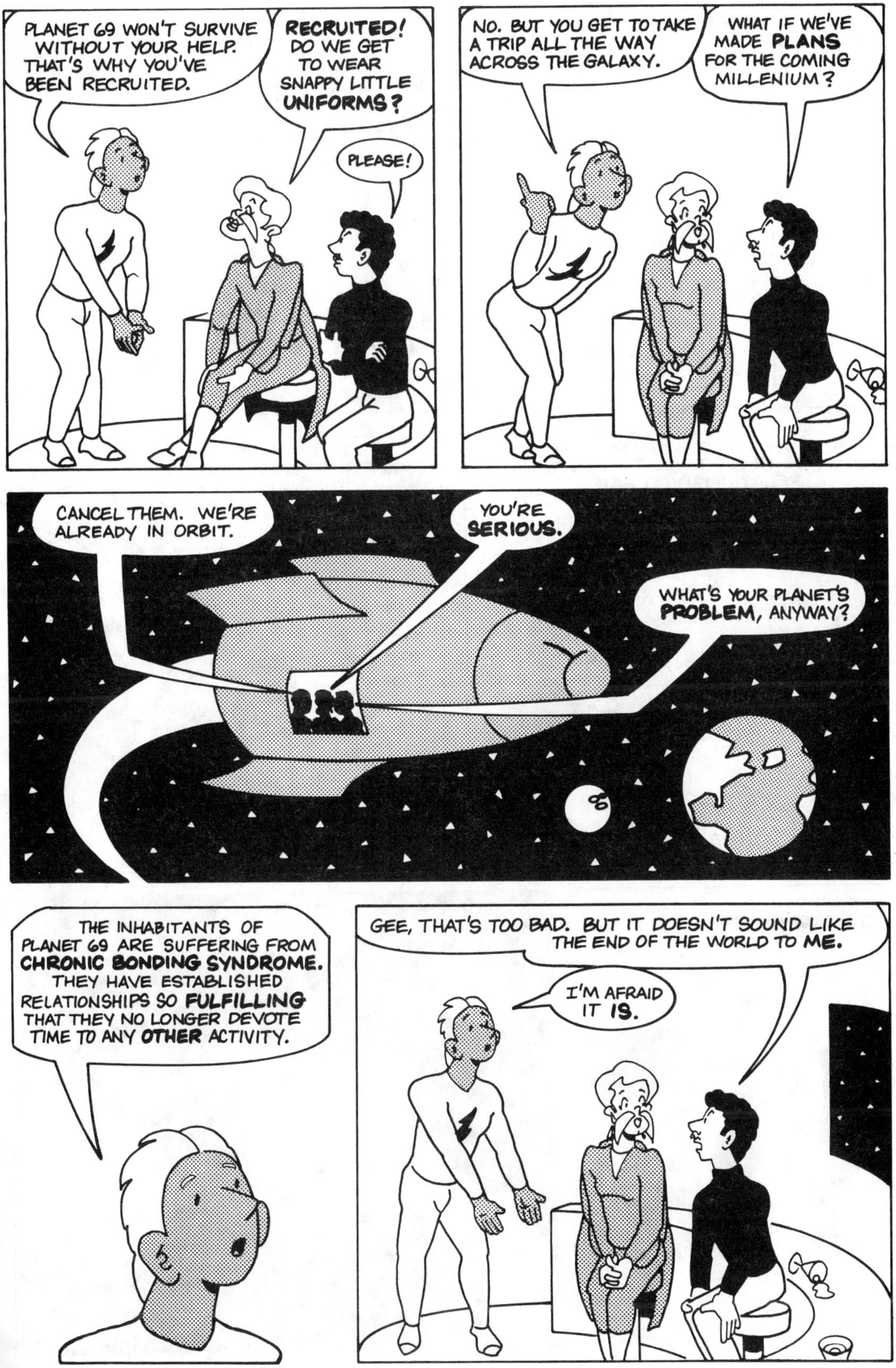

PLANET 69 WON'T SURVIVE WITHOUT YOUR HELP. THAT'S WHY YOU'VE BEEN RECRUITED.
RECRUITED! DO WE GET TO WEAR SNAPPY LITTLE UNIFORMS?
PLEASE!
NO. BUT YOU GET TO TAKE A TRIP ALL THE WAY ACROSS THE GALAXY.
WHAT IF WE'VE MADE PLANS FOR THE COMING MILLENIUM?
CANCEL THEM. WE'RE ALREADY IN ORBIT.
YOU'RE SERIOUS.
WHAT'S YOUR PLANET'S PROBLEM, ANYWAY?
THE INHABITANTS OF PLANET 69 ARE SUFFERING FROM CHRONIC BONDING SYNDROME. THEY HAVE ESTABLISHED RELATIONSHIPS SO FULFILLING THAT THEY NO LONGER DEVOTE TIME TO ANY OTHER ACTIVITY.
GEE, THAT'S TOO BAD. BUT IT DOESN'T SOUND LIKE THE END OF THE WORLD TO ME.
I'M AFRAID IT IS.

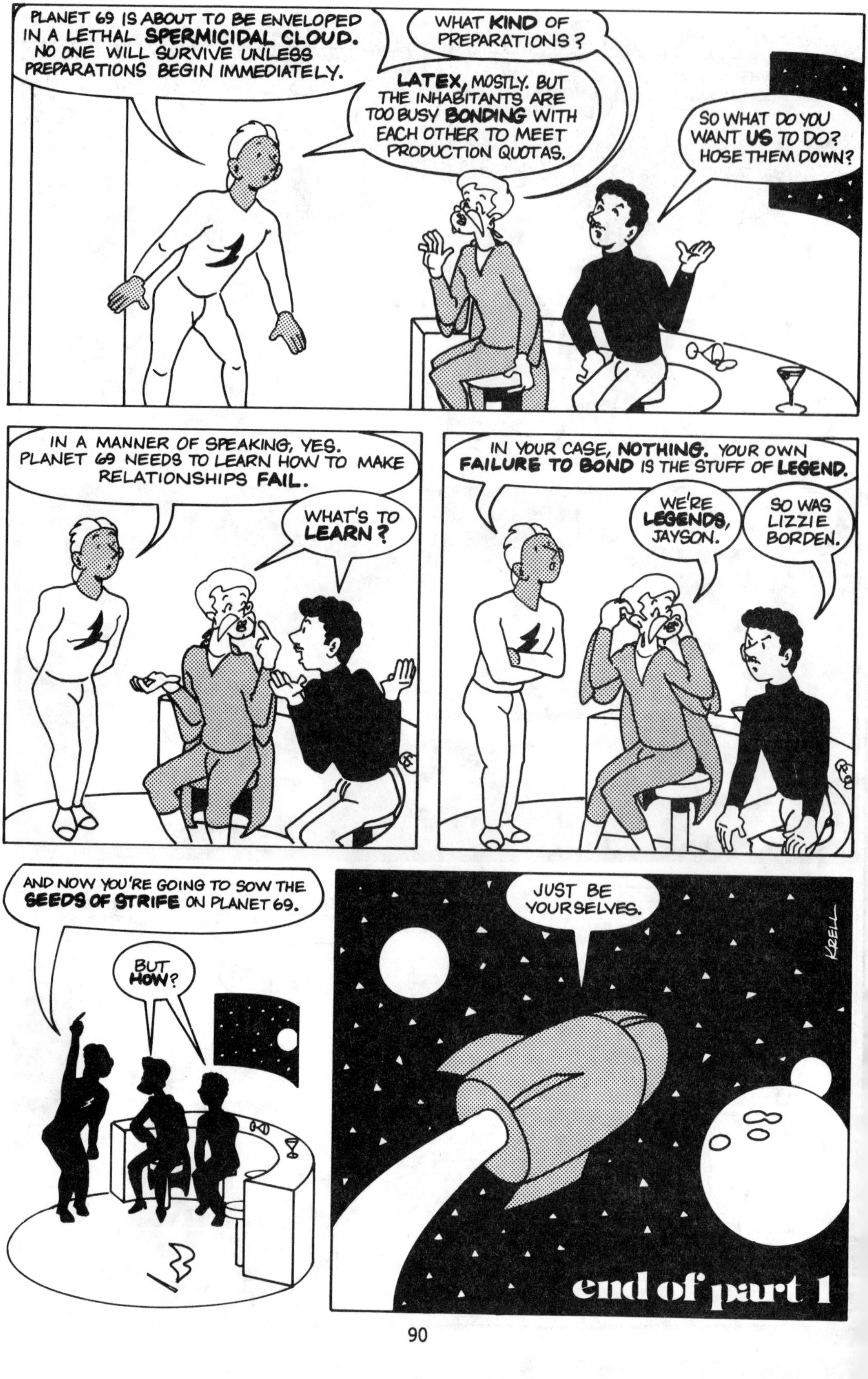
PLANET 69 IS ABOUT TO BE ENVELOPED IN A LETHAL SPERMICIDAL CLOUD. NO ONE WILL SURVIVE UNLESS PREPARATIONS BEGIN IMMEDIATELY.
WHAT KIND OF PREPARATIONS?
LATEX, MOSTLY. BUT THE INHABITANTS ARE TOO BUSY BONDING WITH EACH OTHER TO MEET PRODUCTION QUOTAS.
SO WHAT DO YOU WANT US TO DO? HOSE THEM DOWN?
IN A MANNER OF SPEAKING, YES. PLANET 69 NEEDS TO LEARN HOW TO MAKE RELATIONSHIPS FAIL.
WHAT'S TO LEARN?
IN YOUR CASE, NOTHING. YOUR OWN FAILURE TO BOND IS THE STUFF OF LEGEND.
WE'RE LEGENDS, JAYSON.
SO WAS LIZZIE BORDEN.
AND NOW YOU'RE GOING TO SOW THE SEEDS OF STRIFE ON PLANET 69.
BUT HOW?
JUST BE YOURSELVES.
KRELL
end of part 1

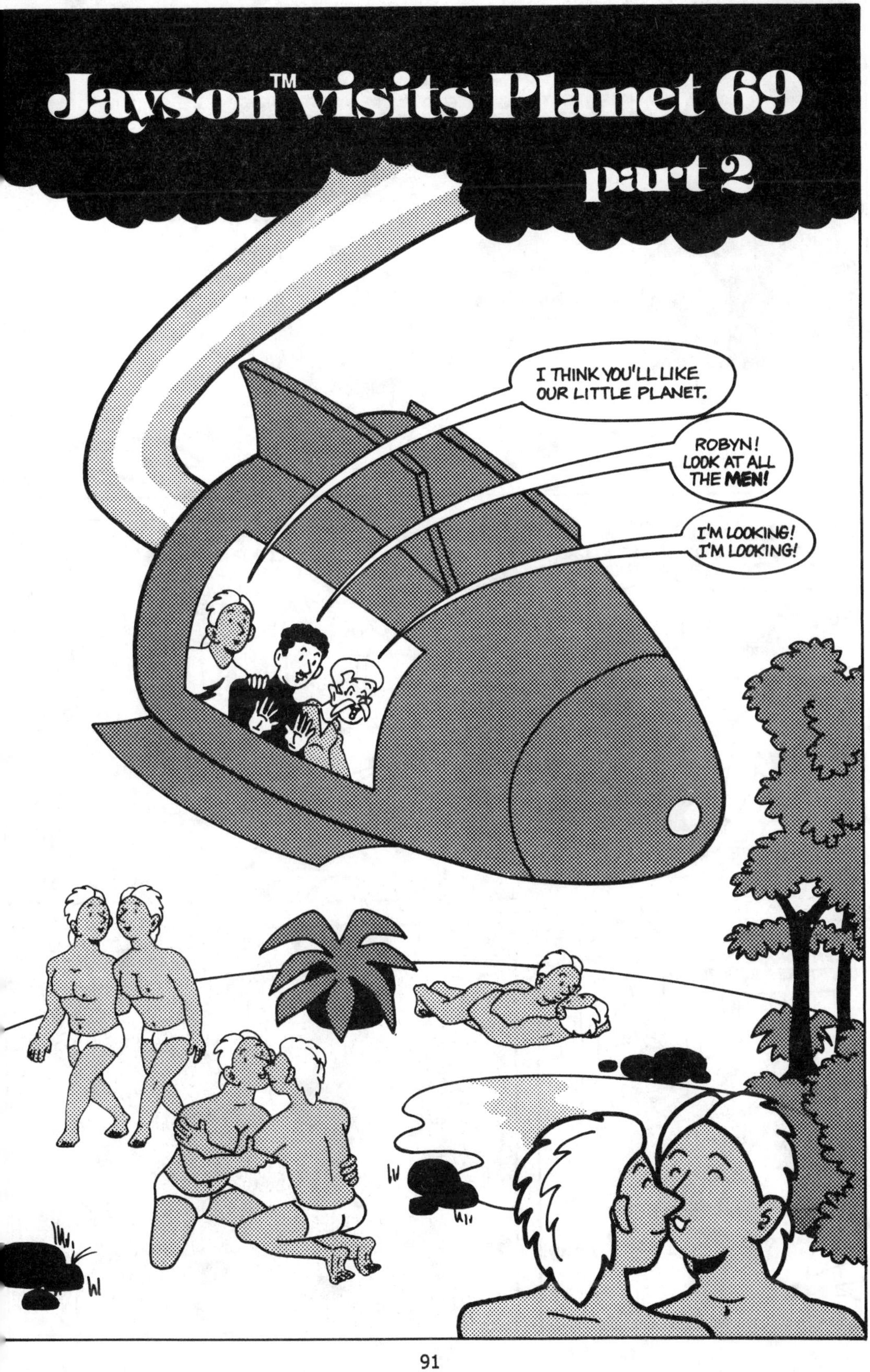
Jayson™ visits Planet 69
part 2
I THINK YOU'LL LIKE OUR LITTLE PLANET.
ROBYN! LOOK AT ALL THE MEN!
I'M LOOKING! I'M LOOKING!

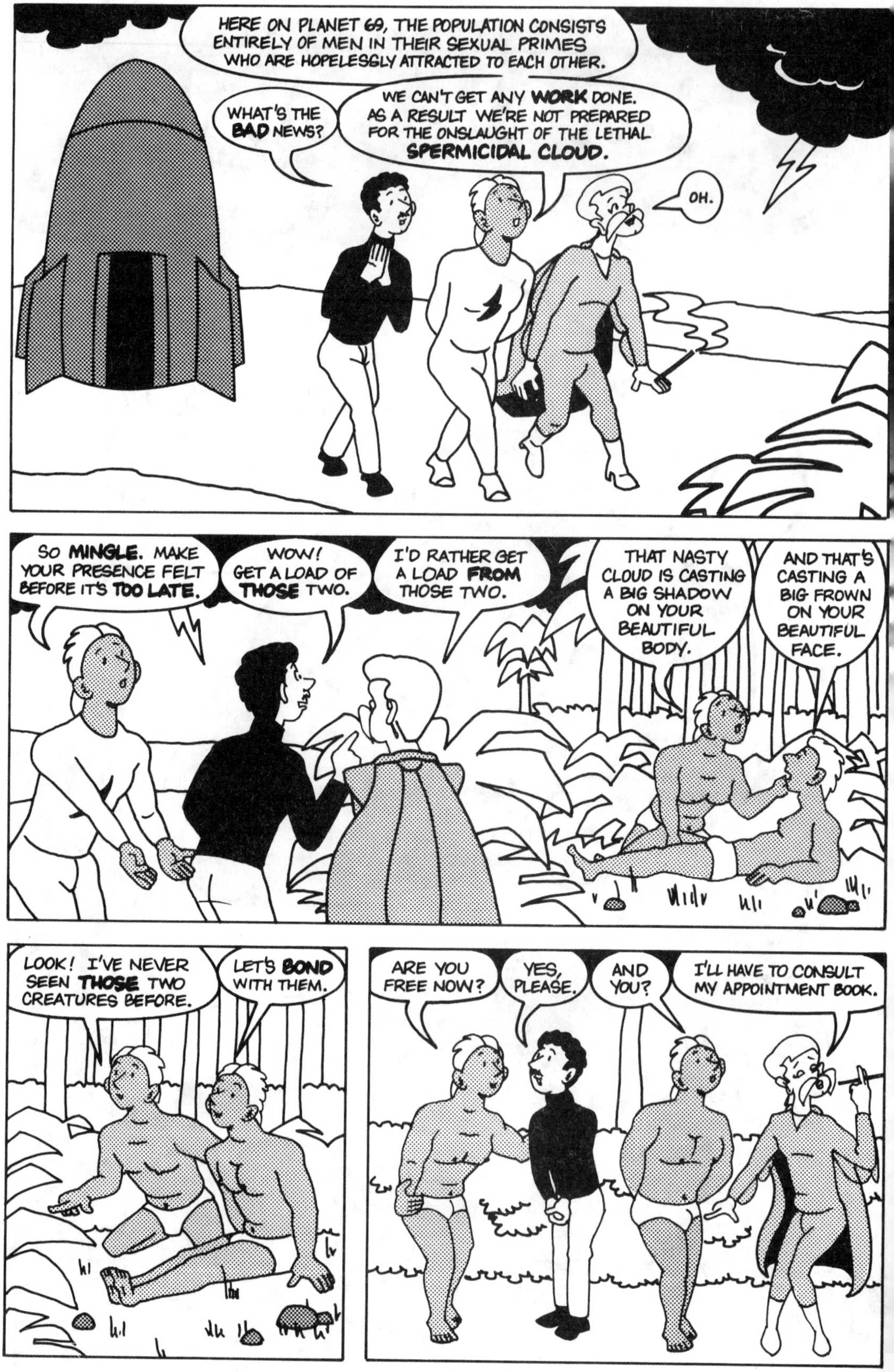
HERE ON PLANET 69, THE POPULATION CONSISTS ENTIRELY OF MEN IN THEIR SEXUAL PRIMES WHO ARE HOPELESSLY ATTRACTED TO EACH OTHER.
WHAT'S THE BAD NEWS?
WE CAN'T GET ANY WORK DONE. AS A RESULT WE'RE NOT PREPARED FOR THE ONSLAUGHT OF THE LETHAL SPERMICIDAL CLOUD.
OH.
SO MINGLE. MAKE YOUR PRESENCE FELT BEFORE IT'S TOO LATE.
WOW! GET A LOAD OF THOSE TWO.
I'D RATHER GET A LOAD FROM THOSE TWO.
THAT NASTY CLOUD IS CASTING A BIG SHADOW ON YOUR BEAUTIFUL BODY.
AND THAT'S CASTING A BIG FROWN ON YOUR BEAUTIFUL FACE.
LOOK! I'VE NEVER SEEN THOSE TWO CREATURES BEFORE.
LET'S BOND WITH THEM.
ARE YOU FREE NOW?
YES, PLEASE.
AND YOU?
I'LL HAVE TO CONSULT MY APPOINTMENT BOOK.

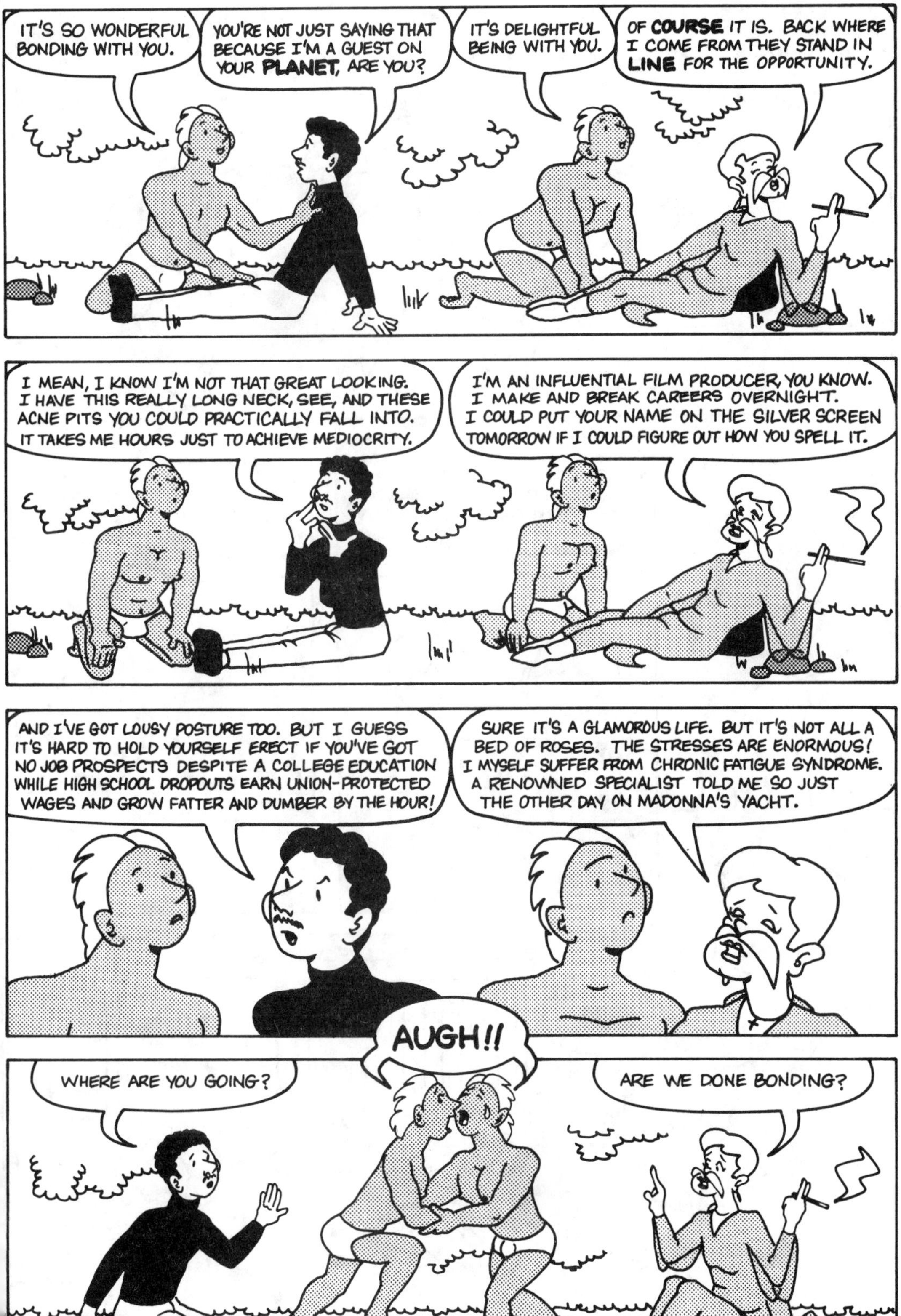

IT'S SO WONDERFUL BONDING WITH YOU.
YOU'RE NOT JUST SAYING THAT BECAUSE I'M A GUEST ON YOUR PLANET, ARE YOU?
IT'S DELIGHTFUL BEING WITH YOU.
OF COURSE IT IS. BACK WHERE I COME FROM THEY STAND IN LINE FOR THE OPPORTUNITY.
I MEAN, I KNOW I'M NOT THAT GREAT LOOKING. I HAVE THIS REALLY LONG NECK, SEE, AND THESE ACNE PITS YOU COULD PRACTICALLY FALL INTO. IT TAKES ME HOURS JUST TO ACHIEVE MEDIOCRITY.
I'M AN INFLUENTIAL FILM PRODUCER, YOU KNOW. I MAKE AND BREAK CAREERS OVERNIGHT. I COULD PUT YOUR NAME ON THE SILVER SCREEN TOMORROW IF I COULD FIGURE OUT HOW YOU SPELL IT.
AND I'VE GOT LOUSY POSTURE TOO. BUT I GUESS IT'S HARD TO HOLD YOURSELF ERECT IF YOU'VE GOT NO JOB PROSPECTS DESPITE A COLLEGE EDUCATION WHILE HIGH SCHOOL DROPOUTS EARN UNION-PROTECTED WAGES AND GROW FATTER AND DUMBER BY THE HOUR!
SURE IT'S A GLAMOROUS LIFE. BUT IT'S NOT ALL A BED OF ROSES. THE STRESSES ARE ENORMOUS! I MYSELF SUFFER FROM CHRONIC FATIGUE SYNDROME. A RENOWNED SPECIALIST TOLD ME SO JUST THE OTHER DAY ON MADONNA'S YACHT.
AUGH!!
WHERE ARE YOU GOING?
ARE WE DONE BONDING?

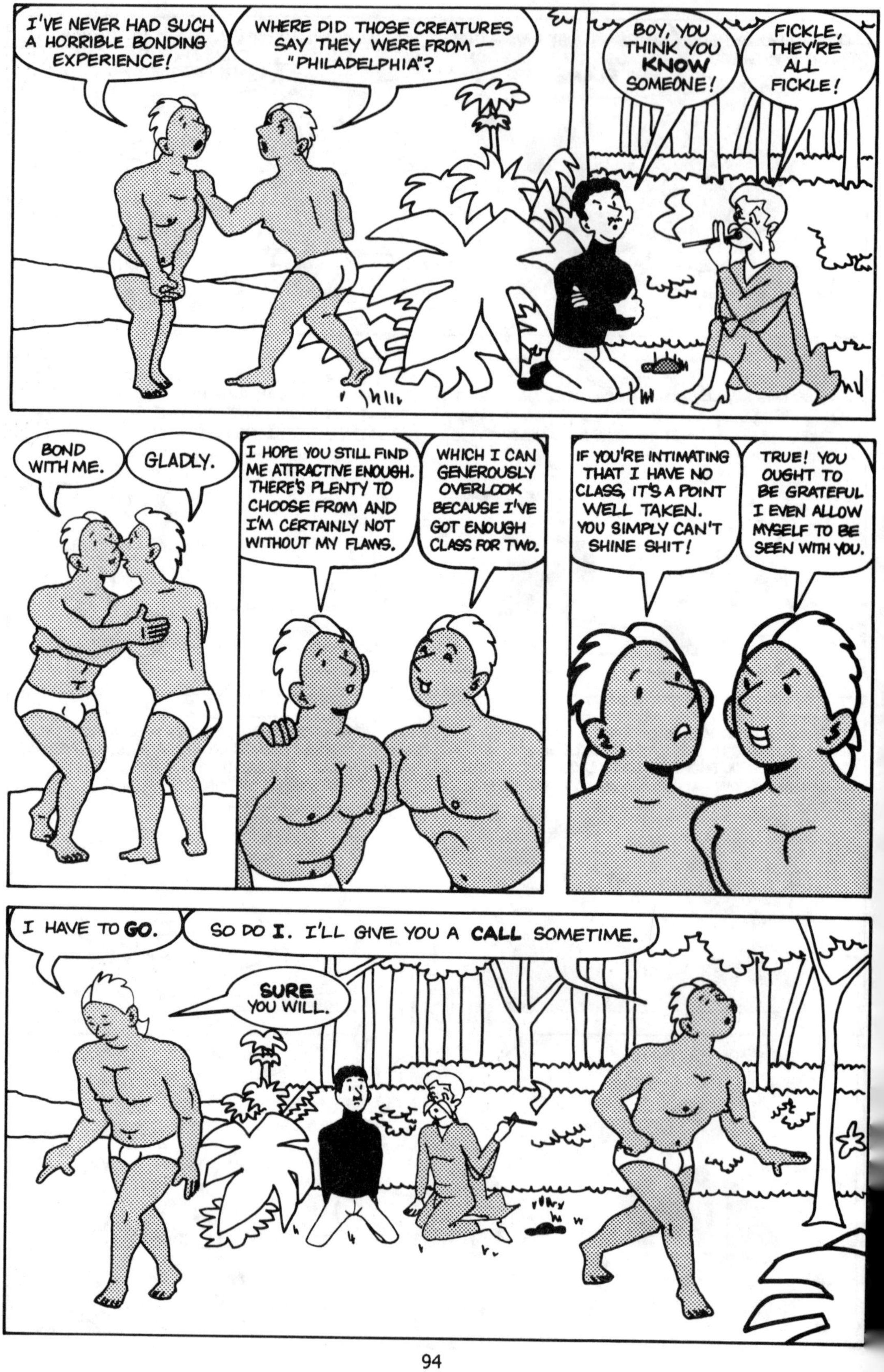

I'VE NEVER HAD SUCH A HORRIBLE BONDING EXPERIENCE!
WHERE DID THOSE CREATURES SAY THEY WERE FROM — "PHILADELPHIA"?
BOY, YOU THINK YOU **KNOW** SOMEONE!
FICKLE, THEY'RE ALL FICKLE!
BOND WITH ME.
GLADLY.
I HOPE YOU STILL FIND ME ATTRACTIVE ENOUGH. THERE'S PLENTY TO CHOOSE FROM AND I'M CERTAINLY NOT WITHOUT MY FLAWS.
WHICH I CAN GENEROUSLY OVERLOOK BECAUSE I'VE GOT ENOUGH CLASS FOR TWO.
IF YOU'RE INTIMATING THAT I HAVE NO CLASS, IT'S A POINT WELL TAKEN. YOU SIMPLY CAN'T SHINE SHIT!
TRUE! YOU OUGHT TO BE GRATEFUL I EVEN ALLOW MYSELF TO BE SEEN WITH YOU.
I HAVE TO **GO**.
SO DO **I**. I'LL GIVE YOU A **CALL** SOMETIME.
SURE YOU WILL.

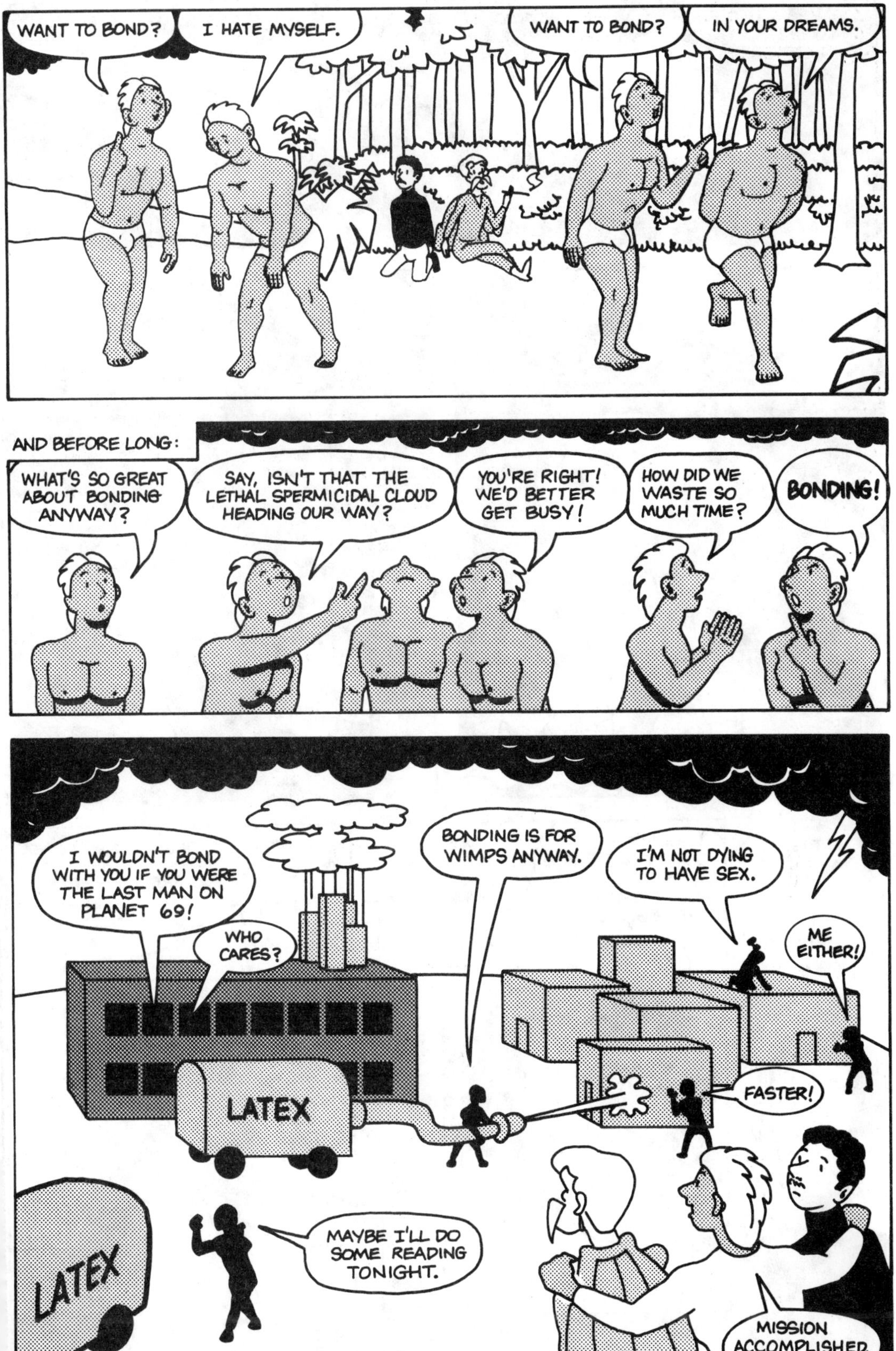
WANT TO BOND?
I HATE MYSELF.
WANT TO BOND?
IN YOUR DREAMS.
AND BEFORE LONG:
WHAT'S SO GREAT ABOUT BONDING ANYWAY?
SAY, ISN'T THAT THE LETHAL SPERMICIDAL CLOUD HEADING OUR WAY?
YOU'RE RIGHT! WE'D BETTER GET BUSY!
HOW DID WE WASTE SO MUCH TIME?
BONDING!
I WOULDN'T BOND WITH YOU IF YOU WERE THE LAST MAN ON PLANET 69!
WHO CARES?
BONDING IS FOR WIMPS ANYWAY.
I'M NOT DYING TO HAVE SEX.
ME EITHER!
LATEX
FASTER!
LATEX
MAYBE I'LL DO SOME READING TONIGHT.
MISSION ACCOMPLISHED.

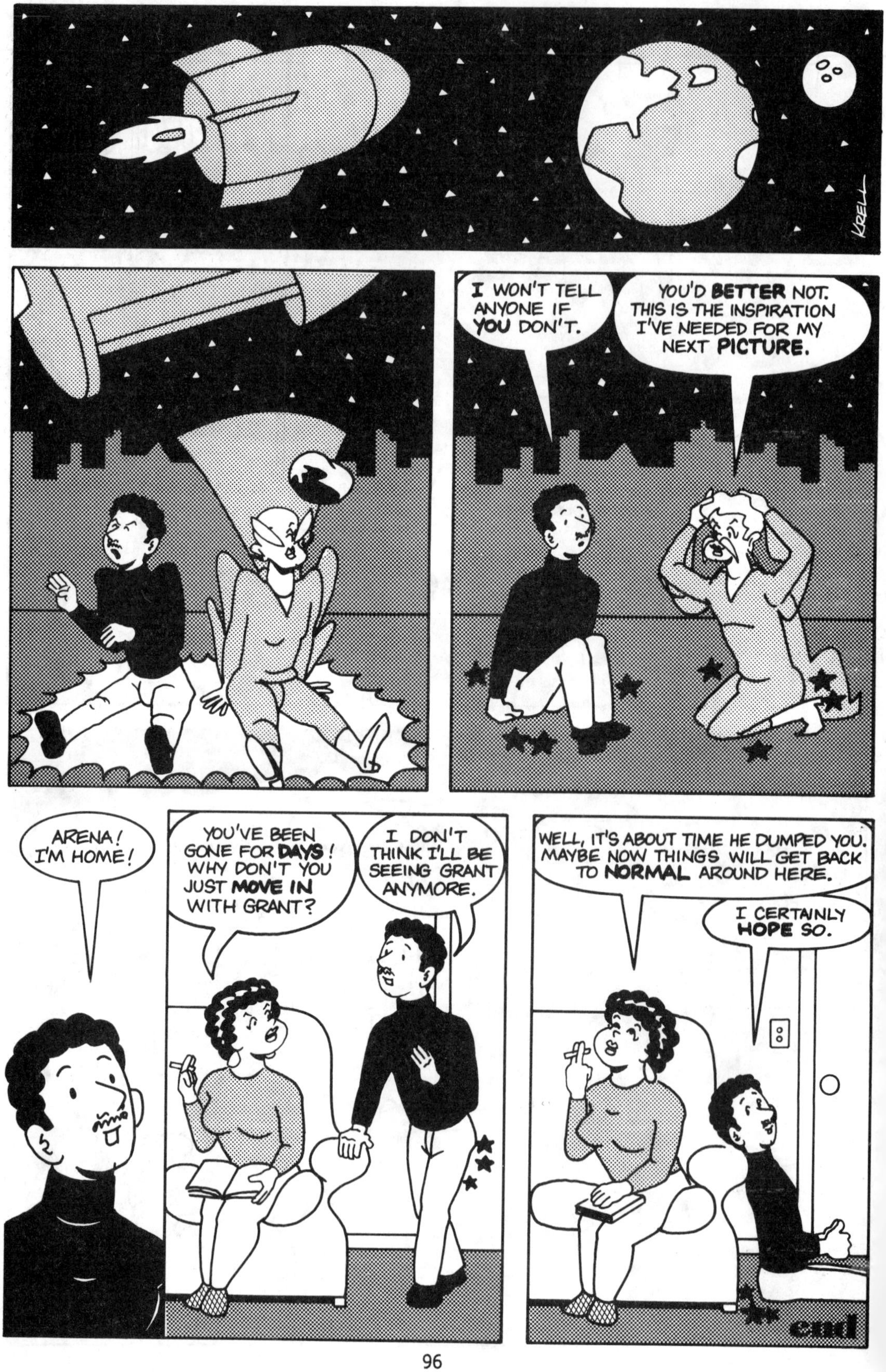
KRELL
I WON'T TELL ANYONE IF YOU DON'T.
YOU'D BETTER NOT. THIS IS THE INSPIRATION I'VE NEEDED FOR MY NEXT PICTURE.
ARENA! I'M HOME!
YOU'VE BEEN GONE FOR DAYS! WHY DON'T YOU JUST MOVE IN WITH GRANT?
I DON'T THINK I'LL BE SEEING GRANT ANYMORE.
WELL, IT'S ABOUT TIME HE DUMPED YOU. MAYBE NOW THINGS WILL GET BACK TO NORMAL AROUND HERE.
I CERTAINLY HOPE SO.
end